W9-BJL-569

DISCARD

# LIFEWAYS·

# The Sioux

## RAYMOND BIAL

MARSHALL CAVENDISH
NEW YORK

SERIES CONSULTANT: JOHN BIERHORST

ACKNOWLEDGMENTS

This book would not have been possible without the generous help of many individuals and organizations that have dedicated themselves to honoring the customs of the Sioux. I am especially grateful to David Clobes, who advised me on my journey through the Black Hills and the Badlands and who provided a number of fine photographs for this book. I would also like to acknowledge the assistance of the National Archives, the Library of Congress, and the Philbrook Museum for furnishing several exquisite illustrations.

I would like to express my appreciation to my editor Kate Nunn for her good cheer and diligence in overseeing this book and others in the *Lifeways* series from concept to finished manuscript. I would like to thank my wife, Linda, and my children Anna, Sarah, and Luke for their faithful support of my work.

Benchmark Books
Marshall Cavendish Corporation
99 White Plains Road Tarrytown, New York 10591-9001
Text copyright © 1999 by Marshall Cavendish Corporation
Map copyright © 1999 by Marshall Cavendish Corporation
Library of Congress Cataloging-in-Publication Data
All rights reserved
Map and illustration by Rodica Prato
Bial, Raymond. The Sioux / Raymond Bial.
p. cm. — (Lifeways) Includes bibliographical references and index.
Summary: Examines the origins, beliefs, language, and culture of the Sioux, also known as the Dakota Indians.
ISBN 0-7614-0804-5 1. Dakota Indians—Juvenile literature. [1. Dakota Indians. 2. Indians of North America—
Great Plains.] I. Title. II. Series: Bial, Raymons. Lifeways.
E99.D1B55 1999 973'.049752—dc2198-2915 CIP AC
Printed in Italy
5 6 4

Cover photos: Raymond Bial

The photographs in this book are used by permission and through the courtesy of: The Philbrook Museum of Art, Tulsa, Oklahoma: 1, 11, 14, 18, 48, 88-89. Raymond Bial: 6, 8-9, 23, 25, 28-29, 60, 64-65, 75, 93, 94-95, 97, 102, 103, 104, 106-107. Library of Congress: 32, 33, 34-35, 52, 57, 62, 70. National Museum of American Art, Washington, D.C./Art Resource: 20-21, 41, 67, 78-79. Joslyn Art Museum, Omaha, Nebraska; Gift of the Enron Art Foundation: 42-43. Special Collections Division, University of Washington Libraries: Neg #UW 18101, 45; Neg #UW 18102, 73. Corbis-Bettmann: 50, 54, 111; UPI/Corbis-Bettmann: 112, 114. National Archives: 61, 81, 84, 86, 90. David F. Clobes: 76. Smithsonian Institution: 115.

This book is respectfully dedicated
to all the people who are working
to help the Sioux people.

# Contents

# Author's Note

At the dawn of the twentieth century, Native Americans were thought to be a vanishing race. However, despite four hundred years of warfare, deprivation, and disease, American Indians have not gone away. Countless thousands have lost their lives, but over the course of this century the populations of native tribes have grown tremendously. Even as American Indians struggle to adapt to modern Western life, they have also kept the flame of their traditions alive—the language, religion, stories, and the everyday ways of life. An exhilarating renaissance in Native American culture is now sweeping the nation from coast to coast.

The *Lifeways* books depict the social and cultural life of the major nations, from the early history of native peoples in North America to their present-day struggles for survival and dignity. Historical and contemporary photographs of traditional subjects, as well as period illustrations, are blended throughout each book so that readers may gain a sense of family life in a tipi, a hogan, or a longhouse.

No single book can comprehensively portray the intricate and varied lifeways of an entire tribe, or nation. I only hope that young people will come away with a deeper appreciation for the rich tapestry of Indian culture—both then and now—and a keen desire to learn more about these first Americans.

# 1. Origins

Sioux country encompasses the Badlands—a
landscape of hard gray rocks and dry gullies that
is strangely beautiful.

GREAT WARRIORS AND BUFFALO HUNTERS, THE SIOUX VALUED STRENGTH and endurance. Yet the Sioux were a deeply spiritual people as well. They viewed themselves as a very small part of a vast universe that reached across the broad prairies to the very edges of the panoramic sky. The sun, the sky, the earth, and the four winds were central to their beliefs, as were the stars—the holy breath of the supernatural.

The Sioux also understood the realities of hardship, having faced cold and hunger, as well as the uncertainty of nature. This direct experience, especially with death in battles and bitter winters, helped to foster their deep beliefs. These beliefs are vividly expressed in stories about their origins. Some stories recount their beginnings in the sacred Black Hills of South Dakota. Others trace the Sioux migration from the forests of Minnesota to the wind-blown plains. Based on ancient oral narratives, the following is a condensed story about how the Sioux came to the earth.

## "The Creation Story"

Long ago, Waziya, the Old Man, lived beneath the earth with his wife, Wakanka. They had a daughter named Ite, who grew to be the most beautiful of women. She was so lovely that she caught the eye of one of the gods, Tate, the Wind. Although she was not a goddess, Ite married Tate, who lived at the entrance of the Spirit Trail. Over time, she bore quadruplets, all boys, who became the North, West, East, and South Winds.

Because his daughter Ite was married to Tate, Waziya was able

**I**n this painting entitled Sioux Telling by Yankton Sioux Oscar Howe, elders recount the history of their people through stories. Pictures depicting heroic deeds were often painted on the sides of tipis.

to mix with the good and helpful gods. However, he yearned to have the power of a true god. Iktomi, the Trickster, who loved to spread discontent, promised Waziya, Wakanka, and Ite enormous power and even greater beauty for Ite, if they would help him make others look ridiculous. He even promised Ite that her beauty would rival that of the goddess Hanwi, the Moon, who was married to the god Wi, the Sun.

The three of them agreed and Iktomi gave Ite a charm, which made her so beautiful that she was less attentive to her four sons. Wi was captivated by her and invited her to sit beside him at the feast of the gods. Ite arrived early and took the vacant seat next to Wi. When Hanwi arrived she saw that her seat had been taken and she was so ashamed that she covered her face with a dark robe to hide from the laughing people—and devious Iktomi who outlaughed everyone.

After the feast, the god Skan, the Sky and judge of all the gods, called a council to expose Wi, who had forsaken his wife; Ite, who dared assume the place of a goddess; Waziya and Wakanka who had vainly wished to be gods; and Iktomi, who had deceived everyone. As punishment, Wi was to lose the comfort of his wife, Hanwi—he was to rule during the day and she would dominate the skies at night. Whenever they came out together, Hanwi would cover her face in shame. Because of her vanity and the neglect of her sons, Ite's next child would be born early and be unlike her other children. Her children were to live with their father, Tate, and she was told to return to the world and live without friends. Half of Ite remained stunningly beautiful, but the other half became so ugly that people were frightened by the sight of her. She became known as Anung-Ite, the Double-Faced Woman.

Waziya and Wakanka were banished to the edge of the world until they learned to help young children. Renamed for their misdeeds, they became known as the Wizard and the Witch. Iktomi was also sent to the edge of the world where he was to be forever without friends. Tate, who was punished for marrying Ite, was told to raise his children properly and to do woman's work. He lived with his four sons, the Winds, and his fifth son, little Yumni, the Whirlwind, beyond the pines in the land of the ghosts. Each day, his sons traveled the earth, swirling in the four directions, according to his instructions.

In the beginning, the Wizard and the Witch, along with Anung-Ite and Iktomi, were the only people on Earth. Iktomi had grown tired of playing tricks on the animals because they never showed any shame over their misfortunes. So he asked Anung-Ite what she most desired. After he swore to abandon tricks and pranks, she told him that she wanted people to come to Earth. She reasoned that if they tasted meat and learned how to make clothes and tipis, they would live where they could have these good things. Iktomi then went to the wolves, again promising to give up his tricks. So, they drove moose, deer, and bears to Anung-Ite's tipi, where she made food, clothing, and shelter to entice the Sioux people.

Iktomi gave a packet of delicious meat and fancy clothing to

**D**ance of Double Woman, *a watercolor by Oscar Howe, shows the magical Double-Faced Woman, who might appear as either beautiful or ugly to those who gazed upon her.*

one of the wolves, who trotted through a cave out of the world and presented the bundle to a young warrior named Tokahe, the First One. When the other Sioux people tasted the food and saw the clothes worn by Tokahe, they were envious and asked how they might acquire such things. Led by the wolf, three men, along with Tokahe, entered the world through the cave to find the source of this bounty. They came to a lake where Anung-Ite had set up her tipi. She appeared to be a lovely young woman to Tokahe and his companions, and, posing as her husband, Iktomi seemed to be a handsome young man. The four young men saw much game, which Iktomi had arranged for the wolves to drive past them, and Anung-Ite gave them tasty foods and fine clothes to take back to their people. Iktomi also told them that he and his wife were really very old, but by consuming this earthly food they had remained young and beautiful.

Returning through the cave to their people, the four young men excitedly described what they had seen. Some people wished to accompany Tokahe, but others thought he was a wizard and doubted such wonders. The chief warned that anyone who ventured through the cave would never be able to come back. Six men and their wives and children joined Tokahe, and, guided by the wolf, they ventured onto the earth. It was not what they expected—they became lost, tired, and hungry.

The babies and small children cried. Anung-Ite appeared and tried to comfort them, but they saw the ugly side of her face and fled in terror. Iktomi then appeared and mocked the people who had been so foolish in coming to the earth. Tokahe was ashamed because he had urged these people to follow him. However, Anung-Ite's hideous face and Iktomi's deceit vanished when the Wizard and the Witch appeared. According to the prophecy, when they were banished to the edge of the earth, the Wizard and the Witch had learned to be tender and merciful to the young. They led the disheartened band to the land of the pines, to the world of the ghosts. They taught them to live as men and women. And this is how Tokahe and his Sioux followers came to be the first people to live on the earth.

Like other native peoples of North America, the ancestors of the Sioux were fur-clad hunters who had most likely trudged across the Bering Strait over a narrow land bridge that connected Asia and Alaska more than 10,000 years ago. Early in their history, tribes of Siouan-speaking people lived in the Southeast—from present-day Florida to Virginia. Around 1500, these restless tribes began to spread over eastern North America. Many Sioux settled in what is now the state of Minnesota, for generations living in the vicinity of Mille Lacs. Others later traveled from the woodlands of present-day Minnesota as far as the Great Plains.

For hundreds of years these hunters and gatherers made their homes in bark lodges among the forests and lakes of the north. They lived on game and wild rice, although in later years they also began to cultivate fields of corn. Men stalked deer, rabbits, and other small animals in the forest and netted fish in the glistening streams. Women glided silently in canoes over lakes, bending over the long grasses and shaking wild rice into their baskets. In the spring, they tapped maple trees for their clear sap, which was cooked down to sweet syrup. When game became scarce, they moved to another part of this country of woods and lakes, using dogs to pull small sleds called travois (trav OY). Occasionally, they killed a buffalo—at that time the large, shaggy beasts roamed as far east as the Appalachian Mountains. Gradually, the Sioux began to realize that the buffalo could provide nearly all their basic needs for food, clothing, and shelter.

There were seven tribes of the Sioux people: Mdewakanton, Wahpeton, Wahpekute, Teton, Sisseton, Yankton, and Yanktonai. These original tribes joined in an alliance called the *Oceti Sakowin*, or Seven Council Fires. Every summer, they came together to talk and perform a Sun Dance. The council of forty-four chiefs discussed future plans for the nation. Four men from among the forty-four were chosen as great chiefs. These chiefs could not inherit their positions; only those who had proven themselves to be exceptionally strong, brave, and wise were considered. At the summer gathering, people also renewed friendships, shared news, and traded articles they had made or acquired from other tribes.

The Teton, from *tetonwan* meaning "Dwellers of the Prairie," were the largest of the seven groups of Sioux people, with seven divisions of its own: Brulé, Oglala, Two Kettles, Miniconjou, No Bows, Hunkpapa, and Sihasapa. The Sioux received their popular name from the Ojibwa, who called the Iroquois, their powerful

*E*very summer the Sioux gathered for the Sun Dance. In this religious celebration, warriors proved their courage by undergoing the terribly painful ordeal of having their chests pierced. Painting by Oscar Howe, a Yankton Sioux.

enemy to the east, "true snakes" and the Sioux to the west "lesser snakes" or "nadouessioux." The French garbled the word "Sioux," a name that is now used for all the Sioux people.

The Sioux may also be divided into three language groups: Dakota, Lakota, and Nakota. Each of these names means "ally" or "friend." A sedentary and agricultural tribe, the Dakotas were known as the Santee or Eastern Sioux, and the Nakotas as the Yankton and Yanktonai or Middle Sioux. The Lakotas were also known as the Teton, the Plains, or Western Sioux.

For years, the Sioux battled the Ojibwa and the Cree in the northern woods. But when the French began to supply their enemies with muskets, or "firesticks," Sioux warriors were suddenly at a tremendous disadvantage. At the same time, they were impressed by the huge buffalo herds that roamed the prairies to the west. In the 1600s, they migrated once again—to the Great Plains of the Dakotas. The Teton were the first to transform themselves into skilled horsemen and buffalo hunters. They fiercely battled other Indian tribes and eventually drove them from the plains.

By 1750, with 30,000 people, the Teton had firmly established themselves in the heart of the northern Great Plains. Most of the Sioux living in the Dakotas today are descended from these Teton. Toward the end of the 1600s, the Nakota also moved onto the broad plains, splitting into the Yankton and Yanktonai branches. The Santee remained in permanent bark homes in the woodlands. In later years, after the Minnesota Sioux Uprising in 1862, some scattered into the Dakotas, Montana, and

To gallop up to a powerful buffalo required skill and courage. Yet men looked forward to the chance to prove themselves in the hunt. Watercolor by Calvin Larvie, a Brulé Sioux.

Nebraska, although most Santee still live on a small reservation in their Minnesota home.

By the early 1800s the Sioux had come to dominate the Great Plains. Excellent horsemen, they were admired as the "finest light cavalry in the world." Flying across the prairie, swift as the wind

on their fine horses, the eagle feathers of their warbonnets streaming after them, they struck fear into the hearts of their enemies. With their sleek horses, they could hunt down enough buffalo in a single day to feed their families for months, leaving war parties of young braves free to sweep across the Great Plains.

# The People and the Land

A wandering people, the Sioux have known many places—from the forests of the Southeast to the land of ten thousand lakes in Minnesota. Yet, for hundreds of years most of the Sioux have lived on vast stretches of the northern prairie—broad, rolling grasslands that flow like waves on the open sea in the unrelenting wind. Much of this landscape is interrupted only by an occasional streambed, a silver vein of water trickling through the ragged V of a ravine. In some places the land is so flat that it appears to be the floor of the sky.

Early explorers described this land as the "Great American Desert," fit only for "wild savages and Indian cattle," which is what they called buffaloes. Millions of the snorting beasts spread over the plains like a deep chocolate-brown blanket as far as one could see. This vast, open country, with neither a tree nor cabin in sight, gave the Sioux an exhilarating sense of space and freedom. Spreading far and wide, the plains were laced with several broad rivers—the Missouri, Platte, Cheyenne, Niobrara, and White. The riverbanks were fringed with stands of the sacred cottonwood trees, which became tattered ribbons of yellow during the autumn months. The Sioux often camped near these clear-flowing waters for protection against enemies and the elements. Otherwise, Sioux country was marked in each direction by the four winds, an overwhelming sky, and not a single other obstruction. It was a country made for great horsemen. Here, a warrior could ride for miles, day after day, with nothing to hinder him.

The Sioux home appears to be more sky than land. In every direction, clouds sweep away into the distance over the broad grazing lands of the buffalo, which the Sioux called tatanka.

The land was also noted for its extreme weather—hot, humid summers and brutal winters. Intense winds roared down from the Arctic, bringing heavy snows and bone-chilling cold. Here, one could get lost in a blizzard, completely blinded by the swirling wall of white, and freeze to death in minutes. Yet the northern plains also knew the tender green of spring, the radiance of summer, and the golden light of autumn. Much of one's time during this joyous warmth was spent getting ready for the next bitterly cold winter.

Much was sacred about this land. Among the luxuriant grasses, the prairie was fragrant with the scent of sage and other herbs used by medicine men in healing rituals. Within the broad prairies were two extraordinary landscapes, one haunted and the other holy— the Badlands and the Black Hills. The Badlands was a place of fantastic, contorted rock sculptures. Most of the colors had been leached from the land by the occasional rains, until it was buff or pale gray, resembling the surface of the moon. It was a strange, mystical place, strewn with the fossil bones of dinosaurs and other ancient creatures. The Sioux believed the Badlands was inhabited by ghosts and monsters. They stayed away from this eroded place.

In higher country, the treeless prairie gave way to sweet meadows enveloped by craggy hills studded with dark pines. There were also clear lakes bordered with spruce and ponderosa pine, as well as juniper and quaking aspen. A sacred place to the Sioux, the *Paha Sapa*, or Black Hills, rose suddenly from the prairie—cool, shadowy, and mysterious. Many rocky landmarks, including the Needles and the Cathedral Spires, thrust upward in the heart of this magical country. Sioux elders told children that

*T he Badlands is rugged country, seemingly unfit for animals or people. The Sioux avoided the eroded hillsides because they thought evil spirits and dreaded creatures lived there.*

the Black Hills were the home of *Wakinyan*, the legendary Thunderbird, whose eyes were bolts of lightning.

Wild animals also made their home in this rugged country. Out on the prairie, birds tended nests hidden carefully on the ground, and the resourceful coyote, always keeping his distance, trotted along the margins of the human world. There were whole towns of prairie dogs, the rodents popping up then diving down into their burrows, and there were waves of buffalo. There were also swift,

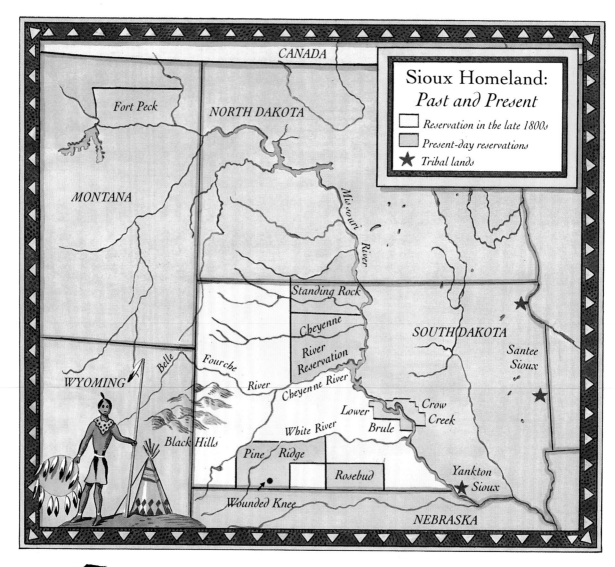

**Sioux Homeland:**
*Past and Present*

☐ Reservation in the late 1800s
☐ Present-day reservations
★ Tribal lands

CANADA

Fort Peck

NORTH DAKOTA

MONTANA

Missouri River

Standing Rock

Cheyenne

River
Reservation

SOUTH DAKOTA

Santee
Sioux

WYOMING

Belle

Fourche

River

Cheyenne River

Crow
Creek

Lower

Brule

Black Hills

White River

Pine Ridge

Rosebud

Yankton
Sioux

Wounded Knee

NEBRASKA

The Sioux ranged east to west, from present-day Minnesota to Montana. They wandered over the Great Plains as far south as Iowa and Nebraska, but often gathered around the Badlands and the Black Hills in what is now South Dakota.

graceful pronghorn antelope springing away as quick and silent as the light. Roaming the Black Hills were elk, moose, mountain sheep, mule deer, bobcats, mountain lions, wolves, brown bears, and grizzlies. If a warrior was brave enough to face the ferocious grizzly with spear and bow, he could proudly wear a bear claw necklace.

Overhead circled vultures, hawks, and eagles, who were the messengers of the Great Spirit in this wild, dramatic land. All the four-leggeds, as the animals were known, and all the winged ones were relatives of the two-leggeds, or humans. Every Sioux prayer ended with the words "Mitakuye oyasin," which means "And all my relations." These relatives included not only people but all living plants and animals, from the smallest insect and the most fragile flower to the sacred buffalo, all of whom were warmed by the same sun and bound together as one in the universe. As expressed in a prayer by the Oglala Sioux holy man Black Elk: "Grandfather, Great Spirit, once more behold me on earth and learn to hear my feeble voice. You lived first, and you are older than all need, older than all prayer. All things belong to you—the two-legged, the four-legged, the wings of the air, and all green things that live."

# 2. A Wandering People

The massive sculpture of Crazy Horse seems to be keeping watch over the Black Hills, which rise up in the heart of Sioux country.

After the Sioux crossed the Missouri River, or *Mni Shoshe* (Big Muddy), they came to depend almost entirely on the buffalo. Moving over the grasslands with the buffalo herds, they hunted whenever they needed food or materials for clothing and shelter. Living in cone-shaped tipis made from wooden poles and buffalo hides, they followed the cycle of the seasons or "moons." Each of these moons reflected a change in weather and activity.

## Lakota Moons

| | |
|---|---|
| January | Moon of the Hard Winter |
| February | Moon of Popping Trees |
| March | Moon of Snow Blindness |
| April | Moon of Tender Grass |
| May | Moon of Green Leaves |
| June | Moon of June Berries |
| July | Moon of Red Cherries |
| August | Moon of Ripening |
| September | Moon of Colored Leaves |
| October | Moon of Falling Leaves |
| November | Moon of Starting Winter |
| December | Moon of Middle Winter |

The Sioux spent the winter at the foot of the Black Hills, which offered shelter from the cold winds sweeping across the plains. April meant spring and the beginning of a new year. Men hunted deer, elk, bear, and antelope, as well as wild turkey, prairie chickens, and rabbits, while the women gathered wild berries and fruit. Before moving out to the plains, they gave the buffalo time to fatten on the tender green grasses.

The Sioux formed themselves into groups, or bands, of family members called *tiyospayes*. Each band had one or more leaders of equal power, usually older men, chosen because of their wealth and wisdom. A chief had to be brave, honest, and intelligent, or he would be replaced by another warrior. In addition to keeping order in the village, these men decided when the group would move to another place, when they should go on a buffalo hunt, and where they would set up camp. They usually consulted medicine men to determine the best time for the hunt and then sent scouts ahead to locate the herds.

In addition to the older men who served as chiefs, young men who had proven themselves in battle became war leaders. No one had to join a war party, but if the leader had been successful, other warriors were usually eager to ride with him. None of the leaders had great authority. Living in small groups, the Sioux did not need an elaborate political organization. They relied primarily on public ridicule and gossip to punish those who broke the rules. Occasionally, a council of older men gathered to make a decision regarding a dispute, but they lacked the authority to enforce their ruling. Those men who had acquired guardian spirits also joined the *Akichita*, a kind of police force that kept order during buffalo hunts and relocations of the camp. Offenders were whipped with a rawhide lash, had their bows broken, or might even have their

**T**his Sioux woman carries a heavy load of firewood through the winter snow. Women worked hard for their families, not only cooking meals and sewing clothes, but making the tipis in which they lived. Photograph by Edward Curtis.

**A** *Sioux medicine man gazes proudly into the prairie sky. Men were expected to face danger and even death with courage, in battle and during the buffalo hunt. Photograph by Edward Curtis.*

tipi and belongings destroyed. Most important, however, were a man's reputation as a hunter and warrior and a woman's merit as a mother and wife. Strength and skill were necessary to survive on the open plains, yet generosity was also revered in "giveaways." A man who owned many horses was honored, yet he was expected to share his food and belongings with the less fortunate members of the band.

*These Brulé Sioux are encamped in Dakota Territory. The Sioux often set up their tipis near streams, which offered a source of water for their horses and themselves. Photograph by John C. H. Grabill, 1890.*

Sioux families included not only children and parents but also grandparents and unmarried aunts and uncles. Grandmothers often helped with household chores and took care of the young children. Although men headed the household, children traced their heritage through both parents. The social order of the *tiyospayes* was formed by male relatives—fathers, sons, and brothers. When a young man married he usually remained with

his father's band. This was partly because large groups of men had to cooperate in many dangerous tasks, notably hunting and warfare. The Sioux believed that men who had grown up together tended to get along better.

Good manners governed the tipi in which several families often made their home. When people gathered around the fire for meals and conversation the men always sat on buffalo rugs on the north side and women on the south side. The head of the household held the place of honor within the circle at the back of the tipi, along with his willow backrest, pipe rack, and sacred things. It was considered impolite to walk between a person and the fire. Men, especially visitors, were always served meals first. Women and children had to wait until the warriors were finished.

The Sioux loved to get together with others, and buffalo humps or other tasty meats were always bubbling in the stew pot. The tipi was a good place to play the moccasin game, to sing sacred songs, to tell stories, or to boast of one's great deeds. Men loved to gamble and seldom undertook a contest that didn't involve a wager on its outcome. Everyone enjoyed guessing games. In the moccasin game a pebble was placed under one of three soft leather shoes. Adults bet on which moccasin covered the pebble. Bragging was not only tolerated but encouraged among the Sioux who needed to be strong and brave to hunt the buffalo, defeat their enemies, and endure the cold winters. Visits usually ended by smoking a pipe, which was passed solemnly from one person to another as the sweet fragrance of tobacco drifted through the tipi.

# Tipis

To make tipis, men traveled to the mountains to cut down long, slender pine trees to make the lodge poles. The strong, light poles were dried in the sun, then hauled to the village. To set up the frame, women tied three of the wooden poles together, raised the end up, and spread out the bottom legs. They next placed eight or ten smaller poles around this frame.

Originally, the Sioux sheathed their lodges with bark, but when they moved onto the plains they began to cover them with buffalo skins. To prepare the skins, women spread fresh hides on the ground and scraped away the fat and flesh with bone or antler blades. After the hides had dried, they scraped off the shaggy hair. After soaking the hides in water for several days, they vigorously rubbed in a mixture of animal fat, brains, and liver to soften the hides. They rinsed the hides and worked them back and forth over a rawhide thong to further soften them. Finally, the hides were smoked over a fire, which gave them a pleasing tan color.

Several women cooperated in making a tipi covering. About fifteen tanned hides were laid out in a shape to cover the tipi and stitched together. The hide covering was tied to a pole and raised, then wrapped around the cone-shaped frame and held together with wooden pins. Two wing-shaped flaps at the top were turned back to make a smoke hole that could be closed to keep out the rain. Always facing east to greet the rising sun, the U-shaped doorway was covered with a hide flap. Sometimes women decorated the top of the doorway with porcupine quills, feathers,

The tipi, seen here from the front and the side, could be easily set up and taken down. Made with wooden poles and buffalo skins, the movable, tentlike homes were well suited to the nomadic life of the Sioux.

and horsetails stitched onto rawhide strips.

The design of the tipi allowed people to remain cool in the summer and relatively warm in the winter. During a heat wave, the bottom edges could be rolled up to allow the cooling breezes to flow over the inhabitants. During the winter, rocks and soil were shoved against the tipi to create a berm, or earthen wall, for greater insulation. Tipis also had a buffalo hide dew cloth hung on the inside walls from about shoulder-height down to the damp ground. Decorated with paintings of battles, dreams, and visions, dew cloths not only kept out moisture, but created pockets of insulating air. With a fire burning in the center of the earthen floor, the tipis stayed warm in the winter. According to an old Sioux saying: "A beautiful tipi is like a good mother. She hugs her children to her and protects them from heat and cold, snow and rain."

The tipi made a very practical home for the nomadic Sioux. Working together, several women could easily set up or take down a tipi in a few minutes. They used the tipi poles as a travois to carry the tipi covering and their other belongings. The poles were strapped to a horse or a large dog's shoulders and the other end dragged along the ground.

Originally, the only Sioux work animals were half-wild dogs—in fact, the dog was the only domesticated animal kept by any Native American tribe. The Sioux raised a large, powerful breed similar to the husky for carrying bundles and pulling travois. These dogs also kept watch at night. A smaller breed of dog was raised for food. Around 1750, the Sioux acquired their first horses from the Cheyennes. By the 1800s, millions of wild horses ranged throughout the American West, and the Sioux used horses rather than dogs as burden carriers.

The Sioux greatly admired horses, which could pull heavier loads than dogs and carry people swiftly across the plains. The Sioux had no word for these animals, so they called them *shunka wakan*, which means the "sacred dog." Men captured and broke wild horses, but preferred to acquire horses that had already been broken. Stealing horses from another tribe became a daring sport among the Plains Indians. A successful raid brought status and war honors, and the size of a family's herd became a symbol of wealth. Generosity was among the highest virtues of the Sioux, and the giving of horses was especially respected. Horses also became a primary means of exchange—a man could trade horses for a wife or a rifle.

Frequently on the move, the Sioux no longer planted corn or made pottery. Why labor in the fields or stalk elusive game in the woods when men could jump on their horses and race after the buffalo herds? In a single hunt, they could provide enough meat to feed their families for months, as well as hides and bones for making tipis and tools. Household goods also had to be light and durable, so they could be carried by a person, a dog, or later a horse. The Sioux did not make pottery because it could be broken on their long journeys. Food, clothing, and other personal belongings were transported in leather pouches called *parfleches*

*R*iding *their swift horses, brave Sioux men pursued the fleeing buffalo and brought down the huge beasts with arrows and spears.*

(par FLESH es). Skins and other animal parts were used to store food and water.

The entire village could be packed up to follow a herd of buffalo in a matter of minutes. The Sioux depended on the buffalo, which gave its life so the people could live. The band might stay in one place for a few weeks, if the herds continued to graze there, or trudge constantly along in pursuit of the thundering beasts. Usually they made camp near streams and woods. They needed water for cooking and drinking and trees for firewood. Constantly at war with the other Plains tribes, the Sioux chose sites that could be defended against attack. They often had favorite camping places to which they returned season after season.

# 3. Lifeways

The Sioux made their homes in temporary clusters of tipis, moving often to follow the herds of buffalo over the broad grasslands of the Great Plains. Painting by George Catlin.

SIOUX LIFE CENTERED ON EXTENDED FAMILIES OF CHILDREN, PARENTS, grandparents, and aunts and uncles. These large families were essential because many parents—both fathers and mothers—died in wars and hunting accidents and from disease and hardship. If children lost one or both of their parents, through either death or divorce, they remained secure because they had many relatives within the band to look after them.

## Cycle of Life

**Birth.** When a woman was about to give birth, she remained in her tipi with one or more older women who served as midwives. Men were not allowed in the tipi during or immediately after the delivery.

Upon the birth of a child, the umbilical cord was put into a beaded bag shaped like a turtle because these shelled creatures enjoyed long lives. The magical bag was fastened to the cradleboard. An identical charm, without the umbilical cord, was placed outside, perhaps in a tree, to fool any evil spirits that might harm the baby.

The birth of a child was a joyous occasion. Within four days, a feast was held to name the newborn, usually after its oldest living grandparent. As children grew up, they would receive additional names based on their character traits.

**Childhood.** Parents did not have more children than they could care for. Often they waited until a child was five or six years old

*Sioux mothers and fathers cared deeply for their children. This photograph of a mother carrying her baby on her back was taken by Edward Curtis in the early twentieth century.*

before having another baby. Families were not large; they usually had four or five children. Parents looked upon their children as their most precious gift. Children were never beaten and rarely punished; they learned to be generous with others and to respect elders. From an early age, they were also treated as adults and allowed to make their own decisions. Yet parents encouraged their children to follow the example of the men who had become the best hunters and warriors, and the women who had become most accomplished in providing food, clothing, and shelter.

Children grew up with aunts and uncles, as well as grandparents and other family members fussing over them and gently encouraging them to follow time-honored beliefs handed down through the generations. The grandparents, other family members, and friends of the family often served as a second set of parents.

Boys usually identified strongly with their father and his family. They were given small bows and arrows to practice shooting at toy buffaloes. Playing with handmade dolls and toy tipis, girls remained close to their mother and her family.

Children were allowed great freedom, and the whole outdoors became their playground. During the summer, girls and boys played in the water and became fine swimmers. They played rough-and-tumble games of running, jumping, and fighting intended to build strength and endurance—traits needed to survive a rugged life as nomadic hunters and warriors. They raced each other on foot and on horseback. Boys formed balls of mud on sticks and flung the mud at each other until the loser was completely covered. In "shooting the buffalo" boys practiced hunting skills by shooting an arrow through a hoop rolled across the prairie grass.

After the buffalo hunt, when their families settled for the winter along wooded streams, the children played "throwing it in," a game in which they spun a top over the ice. They sledded on curved buffalo ribs and slid across the ice on stiff buffalo hides. During these cold months, they also enjoyed stories told by their grandfathers. These stories recounted the adventures of the trickster Iktomi or recalled heroic deeds during battle or on a buffalo hunt. Children learned the history and customs of their people by listening to these legends.

Like other Native Americans, the Sioux did not have a written language; their history was passed down through a rich oral tradition. To help the storytellers remember, old wise men kept the "winter count," picture writing on tanned buffalo hides that recalled the key event of that year. For example, the "winter when the people died of smallpox," was represented by a face with red dots. Some of these winter counts go back over two hundred years.

**Coming-of-Age.** As he approached manhood, a young boy went on a vision quest. This spiritual journey began with purification in a sweat lodge under the guidance of a medicine man. The boy was then taken to a hilltop where he remained alone for four days and nights to "cry for a dream." Some families dug

A grandfather instructs several children in the history of the Sioux people in this 1951 watercolor by Oscar Howe. The Sioux relied on stories to ensure that their ways lived on from one generation to the next.

special vision pits in the hillside. Here, the boy huddled and gazed into the sky for enlightenment.

Sometimes relatives made a flesh offering for the boy. They cut small pieces of skin from their arms, placed them in a gourd, and gave them to the boy. He would be strengthened by knowing that dear friends and relatives had undergone pain for his sake.

Fasting alone, enduring the hot sun or pelting rain during the day, and listening to the howl of wolves at night, the boy sought a vision that would guide him in life. After four days, the medicine man brought him back home and interpreted his dreams for him. Men and sometimes women went on vision quests many times during their lives, but the first "crying for a dream" was the defining time of a boy's life.

At the onset of her first menstrual cycle, a girl also underwent a time of seeking to know herself. An old woman stayed with her for four days while the girl prayed and did her chores. The old woman then took her to the medicine man who interpreted her dreams, after which the old woman bathed and dressed the girl in new clothes. Two or three weeks later, a feast was held for the girl. At this celebration, people danced and sang to honor her becoming a woman.

**Marriage.** Until about 1750, Sioux marriages were often arranged by the parents. Gradually, this custom gave way to young men and women choosing their own partners. A man usually tried to win honors in battle and hunting and acquire many horses before courting a young woman. Visiting her tipi, he sometimes played songs for her on a flute. If he thought she liked him, he would offer one or more horses as a gift to her parents.

Since many warriors lost their lives in battle, it was not uncommon for a man to have two or more wives, especially if he was a man of wealth and standing. Usually sisters, these wives shared housekeeping chores, and their husband had to be able to supply enough meat for his large family. Women were then assured of having a husband, and more children were born in the band.

Marriage was an agreement to live together, with no vows spoken, and an exchange of gifts between the families. Women were encouraged to marry and bear children. Virtue was expected of both men and women. If a woman was unfaithful to her husband, she could be disfigured by having her nose cut off. Marriage was meant to last a lifetime, but divorces did occur. If a couple did not get along, the wife simply placed her husband's belongings outside the tipi. A man who wanted a divorce announced that he had "thrown his wife away" and did not come home.

**Death.** When death came in battle or through old age, people were expected to face the moment with courage. However, after a person died, relatives entered a period of deep mourning.

The body of the deceased was placed in the branches of a tree or on a wooden platform called a burial scaffold. Personal

*The Sioux had great respect for the dead. In this 1880 painting by H. C. Yarrow, the body was carefully wrapped and placed upon a burial scaffold. Raised high up in the air, the deceased would be closer to the spirits.*

belongings and offerings of food were tucked next to the body to comfort the soul. The favorite horse of the deceased was often killed so that its spirit might accompany the departed on its journey to the spiritual world.

## Warfare

Trusted allies of the Cheyenne, the Sioux were continually at war with the Pawnee, Crow, and other tribes that lived at the fringes of their hunting grounds. Warfare among the Plains Indians was an exhilarating, if dangerous sport, much like jousting. Many were killed or seriously wounded, and despite the honor of falling in battle, the primary goal was to come back alive. After a victory, a war chief was humbled if he lost even one man. For young warriors, the main purpose of going into battle was "counting coup," which was as important as scalping dead enemies. Warriors counted coup by getting close enough to an enemy to touch him with a coup stick. Shooting an enemy from a distance was not as heroic or dangerous as riding or running up close enough to touch him with a hand or a stick. Small parties of young men eager to distinguish themselves in battle often joined an experienced leader "whose medicine was good" or who was known for his skill and luck. These war parties made hit-and-run raids on enemy camps to steal horses, which were also a way of counting coup or avenging a relative who had been killed in a skirmish. These young men were usually members of one of the warrior societies, such as the Strong Hearts or the Kit Foxes. The highly renowned Kit Foxes

**W**ith several men in full headdress, this band of warriors gathered on a
rise to plan a raid on a rival group. Photograph by Edward Curtis.

wore a sash, which they staked to the ground during battle. This bold act meant the warrior intended to stand his ground until he defeated his enemies or was killed. The Kit Foxes sang:

*I am a Fox.*
*I am supposed to die.*
*If there is anything difficult,*
*If there is anything dangerous,*
*That is mine to do.*

The Sioux sometimes adopted captured enemies. During one battle, the great chief Sitting Bull encountered an eleven-year-old boy who courageously faced the warriors with his little bow and one last arrow. Sitting Bull shouted, "This boy is brave! I take him for my brother!" Named Jumping Bull, the boy grew up to become a renowned Sioux warrior and Sitting Bull's best friend.

## Buffalo Hunting

Using lances and arrows, men hunted buffalo in several ways. One man might track a single animal. Or small hunting parties might sweep down on several buffalo at once. In the late summer, large communal hunts—carefully planned undertakings—involved the entire band. At this time, men were not allowed to hunt alone and possibly trigger a stampede of the entire herd. Sometimes everyone in the band—men, women, and children—

**H**erds of buffalo once covered the Great Plains, ranging as far eastward as the Appalachian Mountains. The Sioux waited until the buffalo fattened on the tender grass of spring before hunting them.

formed a V and stampeded a herd over a cliff or into a corral made of stones and brush. Another practice was to set a circle of small fires around the buffalo, which were afraid to cross the flames and smoke. The animals were then easily killed. Best known were the big hunts in which all the men in the band galloped after the buffalo, spearing or shooting the animals with arrows as their horses drew alongside them.

Boys took part in the big hunt soon after they learned to ride their spirited horses. Initially, they served as water boys and fire keepers while they learned how the men hunted the magnificent beasts. The killing of his first buffalo was a major, defining event in the life of a teenage boy. Afterward, his father held a feast in his honor and the boy received many gifts. He might also receive a new name to acknowledge his courageous deed.

After the buffalo hunt, the women came to prepare the carcasses, and people enjoyed plenty of fresh meat. The liver and other organs that spoiled quickly in the summer heat, as well as the delicious tongue, hump meat, and ribs, were cooked and eaten right away. Much of the fresh meat, however, was packed on travois and hauled to camp. This red meat was thinly sliced and hung on poles in the sun. Smoke from fires burning beneath the wooden racks helped to keep the flies away and quicken the drying process. Women sometimes pounded the dried meat, called jerky, and mixed it with fat and berries to make pemmican, which men ate on long trips. But most of the dried meat was stored for the lean months of winter. Everyone shared the meat—

giving was very important to the Sioux, especially to those who were the ablest hunters and warriors.

Aside from the buffalo meat, families made use of the horns, hides, and bones. No part of these revered animals was ever wasted. Men made tools—knives, scrapers, and needles—from the bones while the women turned hides into tipi covers, blankets, clothes, and moccasins. Rawhide was made into drums and war shields. Horns were fashioned into spoons, cups, and ladles.

Nearly two hundred different articles could be made from parts of the buffalo's body. Stretched over a frame, the hides became a makeshift boat for river crossings. The thick neck skin made good shields. Scraped to resemble white parchment, skins were folded into parfleches. The hooves were turned into rattles and even the tail made a good flyswatter. Rawhide strips were twisted into sturdy ropes and sinew was used as sewing thread. Bones were made into knives and scrapers, smoking pipes, and toys for the children. Most important, the painted skull became the altar for religious ceremonies.

## Food

In addition to making tipis, hardworking women undertook the arduous tasks of providing food for their families. Women gathered fruits, seeds, and berries, and dug wild potatoes and prairie turnips. Pemmican could be eaten without further preparation, but most meats, whether fresh or dried, had to be roasted over a fire or boiled. To boil food, women dug a pit in the ground which they lined with animal skins and filled with water—or they used the lining of a buffalo stomach. The lining was stretched over the pit between four sticks and filled with water. Heated stones were then dropped into the makeshift pot for cooking meat and vegetables.

Meals often included stew with wild turnips and buffalo meat. One popular dessert was *wojapi*, which is still made by Sioux mothers for their children.

*Women hung strips of buffalo meat on racks to dry in the sun. Using every part of the animal, they also dried skins for making tipi covers, pouches, and other belongings. Photograph by Edward Curtis.*

# Wojapi

Here is a modern version of this dish, which has long been a favorite dessert among the Sioux. It is usually served with fry bread, but you can use pita bread cut into small wedges to dip into the fruit pudding.

### Ingredients:

1 16-ounce can of blueberry
pie filling
Cornstarch (enough to thicken)
Sugar to taste

Traditionally, this dish was made with pounded chokeberries, boysenberries, or blueberries. Today, like Sioux mothers, you can heat blueberry pie filling in a saucepan on the stove. Add a teaspoon or so of cornstarch to thicken the mixture as it heats. Sweeten the pudding with one or two teaspoons of sugar.

# Clothing

Women also made moccasins and clothing for their families from tanned deer or elk hides—knee-length dresses and leggings with buckskin fringes for themselves and sleeveless shirts, breechcloths, and leggings for the boys and men. To keep warm in winter, they wrapped themselves in buffalo robes. Often, the women decorated clothing and moccasins with porcupine quills that had been dyed many colors. The hollow quills were cut into uniform lengths and sewn on like beads. Women embroidered moccasins with quills as a token of love for their husbands, sons, and brothers. Quilling required many hours of painstaking work, and women were admired for the quality of their artistry. When the Sioux began to exchange goods with European traders, they acquired glass beads, which quickly replaced quillwork as decorations.

Men used dyes to paint designs on their clothing. Some people painted or tattooed their bodies; children usually had their ears pierced when they were five or six years old. Men and women also wore necklaces and armbands of beads and bone. Both men and women plaited their hair in two braids, weaving in colorful beads or cloth, although older women often wore their hair down. Some men shaved the sides of their head to make a "roach," or Mohawk-style haircut. Young men wore a single feather in their hair while older war leaders often donned their warbonnets. Notches were clipped in the feathers to indicate the exact deed of the warrior— killed an enemy, killed an enemy and took his scalp, or cut an

**O**n important occasions, including ceremonies and battles, boys and men often wore elaborate quillwork and feathers, as well as jewelry.

**M**en's leather clothing—shirts and leggings—was decorated with fine quillwork. As seen in this Karl Bodmer painting of Big Soldier, a Dakota chief, men also wore feathers in their hair.

**I**n this Edward Curtis photograph, three Sioux chiefs posed on horseback in traditional clothing, including full headdresses made from eagle feathers.

enemy's throat—as well as the number of coups the warrior had counted and the number of times he had been wounded in battle. Feathers were also used to decorate spears, quivers, shields, warbonnets, and pipes.

On special occasions men sewed scalps into their clothing and wore headdresses adorned with many feathers, to show off their prowess as a warrior. In battle, they proudly wore their headdresses. Warriors had risked their lives to earn each of the feathers, which were symbols of honor—counting coup, stealing horses, or saving a person's life. They painted their faces and their horses with bright colors before going into battle to encourage the spirits to protect them.

# 4. Beliefs

Music and dance have always been an important part of religious celebrations among the Sioux. Even today, brightly painted drums keep the rhythm at powwows and other traditional gatherings.

TO THIS DAY, THE SIOUX BELIEVE THAT MANY DIFFERENT KINDS of spirits inhabit the supernatural world, all of whom are *wakan*, or sacred. *Wakan Tanka* (wahKAHN tahnkah), the Great Spirit, or Great Mystery, includes all of these spirits, the most important of which are *Wi*, the sun, *Skan*, the sky, and *Maka*, the earth. The sun and sky are considered male, while the earth is female and the symbol of birth, nurturing, and growth. Other important spirits are the winds, the four directions, the buffalo, and the bear. As Flat-Iron, an Oglala Sioux chief, once said, "From Wakan Tanka, the Great Mystery, comes all power. It is from Wakan Tanka that the holy man has wisdom and the power to heal and make holy charms. Man knows that all healing plants are given by Wakan Tanka, therefore they are holy. So too is the buffalo holy, because it is the gift of Wakan Tanka."

The pipe is still the most sacred of Sioux objects. Representing the flesh and blood of the Sioux, the red stone bowl of the pipe is the head and the wooden stem is the spine, fitted together to make the whole person. There is no balance in the world without this harmonious union of mind and body. The tobacco represents all living green plants. The smoke is the breath of the people rising in prayer to Wakan Tanka. The stem is decorated with porcupine quills and the bowl is carved from red pipestone dug from a quarry in western Minnesota. The quarry is holy ground to native peoples, where one may not raise a weapon. In the past, enemies dug peacefully together, and no one could be attacked as they journeyed to or from the quarry.

The Pipestone Quarry in present-day Minnesota was a sacred place. The Sioux traveled many miles to dig up pieces of red stone, which they fashioned into pipe bowls. Painting by George Catlin.

According to Sioux legend, the sacred pipe was brought to the people by White Buffalo Woman. Along with the pipe, she brought rituals to guide the people on the right way of life. After she had presented her gifts, she bid farewell, strode over a hill into the sunset, and changed into a white buffalo. Here is the story, adapted from a version told by Dakota chronicler Iron Shell, which recounts the origin of the pipe and the seven sacred ceremonies.

## "White Buffalo Calf"

And so it was, Whope, the daughter of Wi, the Sun, and Hanwi, the Moon, dressed in lovely clothes, appeared to two young scouts. So radiant was her countenance, so perfect was her figure, that the two men fell in love with her.

As they beheld her, she spoke to them, "I am of the Buffalo People. I have been sent to this earth to talk with your people. Go to your leader and tell him to have a council tipi set up in the center of the village. The door of the tipi must face east. Spread sage at the place of honor. Behind the fireplace, soften a square of the earth and place a buffalo skull there with a small rack behind it. I have matters of great consequence to share with your people. I shall come to the village at dawn."

As she spoke, one of the scouts was so struck by her charm that he approached Whope. There was a crash of thunder and a cloud enveloped them both. As the cloud drifted away, the other scout beheld the lovely woman standing untouched, but at her feet lay the skeleton of the young warrior. She then directed the scout to carry her message to his people.

The scout returned to the camp and told the chief, Buffalo-Who-Walks-Standing-Upright, about his encounter with the woman. Preparations were made for welcoming this mysterious stranger according to her instructions. An escort of virtuous young men was chosen to lead her through the village to the tipi. By daybreak, a large group of people had gathered around the council tipi in anticipation of her arrival.

As the sun rose in the east, the beautiful woman appeared over the horizon. She carried a pipe stem in her right hand and a red pipe bowl in her left hand, which she joined together. In a stately manner, she walked through the village, entered the council tipi, circled to the left of the door, and sat down at the place of honor. When she was seated, the chief welcomed her.

Arising and holding the pipe, the woman told them that Wakan Tanka was pleased with the Sioux people, and that she, as a representative of the Buffalo People, was proud to be their sister. She told them that because they had preserved good against evil and harmony against conflict, the Sioux had been chosen to receive the pipe, which she held on behalf of all mankind. The pipe was to be the symbol of peace and was to be used as such between men and nations. Smoking the pipe was to be a bond of good faith, and a holy man smoking the pipe would be in communion with Wakan Tanka.

She addressed the women as her sisters, saying that in life they bore great difficulties and sorrow, but in their kindness they comforted others in time of trouble and grief. By giving birth to

*S*tanding by their tipi, two Sioux men call upon the great spirits. The Sioux honored their heritage through religious ceremonies and stories such as "White Buffalo Calf." Photograph by Edward Curtis.

children, by clothing and feeding them, by being faithful as wives, they maintained their families. Wakan Tanka had planned it so, and he was with them in their times of sorrow. Next she spoke to the children as little brothers and sisters and told them to respect their parents who loved them and made sacrifices on their behalf.

To the men she spoke as a sister, telling them that all things upon which they depended came from the earth, the sky, and the four winds. The pipe was to be used to offer sacrifices and prayers to Wakan Tanka for all the blessings of life—and it was to be offered daily. She told them to be kind and loving to their women and children.

Whope told the chief it was his duty to honor the pipe, since through the pipe the nation lived. As a sacred object, the pipe was to be used in times of war, famine, sickness, or any other extreme need. She instructed Buffalo-Who-Walks-Standing-Upright in the proper use of the pipe, and she revealed the seven sacred ceremonies that the Sioux were to practice: purification, vision seeking, the Sun Dance, the ball throwing, making a buffalo woman, making as brothers, and owning a spirit. She stayed with the people for four days. Before leaving, she lit the pipe with a buffalo chip and offered it first to Skan, then to Maka, then to Four Winds. She smoked and passed the pipe to the leader. When he had smoked, she announced that her mission was completed, and laying the pipe against the rack, she left the tipi.

As she walked away from the village, fading into the distance, she became a White Buffalo Calf. In this way, Whope, the daughter of Wi and Hanwi, had returned to the earth to teach mankind. From that day forward, whenever a white buffalo appeared in a herd, no kills were made in that herd. The herd was sacred. And for more than ten generations the descendants of Buffalo-Who-Walks-Standing-Upright have cared for the sacred pipe on behalf of the Sioux people.

## Ceremonies and Dances

Most Sioux boys were brought up to be warriors, but they could become holy men as well. These medicine men were honored for their ability to interpret dreams and visions. Among the most curious were the *heyokas*, who were also known as the thunder-dreamers, or forward-backward men. If a young man dreamed of the Thunderbird, thunder, or lightning, he had to act out his dream by becoming a *heyoka*. He had to do everything backward—say "good morning" in the evening and ride his horse backward—no matter how embarrassing. He became the sacred clown. But he also helped people to interpret their dreams, which is how the Sioux believed messages were received from the spirits. Despite his supernatural powers, a *heyoka* led a very difficult, unhappy life. To be freed of this role, a *heyoka* plunged his bare arm into a kettle of boiling water and retrieved a chunk of meat. He was not burned, probably because his arm had been smeared with a special herbal salve.

Many religious ceremonies were held in the sweat lodge, a small, domed hut made by draping buffalo skins over bent willow

*T*hree Oglala Sioux men gathered before an altar in a tipi in this Edward Curtis photograph. The buffalo skull in the foreground was the most important part of the altar.

branches. Inside the sweat lodge, people chanted songs, spoke their deepest thoughts, and prayed to Wakan Tanka. Four times the water was poured over the hot stones and four times the entrance flap was lifted, because, like the four winds and the four directions, this number was sacred. The pipe was passed from hand to hand, and the fragrance of sweet tobacco blended with the vapor within the lodge.

Sweat lodge rituals included purification when a boy embarked on a vision quest. An adult relative or medicine man usually guided the boy on his first "sweat." Participants huddled around a pit in the absolute dark of the sweat lodge. Outside, rocks were heated in a fire until they glowed red-hot. Then, they were carried on sticks, one by one, into the sweat lodge. As the medicine man prayed and poured water over the stones, the sweat lodge filled with hot steam—the sacred breath of Wakan Tanka. This steam cleansed the body and the soul. If the heat became too intense, the boy might cry out, "All my relations!" and the entrance flap was opened.

Among the important Sioux ceremonies was the *yuwipi*. Participants first cleared the tipi and laid out a sacred square with many small bundles of tobacco. They set up an altar consisting of a buffalo skull, a black and red staff, an eagle feather, and a deer tail. The floor was then strewn with sacred sage. Everyone had a twig of sage in their hair to receive the words from the spirits. In this ceremony, the medicine man, as interpreter between the spirits and the people, was rolled up in a blanket. The yuwipi took place in utter darkness. The only sounds were the rhythmic beat of the drum and a singer's chant, but soon eerie noises surfaced from the dark—high, birdlike, otherworldly. People heard the cry of the eagle and felt the touch of its wings on the walls. Tiny ghostly lights danced through the dark, and someone announced, "The spirits are here." At the end of the solemn ceremony, the yuwipi man was unwrapped and he explained the messages of the spirits who had visited them.

Whether settled in winter camp or wandering the wide prairie, Sioux bands usually lived far away from each other. However, at

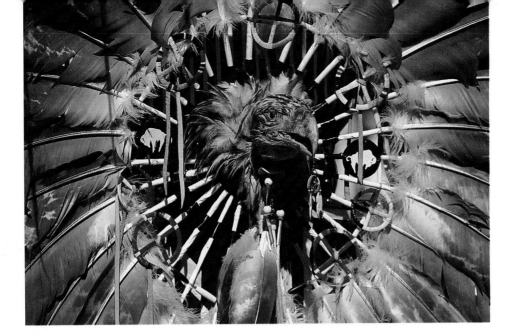

*F*lying high in the air where the spirits lived, the eagle has long been a sacred creature to the Sioux. Here, a dancer has drawn upon the spiritual power of the bird in the design of his war shield.

midsummer, the tiyospayes gathered on the plains for the Sun Dance, the greatest of Sioux ceremonies. They arranged their tipis in a circle, leaving the center open for visiting, ceremonies, songs, and games. Bands shared news about friends and enemies, as well as locations of the buffalo herds. Young people courted and old people gossiped at the large gathering. The men shared the sacred pipe and, with the rising smoke, sent promises upward to Wakan Tanka.

But the Sun Dance was the primary reason they had come together. This twelve-day event was a prayer to the sun and its warming rays, the source of life and renewal. It was also a sacrifice in which men showed courage and the ability to withstand excruciating pain. At the center of the dance circle stood the

For hundreds of years, the Sioux have celebrated their way of life in dance and prayer. Here, a young man silhouetted against the setting sun continues the proud traditions of his people.

Sacred Pole, a forked cottonwood tree. Flags of the sacred colors of red, white, black, and yellow, which represented the four directions, fluttered from the pole.

The men wrapped red skirts around their waists and placed sage wreaths in their hair. Gazing at the sun and rhythmically blowing eagle bone whistles, they danced for four days. The skin of their chests was then pierced with sharp sticks tied to rawhide thongs and the Sacred Pole. At the end of the dance, the men had to tear themselves loose, the sticks ripping through their flesh. Women also pierced their wrists or collarbones. Sun Dancers underwent these ordeals to help unfortunate friends and relatives by assuming their pain.

To this day, most Sioux people have kept their religion, their language, and many of the old customs. They still follow many of the rituals and consult the medicine men. They also continue to believe in the sacred circle, as eloquently expressed by Black Elk: "You have noticed that everything an Indian does is in a circle, and that is because the Power of the World always works in circles, and everything tries to be round. . . . The Sky is round, and I have heard that the earth is round like a ball, and so are all the stars. The wind, in its greatest power, whirls. Birds make their nests in circles, for theirs is the same religion as ours."

# 5. Changing World

This gathering of hundreds of tipis near Fort Pierre in present-day South Dakota was painted by George Catlin.

THE SIOUX WERE FRIENDLY WITH THE EXPLORERS, TRAPPERS, and traders who first ventured onto the plains. The fiercely independent trappers came to prefer the wilds of the prairies and mountains to the cities of the East. They learned the native languages, lived and dressed like Native Americans, and many of the men married Indian women. The traders brought wonderful new goods, which quickly became essential to the Sioux—rifles, gunpowder, lead, matches, blankets, coffee, and sugar. They exchanged steel knives and axes, iron kettles, cloth, and blankets, as well as glass beads and ribbons for furs and hides. Unfortunately, the traders also brought whiskey, which destroyed the body and soul of the Indian, and disease—smallpox and measles—which wiped out entire villages.

During the American Revolution and the War of 1812, the Sioux sided with the British. In 1815, however, the eastern tribes signed friendship treaties with the United States. Ten years later, another treaty acknowledged that Sioux territory included much of present-day Wisconsin, Minnesota, Iowa, Missouri, the Dakotas, and Wyoming. However, in 1837, the Sioux were pressured into selling all their land east of the Mississippi River to the United States. Even more land was sold in 1851.

Out on the Great Plains, the Sioux generally remained at peace with the whites—until settlers on their westward journey began to cross Sioux hunting grounds in long wagon trains. As they traveled, kicking up dust and hunting to supply themselves with fresh meat, they disturbed the great herds of buffalo upon which

$\mathbf{F}$ollowing an attack on a Brulé Sioux village, thousands of people met in a council near Bear Butte to discuss whether or not to go to war with the settlers and soldiers. With the arrival of whites, the Sioux way of life changed forever.

the Sioux depended. Then people began to homestead on the prairie, laying claim to land that the Sioux had hunted for generations. The Sioux did not like the stream of settlers or the forts the army was building deep in their home country to protect the homesteaders.

Among the settlers was a young Mormon who had lost a lame cow on the range in the summer of 1854. A Sioux man killed and butchered the stray animal, after which the settler complained to Lieutenant John Grattan, who commanded Fort Laramie. The lieutenant was eager to make a name for himself and get promoted. He rode to the Sioux camp by the Platte River with thirty soldiers and two howitzers and demanded the surrender of the warrior who had killed the cow. Refusing to hand over the man, Sioux chief Conquering Bear agreed to pay for the cow, but Grattan rejected his offer and ordered his men to fire, killing Conquering Bear. Angry warriors rushed from their tipis and wiped out Grattan and his troops, sparking the Great Sioux War that swept over the territory like a prairie fire for the next thirty-seven years.

The pattern of this war was one of raids and surprise attacks by the Sioux as they fiercely resisted the westward advance, and brutal retaliation by American soldiers. For the most part, the war was not fought in the Plains Indian way of counting coup and winning eagle feathers. The soldiers zealously slaughtered women and children, as well as warriors. It became clear that the goal of the United States government was not simply to win the war but to annihilate the Sioux people.

In Minnesota, the Santee were already living on reservations, but they were starving because they had no rations. They protested to the agent, but he laughingly told them to eat grass. In what came to be known as the Minnesota Sioux Uprising of 1862, the Sioux revolted and many were killed, including several hundred settlers and soldiers. The cruel agent was the first to be shot dead. He was found with his mouth stuffed with grass. The uprising was put down, and thirty-eight Santee men were hanged in the largest mass execution in United States history.

Again and again, a truce was declared and men on both sides came together to sign a treaty. The Sioux always agreed to give up more of their land, and the Americans always promised that the Sioux would be allowed to live peacefully on their remaining land—and the treaties were always broken. In 1866, gold was discovered in Montana and in violation of the treaty, the Americans built a road through Sioux land. They also established forts to protect the prospectors along what came to be called the Bozeman Trail by the Americans and Thieves' Road by the Sioux.

In defense of their land, Red Cloud, a great Oglala Sioux chief, led three thousand warriors against Fort Philip Kearny. Captain William J. Fetterman, one of the leaders of the fort, was spoiling for a fight. One day the warriors attacked a company that had been sent out to cut firewood, and Captain Fetterman agreed to rescue the men. However, he and his men were led into an ambush and everyone, including Fetterman, was killed. Among the warriors was a young man who fought with distinction. He wore a magic pebble behind his ear and sprinkled sacred gopher dust on his

*T*he Red Cloud delegation, left to right: Red Dog, Little Wound, John Bridgeman (interpreter), Red Cloud, American Horse, and Red Shirt. The photograph was taken around the time of the battle over the Bozeman Trail.

horse to make him bulletproof. His name was Crazy Horse.

After the Fetterman Massacre, representatives negotiated another agreement with the Sioux, which became known as the Fort Laramie Treaty of 1868. The Sioux had to give up all the land west of the Missouri River and south of the Niobrara River. Again government officials assured the Sioux that neither white settlers nor gold seekers would be allowed on their land "as long as the sun shall shine and as long as the grass shall grow."

However, another controversial figure soon galloped onto the scene. General George Armstrong Custer was known as the Boy General and the Glory Hunter, but the Plains Indians simply called him Long Hair. Vain and ambitious, Custer surrounded himself with reporters. With one or two victories over the Indians, he expected to be nominated for the U.S. presidency. In 1873, he led an expedition through the Black Hills and reported, "There is gold at the grass roots." Gold seekers swarmed over the Black Hills, digging into the sacred land, and the government did nothing to stop them. In fact, the government ordered all Indians, including the Sioux, to abandon their nomadic way of life, settle on reservations in Dakota territory, and "walk the white man's road." They set a deadline of January 1876, after which all Indians not on the reservations would be considered "hostile."

Since the Sioux did not travel much in the winter, many didn't receive word of the order and those who had simply ignored it. Open season was declared upon the Sioux who joined with the Cheyenne under the leadership of Sitting Bull, who had been a great Sioux warrior but now guided his people as a medicine man. Among the war chiefs were Gall, Rain-in-the-Face, and Crazy Horse. The army planned a three-pronged attack to kill or capture the "hostiles" under the leadership of Generals Crook, Terry, and Custer.

In June 1876, the Sioux and Cheyenne held their annual Sun Dance at Medicine Rocks in Montana. Sitting Bull offered sacrifices to the Great Spirit and received a vision in which he saw many soldiers falling down. He told his people: "We will have a great victory." Soon after the celebration, the Sioux were attacked by U.S. soldiers. General Crook's troops first encountered the warriors, but after incurring losses and seeing the large number of Indians he retreated.

**I**n ceremonial dress, Sitting Bull, the proud, dignified Hunkpapa Sioux leader, sat for this portrait by David F. Barry in 1885. Sitting Bull was a great chief who later became a visionary medicine man.

On June 25, Custer approached the Indian encampment near Greasy Creek. Scouts advised him that there were too many warriors, but the arrogant Custer believed that his 7th Cavalry could defeat all the Indians of the Great Plains in a single battle. He was ordered to join General Terry at the Little Bighorn River on the twenty-seventh, but rushed to engage the Indians the day before because he wanted all the glory for the anticipated victory. Dividing his troops into several companies, he attacked the village, but was surprised to encounter so many warriors. Each of the companies was routed and Custer retreated up a hill. "Brave hearts follow me!" Crazy Horse shouted as he led his warriors against Custer. In less than a quarter of an hour, Crazy Horse and his warriors killed Custer and his 225 men. Only a horse named Comanche survived the fierce battle. A young warrior named White Bull, Sitting Bull's nephew, most likely dealt the death blow to Custer at the Little Bighorn. The fierce battle became the largest—and the last—victory for the Plains Indians.

Buffalo hunters did as much as soldiers to destroy the Sioux way of life. "Send them powder and lead, and let them kill, skin, and sell until they have exterminated the buffalo," urged General Phil Sheridan. "Then your prairies will be covered by speckled cattle and the festive cowboy, who follows the hunter as a second forerunner of civilization." Soon the prairie winds carried the stench of rotting carcasses as hunters killed thousands of the huge beasts. "Where have all the buffalo gone?" the Sioux began to ask themselves, hoping the great herds would again come thundering

*T*his depiction of the Battle of the Little Bighorn was painted by Stephen Standing Bear, a Lakota Sioux, who took part in the conflict. Every American soldier, including Colonel George Armstrong Custer, was killed in this battle.

over the horizon. But the buffalo had vanished, and the proud warriors were forced to surrender. If they did not, their women and children would have starved.

The free-spirited Sioux were shocked by reservation life in which they were imprisoned within barbed wire fences. Not only was their spirit ravaged, they were cold, hungry, and sick. The government had promised rations, blankets, and tools, but dishonest officials frequently stole everything. These were tragic days for the Sioux. "Friendly" Indians were turned against "hostiles," who wished to continue the old way of life. "One does not sell the land people walk on," Crazy Horse once said. He was

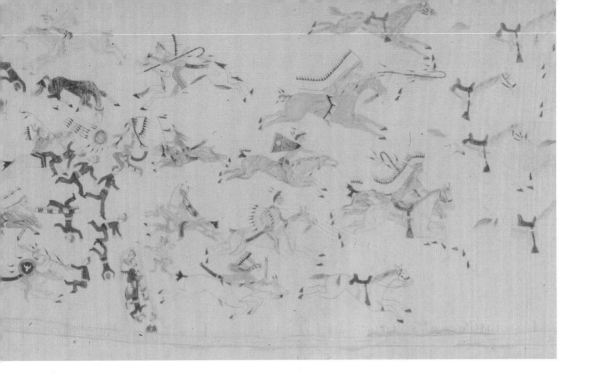

jailed in a small cell but fought for his liberty. As Crazy Horse tried to break away, two or three men grabbed his arms, and a soldier stabbed him with a bayonet. His family placed Crazy Horse's body on his horse and fled to the hills, where they buried the great chief. To this day, no one knows the location of his grave.

Without their leader, cold and starving, the Sioux plunged into despair. Then they heard a message that, far to the south, a Paiute medicine man name Wovoka, had died and come to life again. The spirits had given him a song and a dance that would bring all the slain warriors and the buffalo back to life. Wovoka's message became known as the Ghost Dance Religion, and it fired desperate hopes across the prairies.

*T*heir way of life coming to an end, this band of Sioux dancers under the leadership of Big Foot posed for this photograph taken by John C. H. Grabill on August 9, 1890, near the Cheyenne River in present-day South Dakota.

> *A new nation is coming,*
> *A new nation is coming,*
> *The buffalo nation is coming.*
> *We will live again,*
> *Says the father,*
> *Says the father.*

Dancers whirled feverishly in the Ghost Dance until they went into a trance. When they awoke, they told of seeing the buffalo rising from a hole in the earth. They saw the white people's fences and buildings rolling up in a carpet, under which lay the prairie of their ancestors. The Ghost Dance was based on prayer, dance, and song—not violence. Yet, late in 1890, the agent at the Pine Ridge Reservation called for soldiers to put down the dance of lost hopes. Among the soldiers was the 7th Cavalry, Custer's old regiment, who sought bloody vengeance against the Sioux.

On December 15, 1890, Indian police surrounded Sitting Bull's home. They tried to arrest the great chief and holy man, but a gun battle broke out. Sitting Bull, his young son Crow Foot, several of his followers, and six Indian police were killed in the ensuing outbreak. When word of Sitting Bull's death reached the Cheyenne River, the band of Ghost Dancers camping there under the leadership of Big Foot panicked. They fled toward Red Cloud, who was living at Pine Ridge. They hoped the great chief, a friend of the whites, would protect them.

The soldiers engaged the Ghost Dancers eighteen miles from Pine Ridge at a place called Wounded Knee. Big Foot and his people surrendered peacefully and made camp, surrounded by several hundred soldiers, among them the 7th Cavalry. The next morning, December 29, 1890, a shot rang out—no one knows if it came from a soldier or an Indian, or if there really was a shot at all on that bitterly cold day. With Hotchkiss cannons and repeating rifles, the soldiers fired upon the Sioux. Women and children tried to hide in a nearby ravine, but they were hunted down and ruthlessly murdered by the soldiers. By the time the soldiers stopped firing their guns, they had killed two hundred people. Afterward, the frozen bodies were stacked like firewood and buried in a mass grave.

The great Sioux holy man Black Elk, who was at Wounded Knee, later reflected: "When I look back now from this high hill of my old age, I can still see the butchered women and children lying heaped and scattered all along the crooked gulch as plain as when I saw them with eyes still young. And I can see that something else died there in that bloody mud . . . a people's dream died there . . . for the nation's hoop is broken and scattered. There is no center any longer and the sacred tree is dead."

## After the Indian Wars

From 1890 to 1934, destitute and forgotten, the Sioux barely survived. Living on the edge of starvation, with poor health care, they had shorter lives than other Americans. Schools were inadequate—some had only three grades—and there were few jobs on or near the reservations. Many men, once great warriors, sank into the despair of drink. Sioux traditions and religious beliefs were discouraged or outlawed. Rituals took place in secret. Forbidden as "self-torture," the Sun Dance was performed in hidden, out-of-the-way places. There was no freedom of religion for the Sioux people.

However, when Franklin Roosevelt was elected president, he appointed two men who were sympathetic to the plight of Native Americans: Harold Ickes as secretary of the interior and John Collier as commissioner of Indian affairs. The Sioux were allowed to openly practice their religion, and under the provisions of the Indian Reorganization Act of 1934 they were permitted to at least partly govern themselves. In addition to the tribal leadership, there was also a white superintendent on each reservation who exercised greater authority than the council. Major crimes were still handled by the F.B.I. and off-reservation courts. But tribal presidents and council members were popularly elected and tribal courts were established, along with tribal police forces. The Sioux gradually came to realize that they might once again have control over their own destinies.

*Over the course of the summer, the Sioux now hold powwows on their reservations in North and South Dakota. Here, a boy dances at a powwow held by the Brulé Sioux near Mitchell, South Dakota.*

# 6. New Ways

Powwows are an important way the Sioux preserve their identity as a native people. Here, a man is elaborately outfitted in fur and feathers, including a magnificent headdress.

IN 1968, THE AMERICAN INDIAN MOVEMENT (AIM) WAS FOUNDED in the impoverished neighborhoods of St. Paul, Minnesota, because native languages, religion, and traditions were being lost. Most of AIM's activist members were young urban Indians, including many Sioux. These young people began to visit Sioux medicine men in South Dakota to learn about their past. One of the foremost leaders was Russell Means, an Oglala Sioux from Pine Ridge, South Dakota. Crow Dog, a Brulé Sioux from Rosebud, South Dakota, became the medicine man for AIM. The Sioux also took a leading role in organizing the Trail of Broken Treaties, in which tribal representatives marched to Washington in 1972, occupied the Bureau of Indian Affairs building, and presented a number of demands for human rights.

The climax of the movement was the occupation of Wounded Knee, a village on the Pine Ridge Reservation in South Dakota, in February 1973 by several hundred people, mainly Sioux. They were protesting the deplorable living conditions on reservations, especially at Pine Ridge. For seventy-one days, the protesters held off a heavily armed group of F.B.I. agents, marshals, and Indian police. Two Indians were killed during the siege, including Buddy Lamont, a Pine Ridge Sioux and ex-marine, who was buried next to the Ghost Dancers of 1890. If nothing else, the protesters showed that they were proud to be warriors once again.

Since that time, Indian activists have become educators and founded schools to help children learn English. They have also run for tribal offices to help their people on the reservation. They have

*T*he tragedy of Wounded Knee is very painful to the Sioux. Many still make the pilgrimage to the sacred, windblown hilltop where so many innocent people were killed.

won lawsuits, including a $105 million payment for their removal from the Black Hills, although many Sioux would still like to have the sacred land returned to them.

They have also worked to preserve their language and culture in a larger white society. Among the Sioux, there are three principal language groups—Dakota, Nakota, and Lakota. In the Dakota language there are four dialects: Assinoboin, Santee, Teton, and Yankton. Missionaries once zealously tried to destroy Sioux beliefs and language, but recently Franciscan fathers have worked to preserve the Sioux language by preparing Lakota dictionaries and grammar textbooks.

Here are some examples of the Dakota language, which has been kept alive to the present day. The words may appear a little difficult, but, if you follow the pronunciation key, you will be able to gain some understanding of how words are pronounced in the Dakota language. These examples are based primarily on *An English-Dakota Dictionary* by John P. Williamson and to an extent on *Everyday Lakota: An English-Sioux Dictionary for Beginners* edited by Joseph A. Karol and Stephen L. Roxman.

Some Sioux words are nasalized, or spoken through the nose. These words are indicated by the "ñ." Here is the Dakota alphabet along with examples of the pronunciation. All of the vowels and consonants are spoken as in English, except for the following:

| a | (ah) as in far |
| c | (che) as in **ch**ew |

| ç | a strong, exploded **c** not found in English |
|---|---|
| e | (e) as in th**ey** |
| g | (ghe) as in **g**ive |
| g | a guttural sound, not in English |
| <u>h</u> | sound of **ch** as in German **ach** |
| i | (ee) as in mach**i**ne |
| n | a nasalized sound, similar to i**n**k |
| o | (oh)   as in g**o** |
| <u>s</u> | (she)  as in **sh**e |
| <u>t</u> | an exploded **t**, not in English |
| u | (oo)   as in **oo**ze |
| <u>z</u> | as in a**z**ure |

A few letters are followed by a break or brief pause indicated by '.

Here are some words spoken by the Sioux, some of which are especially important to them. Others are everyday words that show some of the things you may have in common with Sioux children.

## Dakota Language

| boy | ho<u>ks</u>idañ |
|---|---|
| brother | huñkawañ<u>z</u>i |
| buffalo | tatañka |
| child | hwk<u>s</u>iyopa |
| corn | wamnaheza |

| | |
|---|---|
| dog | su̲ñ'ka |
| earth | maka |
| father | atkuku |
| forest | coñ'tañka |
| friend | koda |
| girl | wiciñyañna |
| home | ti'pi |
| horse | su̲ñktañka |
| mother | huñ'ku |
| no | hiya |
| prairie | tiñ'ta |
| prairie dog | piñspiñza |
| rain | maga̲zu |
| river | wakpa |
| school | wayawapi |
| sister | ta'winoh̲tiñ |
| sky | mah̲piyato |
| sun | añpetuwi |
| water | mini |
| yes | hañ |

## "We Shall Live Again"

The Sioux have not disappeared from the Great Plains. Today, like their ancestors, girls and women make lovely beaded moccasins, purses, belts, and medallions. They have brought back the tradition of quilling, using naturally dyed porcupine quills for decoration instead of beads. Boys learn to ride horses as soon as they begin to walk, and many grow up to herd cattle instead of hunting buffalo. The tribes own several million acres of grazing land, but lack the financial resources to build their own cattle business. So, they lease their land to white ranchers who keep most of the profit. A handful of Sioux now have their own small ranches, but at least 80 percent of Sioux grazing lands are leased to white ranchers. Expert horsemen, many young Sioux work as ranch hands off the reservation and compete for prize money at local rodeos. Yet many Sioux still live in deep poverty. After completing high school, most young people leave the reservation in search of jobs. They tend to find only seasonal jobs, though, putting in fence posts, painting barns, and herding sheep; they pick beets and potatoes, as well as fruit—anything to earn a few dollars and get by.

In recent years, larger numbers of Sioux men and women have been able to attend college and gradually assume professional positions as teachers, nurses, doctors, lawyers, engineers, and reservation administrators. Even so, they do not forget their origins. A computer programmer, living in a modern house, may consult a medicine man as well as a modern doctor. A woman might attend a Christian church, but also take part in a traditional ceremony. Her husband may purify himself in a sweat lodge ceremony.

Because of their generosity many Sioux do not save money or manage their personal finances with care. To honor a dead relative, families still hold a giveaway feast in which they feed all comers and hand out many valuable gifts to the poor. Just as the hunter of the past donated a portion of his game to the helpless people—the old folks, the widows, and the orphans—the Sioux still share their income and food with the needy. This is an admirable philosophy, but it does not help their families if they give away so much that they are left impoverished themselves.

*Often held at the local fairgrounds, powwows are exciting events for young and old alike. Spectators gather around the dance circle to*

Recently, powwows have become a means of strengthening native roots. Traditionally, the Sioux gathered in the spring to celebrate the seasonal renewal of life. People sang, danced, and prayed to Wakan Tanka. Today the powwow is central to the Sioux way of life. Many families get together on weekends from April through September and enjoy traditional activities.

The powwow begins with the grand entry, in which the eagle

*watch boys, girls, men, and women dance through the afternoon and again in the evening.*

staff, along with the U.S., state, and tribal flags are carried into the circle. Invited dignitaries and all the participants then dance in a circle, clockwise. Accompanied by drum music and songs, the dancers then perform in different categories: men's traditional dance, grass dance, and fancy dance; women's fancy dance, jingle dress dance, and intertribal dance. There are also honor songs and giveaways acknowledging the past when a chief would donate horses, food, blankets, and other possessions to the needy.

The Sioux population continues to grow steadily; today, there are over 100,000 Sioux in the United States and Canada. Most live on reservations in the Dakotas, as well as in Minnesota, Montana, and Nebraska. The health of the Sioux has improved and life expectancy has increased. But unemployment remains high, and housing continues to be substandard. Yet the Sioux have cause to be hopeful. They have committed themselves to keeping alive the language, beliefs, and traditions of their ancestors because "a people without history is like wind in the buffalo grass." Proud warriors and powerful women, they have endured the most outrageous abuse, including wholesale slaughter of their people. If they can survive such mistreatment, the Sioux believe they can once again prosper as a people. Just as the noble buffalo have come back to the windblown plains, so too the Sioux sing: "We shall live again. We shall live again."

*More and more Sioux children are seeking an education while still preserving many of the old ways. They may grow up to become a doctor or a teacher, but they will always be Hunkpapa or Brulé.*

# More About

# the Sioux

# Time Line

**1500s** Siouan tribes migrate from eastern North America and settle in what is now Minnesota.

**mid-1600s** Many Sioux begin to migrate to the Great Plains from present-day Minnesota.

**mid-1700s** The Sioux acquire horses and learn to use them expertly. Nomadic buffalo hunters, the Sioux dominate the other tribes of the Great Plains.

**1800s** The Great Sioux Nation dominates the northern plains, including the present-day Dakotas, northern Nebraska, eastern Wyoming, and southeastern Montana.

**1803** The United States purchases the Louisiana territory from France, a vast area that includes Sioux home country. In the following years, trading posts are established throughout the West.

**1804** The Sioux encounter the Lewis and Clark expedition of 1803-1806.

**about 1831** Sitting Bull is born.

**1837–1870** At least four smallpox epidemics ravage the tribes of the Great Plains.

**about 1842** Crazy Horse is born.

**1849** The United States government purchases Fort Laramie from the American Fur Company and brings in troops.

**1851** The Eastern Sioux are forced to sell their land in Minnesota and move to reservations. The first of the Fort Laramie treaties is signed with the Sioux and other tribes. Miners and wagon trains of settlers travel over what becomes known as the Bozeman Trail.

**1854** The Sioux first encounter U.S. military forces. John L. Grattan and U.S. soldiers are wiped out at the North Platte River, thus beginning the Great Sioux Wars.

**1855** Brulé chief Conquering Bear is killed in a dispute over a cow. His people avenge his death by killing thirty soldiers. In retaliation, Colonel William Harney leads 1,300 troops in a massacre of an entire Brulé village.

**1862** The Homestead Act leads to a flood of settlers on Indian lands. The Eastern Sioux fight back in the Great Sioux Minnesota Uprising of 1862. Following the revolt, thirty-eight Sioux men are executed.

**1864** Colonel Chivington leads an attack against Black Kettle's camp in Colorado, slaughtering 105 Cheyenne women and children and 28 men, in what became known as the Massacre at Sand Creek.

**1865** General Patrick Connor organizes an invasion of the Powder River Basin, from the Black Hills to the Bighorn Mountains. They had a single order: "Attack and kill every male Indian over twelve years of age." In late autumn, nine treaties are signed with Sioux tribes.

**1866** Young Sioux warriors, including Crazy Horse, ambush troops under the command of Captain Fetterman and kill eighty soldiers in the Battle of the Hundred Slain, also known as the Fetterman Massacre.

**1866–1868** Chief Red Cloud leads a successful battle to close the Bozeman Trail, a trail to the gold mines of Montana that crossed Teton hunting grounds.

**1868** The Great Sioux Reservation, encompassing most of South Dakota west of the Missouri River, is established. The United States promises to keep settlers out of this territory, including the Black Hills.

**1874** The Sioux people defend their homes and way of life from a flood of prospectors seeking gold in the Black Hills.

**1875** The United States government orders the Sioux to report to reservations by January 1876 or be declared "hostile."

**1876** General Custer attacks Crazy Horse's large winter camp. In late June, Sitting Bull, Crazy Horse, Gall, and several Cheyenne leaders defeat Custer and the 7th Cavalry at the Battle of Little Bighorn.

**1877** Sitting Bull escapes to Canada. Crazy Horse surrenders at Fort Robinson, and a small band of Miniconjou Sioux is defeated by General Nelson Miles. On September 6, Crazy Horse is killed. The United States takes over the Black Hills.

**1881** Sitting Bull and 186 followers surrender at Fort Buford. He is imprisoned at Fort Randall for two years instead of being pardoned, as promised.

**1887** The General Allotment Act reduces the land of Indian nations by giving 160 acres to each family and 80 acres to individuals.

**1889** An act of Congress divides the Great Sioux Reservation into six regions. Some tribes begin the Ghost Dance, a religious ceremony to restore their way of life on the plains. Late in the year, South Dakota is admitted into the Union.

**1890** Sitting Bull is murdered on the Standing Rock Reservation, prompting Big Foot and his band to flee to Pine Ridge for protection under Red Cloud. Two hundred people in Big Foot's band are massacred by the 7th Cavalry at Wounded Knee on December 29, thus ending the Great Sioux Wars.

**1910** The United States government prohibits the Sun Dance of the Plains Indians.

**1924** The United States recognizes all Native Americans born within the states and territories as citizens.

**1934** The Indian Reorganization Act recognizes tribal governments and provides financial assistance.

**1973** Members of the American Indian Movement seize the village of Wounded Knee on the Pine Ridge Reservation.

**1980** The United States Supreme Court orders the federal government to pay the Sioux tribes for land taken illegally.

**1982** The Sioux lose a supreme court case to regain ownership of the Black Hills of South Dakota.

**1990** South Dakota governor George S. Mickelson and tribal representatives proclaim 1990, the hundred-year anniversary of Wounded Knee, as a Year of Reconciliation. A Century of Reconciliation is declared a year later, in 1991.

# Notable People

**Black Elk** (1863–1950) was born on the Little
Powder River in eastern Wyoming. At the age
of five, he had his first vision and another
when he was nine. He interpreted these
visions to mean that he was to work to keep
the Sioux religion alive. At thirteen, he took
part in the Battle of Little Bighorn, after which
his family joined Crazy Horse. Following the
death of the great war chief in 1877, his family
went with Sitting Bull to Canada.

*Black Elk*

About this time, Black Elk was recognized
as a holy man. He went with his family to the
Pine Ridge Reservation, where he was often
consulted for his visions. From 1886 to 1889,
he toured the eastern United States and Europe with Buffalo Bill Cody's
Wild West Show. At first he did not believe in the Ghost Dance. Yet
gradually his feelings changed. Tormented by the massacre at Wounded
Knee, he became convinced that all people must live in harmony and that
the new religion held an important message for the Sioux.

In 1930, Nebraska poet John G. Neihardt visited Black Elk at Pine
Ridge and the next year recorded his oral history. The holy man's account
was published in *Black Elk Speaks: Being The Life Story of a Holy Man of the
Oglala Sioux*. Black Elk's wise and poetic words have since been widely
published throughout the world.

**Gertrude Bonnin** (1876–1938) was born in the same year as the Battle of the
Little Bighorn. Although she distrusted most non-Indians, she sought an
education against her mother's wishes. Attending the Boston
Conservatory of Music, she became an accomplished violinist. She later
began to publish articles and poems in popular magazines. Her
autobiographical book, *American Indian Stories* (1921) describes her
changing views of the European-American world and her acceptance of
Christianity. She also published *Old Indian Legends* (1901).

*Gertrude Bonnin*

With Charles Eastman, she co-founded the Society of American Indians, which worked on behalf of Native Americans from 1911 to the mid-1920s. Bonnin also taught for a while at Carlisle Indian School in Pennsylvania. Under the pen name of Zitkala-sa, she investigated white settlers who had swindled the Indians of Oklahoma. An advisor to the Meriam Commission in the 1920s, she remained active in Indian causes until her death.

**Elizabeth Cook-Lynn** (1930–   ) was born on the Crow Creek Reservation at Fort Thompson, South Dakota. Her grandfather was a Sioux linguist who helped to prepare early dictionaries of the Dakota language. Educated at South Dakota State College, the University of South Dakota, the University of Nebraska, and Stanford University, she became a highly regarded poet, editor, and professor. For many years, she has edited *Wicazo Sa Review*, a leading journal of Native American studies.

She has widely published in literary journals and anthologies. Her published works include *Then Badger Said This (1978); Seek the House of Relatives (1983); The Power of Horses & Other Stories (1990);* and *From the River's Edge (1991).* Retired as professor emerita from Eastern Washington State University, she continues to write and teach as a visiting professor.

**Crazy Horse** (about 1842–1877) was born on Rapid Creek not far from present-day Rapid City, South Dakota. His father was an Oglala medicine man and his mother was a Brulé who died when he was still young. Just before he turned twelve, Crazy Horse killed a buffalo and received his first horse. About this time he witnessed the brutality of American soldiers against Sioux people, after which he went on a vision quest. He dreamed of a rider in a storm, a great warrior with long unbraided hair and a zigzag lightning design on his cheek. Afterward, he received his father's name of Crazy Horse.

At age sixteen, Crazy Horse took part in his first battle—a raid against the Crow. He showed great courage and skill in the War of the Bozeman Trail of 1866–1868. He became war chief of the Oglala Sioux in 1868 and led attacks against railroad surveyors, gold prospectors, and soldiers for the next ten years. At the Battle of Little Bighorn, Crazy Horse led the attack on General George Armstrong Custer's troops from the north and west. Crazy Horse led his eight hundred warriors in other skirmishes, but exhausted and starving, he surrendered in 1877. His people never received the reservation promised them and on September 5, 1877, Crazy Horse was bayoneted by a soldier, supposedly for resisting arrest.

**Ella Deloria** (1888–1971) was born on the Yankton Sioux Reservation. Her father was an Episcopal minister of French descent and her mother was a Yankton Sioux. She attended boarding school in Sioux Falls, South Dakota, and later Oberlin College and Columbia University. While attending Columbia, she worked with anthropologist Franz Boas in translating a number of Lakota stories. Over the years, she continued to work with Boas on traditional Lakota stories and Dakota grammar. Much of her work is unpublished, including "Dakota Autobiographies" and "Dakota Speeches," both of which were written in the late 1930s. Among her published works are *Waterlily*, a fictional study of her culture written in the 1940s but not published until 1988, and *Speaking of Indians* (1944), an essay about Sioux lifeways. In most of her writing, Deloria deals with the difficulty of relationships and cultural conflict between Native and European-American viewpoints.

**Vine Deloria Jr.** (1933–    ), a Standing Rock Sioux, was born on the Pine Ridge Reservation in South Dakota. Educated at Iowa State University and the University of Colorado Law School, Deloria became a well-known public speaker on Indian issues. A highly regarded author, he has published *Custer Died for Your Sins* (1969); *We Talk You Listen: New Tribes, New Turf* (1970); *God Is Red* (1973), and *Red Earth, White Lies: Native Americans and the Myth of Scientific Fact* (1995).

In the 1980s, Deloria supported Sioux efforts to return the sacred Black Hills to his people. He has served as executive director of the

*Russell Means*

National Congress of American Indians. Currently a university professor, he continues to write books about Indian concerns.

**Little Crow** (about 1810–1863) became leader of his Sioux band when his father, who was chief, died in 1834. He maintained good relations with the whites who had settled near his home at present-day St. Paul, Minnesota. In 1851, he signed a treaty, giving up much of his people's land in exchange for a reservation on the upper Minnesota River. In 1857, he and his warriors attacked a renegade band of Wahpekute Sioux, and a year later he joined a Sioux treaty delegation that went to Washington, D.C.

However, the Sioux became angry as more settlers moved into the region and threatened the Sioux way of life. At first, Little Crow sought peace, but then he assumed leadership in the Minnesota Uprising of 1862. Many settlers were killed or taken captive, but by year's end the revolt was put down. More than three hundred people were sentenced to be die on the gallows, but President Abraham Lincoln pardoned most of the men. Still, thirty-eight warriors were hanged, the largest mass execution in United States history.

Little Crow and his son escaped, but while picking berries they were ambushed by settlers who wanted the $25 bounty on Sioux scalps. His son managed to get away, but Little Crow was murdered. Later, the Minnesota Historical Society put his skeleton and scalp on display, but eventually his remains were returned to the Sioux for proper burial.

**Russell Means** (1940–    ) was born in Porcupine, South Dakota, on the Pine Ridge Reservation and raised in Oakland, California. His mother was Yankton Sioux and his father was part Oglala and part Irish. In addition to a career as a public accountant, Means became an Indian dancer and rodeo rider before returning to the Rosebud Reservation in South Dakota. After moving to Cleveland, Ohio, he became director of the Cleveland Indian Center and worked to transform the organization into a chapter of the American Indian Movement (AIM). Outspoken and charismatic, Means quickly emerged as one of AIM's principal leaders. In the early 1970s, he was involved in several protests, including the 1973 siege of Wounded Knee in which two Indians were killed.

From 1973 to 1980, Means was tried in four cases related to his political activities. Imprisoned for a year in South Dakota, he survived stabbings and shootings by inmates. He has continued to take a leading role in political protests, including Yellow Thunder Camp, a settlement in the Black Hills. He has also begun an acting career and has appeared in several popular movies.

**Red Cloud** (about 1822–1909) was born near the Platte River in present-day north-central Nebraska. Because of his bravery, he became chief of his band and over his lifetime counted eighty coups. During the 1860s, prospectors traveled across buffalo hunting grounds on the Oregon Trail and a branch called the Bozeman Trail that led to eastern Montana. Red Cloud and his Oglala Sioux joined other Sioux and Cheyenne bands to attack wagon trains and military patrols on both trails. In 1866, Red Cloud rode into Fort Laramie to sign a peace treaty, but left when the government would not agree to stop building forts on the Bozeman Trail. Two forts were completed and came under siege, culminating in 1866 in the Fetterman Massacre in which Captain Fetterman and eighty of his men were killed.

*Red Cloud*

In the Fort Laramie Treaty of 1868, the government promised to abandon its posts along the Bozeman Trail and established the Great Sioux Reservation, and Red Cloud and the other leaders agreed to cease their raids on army forts and wagon trains. The Sioux celebrated by burning the forts soon after they were evacuated. Red Cloud traveled to Washington to meet with President Ulysses S. Grant and Seneca commissioner of Indian affairs Ely Parker. However, in 1874, General George Armstrong Custer violated the treaty by leading a mining expedition into the Black Hills, which led to a rush of miners and more conflict.

Despite the restless spirit of his warriors, Red Cloud advocated peace with the whites. After the victory at Little Bighorn, in which his son Jack and others in his band took part, government officials accused Red Cloud of aiding militant Sioux and relocated him to the Pine Ridge agency in 1878. He was deposed as chief of Pine Ridge in 1881. When the Ghost Dance swept the Great Plains, he still favored peace but was unable to control his warriors. Suffering from poor health in his later years, he died in 1909.

**Sitting Bull** (about 1831–1890) was born along the Grand River near present-day Bullhead, South Dakota. A Hunkpapa Sioux, as a young man, he proved himself a fine warrior and hunter, killing his first buffalo at age ten and counting his first coup against a Crow at age fourteen. Following his vision quest, he was accepted into the Strong Hearts, a warrior society of which he became chief at the age of twenty-two. During the 1850s, he distinguished himself in battle against other tribes, but avoided confrontations with the whites who were coming into the region.

Following the Minnesota Uprising of 1862, Sitting Bull and his band attacked army scouting parties. During the War of the Bozeman Trail of 1866–1868 and the War for the Black Hills of 1876–1877, he and the Strong Hearts attacked small parties of settlers and prospectors. Around this time, Sitting Bull came to be recognized as a spiritual leader as well as a great warrior. In mid-June of 1876, Sitting Bull held a three-day Sun Dance in which he had a vision of soldiers falling dead. On June 17, the forces of Sitting Bull and Crazy Horse allied to defeat General Crook in the Battle of the Rosebud River. Just eight days later, the Sioux and Cheyenne defeated George Armstrong Custer at the Battle of the Little Bighorn. The victory, however, led to a stepped-up military campaign against the Plains Indians. After a series of defeats, many of the Sioux surrendered, but Sitting Bull and some of his followers went to Canada.

When Canada refused to help him, he and his followers returned to the United States and surrendered in 1881. Held prisoner for two years, he was finally allowed to settle on the Standing Rock Reservation in North

Dakota in 1883. For a year, during 1885–1886, he toured with Buffalo Bill Cody's Wild West Show but was disgusted by the disrespectful audiences and returned to the reservation. Because of his opposition to the further breakup of the Sioux reservation and his resistance to white customs and policies, he came into conflict with Indian agent James McLaughlin. When Sitting Bull invited a group of Ghost Dancers to the reservation, the unscrupulous McLaughlin ordered his arrest. Sitting Bull was killed in a gun battle between Indian police and his supporters. Because of this tragic incident, Big Foot and his band fled the reservation which led to the Wounded Knee Massacre of 1890.

# Glossary

**counting coup**  Touching an enemy in battle to prove one's bravery.

**Dakota**  A Siouan word meaning "friend." Also the language spoken by the Santee Sioux.

**Ghost Dance**  A religion that swept across the tribes of the Great Plains in the late 1800s.

**Lakota**  A Siouan language spoken by the Teton Sioux. Also the name of the Tetons.

**moccasins**  Soft leather shoes often decorated with colorful beads or quills.

**nomadic**  Moving seasonally from one place to another.

**pemmican**  Pounded dry meat mixed with fat and berries used as "energy food" when warriors went on long journeys.

**Paha Sapa**  Sioux name for the sacred Black Hills of South Dakota.

**Sun Dance**  The most important Sioux ceremony, held each summer.

**sweat lodge**  Dome-shaped hut covered with buffalo skins in which purifications and other sacred ceremonies are held.

**tiyospaye**  A group of families belonging to the same Sioux band.

**travois**  A sled made of two poles lashed together and pulled by a dog or horse.

**Tribal Council**  The legal governing body for each of the Sioux reservations.

**vision quest**  A coming-of-age ceremony of solitary fasting for four days to induce dreams in young people.

**Wakan Tanka**  The Great Spirit who watches over all living things.

**warbonnets**  Feathered headdresses worn by great Sioux warriors.

# Further Information

Many fine books have been written about the Sioux who today live on the northern Great Plains. Among them, the following titles were very helpful in researching and writing *The Sioux*. "The Creation Story" is based upon narratives collected by J. R. Walker and published in *The Sun Dance and Other Ceremonies of the Oglala Division of the Teton Dakota Sioux* and other accounts. The White Buffalo Calf legend is adapted from *The Sioux: Life and Customs of a Warrior Society* by Royal B. Hassrick.

Brown, Dee. *Bury My Heart at Wounded Knee*. New York: Holt, Rinehart & Winston, 1970.

Curtis, Edward S. *The North American Indian: Being a Series of Volumes Picturing and Describing the Indians of the United States and Alaska*. New York: Johnson Reprint Corp., 1970.

Edmonds, Margot, and Clark, Ella E. *Voices of the Winds: Native American Legends*. New York: Facts on File, 1989.

Erdoes, Richard. *Native Americans: The Sioux*. New York: Sterling Publications, 1982.

Ewers, John. C. *Five Indian Tribes of the Upper Missouri*. Norman, OK: University of Oklahoma Press, 1961.

Griffin-Pierce, Trudy. *The Encyclopedia of Native America*. New York: Viking, 1995.

Hassrick, Royal B. *The Sioux: Life and Customs of a Warrior Society*. Norman, OK: University of Oklahoma Press, 1964.

Hedren, Paul L. *Traveler's Guide to the Great Sioux War: The Battlefields, Forts, and Related Sites of America's Greatest Indian War*. Helena, MT: Montana Historical Society, 1996.

Johansen, Bruce E., and Grinde, Donald A. Jr. *The Encyclopedia of Native American Biography*. New York: Henry Holt and Co., 1997.

Johnson, Michael G. *The Native Tribes of North America: A Concise Encyclopedia*. New York: Macmillan Publishing Co., 1994.

Karol, Joseph S., and Rozman, Stephen L. *Everyday Lakota: An English-Sioux Dictionary for Beginners*. St. Francis, SD: Rosebud Educational Soc.,1971.

Langer, Howard J. ed. *American Indian Quotations*. Westport, CT: Greenwood Press, 1996.

Lyford, Carrie A. *Quill and Beadwork of the Western Sioux*. Boulder, CO: Johnson Books, 1979.

Neihardt, John G. *Black Elk Speaks: Being the Life Story of a Holy Man of the Oglala Sioux*. Lincoln: University of Nebraska Press, 1961.

Powers, Marla N. *Oglala Women: Myth, Ritual, and Reality*. Chicago: University of Chicago Press, 1986.

Schult, Milo J. *Where Buffalo Roam*. Interior, SD: Badlands Natural History Association, 1979.

Shanks, Ralph, and Shanks, Lisa Woo. *The North American Indian Travel Guide*. Petaluma, CA: Costano Books, 1993.

Sneve, Virginia Driving Hawk. *They Led a Nation: The Sioux Chiefs*. Sioux Falls, SD: Brevet Press, 1975.

Standing Bear, Luther. *Land of the Spotted Eagle* Lincoln: University of Nebraska Press, 1978.

Waldman, Carl. *Encyclopedia of Native American Tribes*. New York: Facts on File Publications, 1988.

Walker, J. R. *The Sun Dance and Other Ceremonies of the Oglala Division of the Teton Dakota Sioux*. New York: AMS Press, 1979.

Williamson, John Poage. *An English-Dakota Dictionary*. St. Paul, MN: Minnesota Historical Society Press, 1992.

Writers' Program. South Dakota. *Legends of the Mighty Sioux*. Interior, SD: Badlands Natural History Association, 1987.

Young people who wish to learn more about the Sioux will enjoy these excellent books for children:

Bonvillain, Nancy. *The Teton Sioux*. New York: Chelsea House Publishers, 1994.

Brooks, Barbara. *The Sioux*. Vero Beach, FL: Rourke Publications, 1989.

Densmore, Frances. *Teton Sioux Music and Culture*. Lincoln: University of Nebraska Press, 1992.

Hoover, Herbert T. *The Yankton Sioux*. New York: Chelsea House Publishers, 1988.

McGinnis, Mark W. *Lakota & Dakota Animal Wisdom Stories*. Chamberlain, SD: Tipi Press, 1994.

McGovern, Ann. *...If You Lived with the Sioux Indians*. New York: Scholastic, Inc., 1994.

Nicholson, Robert. *The Sioux*. New York: Chelsea House Publishers, 1994.

Sneve, Virginia Driving Hawk. *The Sioux*. New York: Holiday House, 1993.

Standing Bear, Luther. *Stories of the Sioux*. Lincoln: University of Nebraska Press, 1988.

Wolfson, Evelyn. *The Teton Sioux: People of the Plains*. Brookfield, CT: Millbrook Press, 1992.

## Organizations

Cheyenne River Sioux Tribal
Council
P.O. Box 590
Eagle Butte, SD 57625
(605) 964-4155
Fax (605) 964-4151

Crow Creek Sioux Tribal Council
P.O. Box 658
Fort Thompson, SD 57339
(605) 245-2221
Fax (605) 245-2216

Devils Lake Sioux Tribal Council
Sioux Community Center
Fort Totten, ND 58335
(701) 766-4221
Fax (701) 766-4854 BIA

Flandreau Santee Sioux Executive
Committee
Flandreau Field Office
P.O. Box 283
Flandreau, SD 57028
(605) 997-3891

The Heritage Center
Red Cloud Indian School
P.O. Box 100
Pine Ridge, SD 57770
(605) 867-5491
Fax (605) 867-1291

Lower Brule Sioux Tribal Council
Lower Brule, SD 57548
(605) 473-5561

Lower Sioux Agency Interpretive
Center
Route 1, Box 125
Morton, MN 56270
(507) 697-6321

Oglala Sioux Tribal Council
Pine Ridge, SD 57770
(605) 867-5821
Fax (605) 867-5582

Prairie Island Community
Council
5750 Sturgeon Lake Road
Welch, MN 55089
(612) 388-8889

Rosebud Sioux Tribal Council
P.O. Box 430
Rosebud, SD 57570
(605) 747-2381
(605) 747-2243

Santee Sioux Tribal Council
Route 2
Niobrara, NE 68760
(402) 857-3302
Fax (402) 857-3307

**Sisseton-Wahpeton Sioux Tribal Council**
Route 2, Agency Village
Sisseton, SD 57262
(605) 698-3911
Fax (605) 698-3708

**Shakopee Sioux Community Council**
2330 Sioux Trail N.W.
Prior Lake, MN 55372
(612) 445-8900
Fax (612) 445-5906

**Standing Rock Sioux Tribal Council**
Fort Yates, ND 58538
(701) 854-7231
Fax (701) 854-7299

**Upper Sioux Community Board of Trustees**
P.O. Box 147
Granite Falls, MN 56241
(612) 564-2360
Fax (612) 564-3264

**Yankton Sioux Tribal Business and Claims Committee**
P.O. Box 248
Marty, SD 57361
(605) 384-3641

## Native American Newspapers

There are several highly regarded Native American newspapers. Among them, these two nationally published newspapers include a great deal of information about the Sioux:

*News from Indian Country*
Route 2, Box 2900-A
Hayward, WI 54843
(715) 634-5226

*Indian Country Today*
1920 Lombardy Dr., P. O. Box 2180
Rapid City, SD 57701
(605) 341-0011

# Websites

Over the past few years, Native Americans have established themselves on the Internet. Here are some of the best and most interesting websites to visit for more information about the Sioux Indians and other native peoples.

**Capucine's Native Resources**
http://www.klingon.org/native/pages/nations.html

**Cheyenne River Sioux Tribe**
http://www.cheyenneriversioux.com/index.htm.html

**Fort Peck Tribes**
http://www.usd.edu/iais/siouxnation/FtPeck/fortpeck.html

**The Great Sioux Nation**
http://www.historychannel.com/community/sioux/

**The Harry V. Johnston Lakota Cultural Center**
http://crstis2.crst.nsn.us/lakotaculture/default.html

**Index of Native American Resources on the Internet**
http://hanksville.phast.umass.edu/misc/NAresources.html

**The Journey Museum**
http://www.sdsmt.edu/journey/

**Lakota Information Home Page**
http://maple.lemoyne.edu/~bucko/lakota.html

**Lakota Sioux**
http://www.blackhills-info.com/lakota_sioux/

**North Dakota Tribes**
http://indy4.fdl.cc.mn.us/~isk/maps/dakotas/nd.html

**Oglala Lakota College**
http://www.olc.edu/olc.home3.html

**Sisseton Wahpeton Community College**
http://swcc.cc.sd.us/CC.HTM

**Sisseton Wahpeton Sioux Tribe**
http://swcc.cc.sd.us/homepage.htm

**Tribute to the Oglala Lakota Sioux, their history, culture, and leaders**
http://www.geocities.com/Athens/Acropolis/3976/Hawk.html

**Yankton Sioux People**
http://www.usd.edu/iais/siouxnation/yankton.html

# Index

Page numbers for illustrations are in **boldface**.

# Raymond Bial

HAS PUBLISHED OVER THIRTY CRITICALLY ACCLAIMED BOOKS OF PHOTOGRAPHS for children and adults. His photo-essays for children include *Corn Belt Harvest, Amish Home, Frontier Home, Shaker Home, The Underground Railroad, Portrait of a Farm Family, With Needle and Thread: A Book About Quilts, Mist Over the Mountains: Appalachia and Its People, Cajun Home,* and *Where Lincoln Walked.*

He is currently immersed in writing *Lifeways*, a series of books about Native Americans. As with his other work, Bial's deep feeling for his subjects is evident in both the text and illustrations. He travels to tribal cultural centers, photographing homes, artifacts, and surroundings and learning firsthand about the lifeways of each of these peoples.

A full-time library director at a small college in Champaign, Illinois, he lives with his wife and three children in nearby Urbana.

# BROWN GIRL
## IN THE RING

# BROWN GIRL
## in the RING

AN ANTHOLOGY OF SONG GAMES

FROM THE

EASTERN CARIBBEAN

COLLECTED AND DOCUMENTED BY

# ALAN LOMAX, J.D. ELDER,
# AND BESS LOMAX HAWES

PANTHEON BOOKS  NEW YORK

Copyright © 1997 by Alan Lomax

All rights reserved under International and Pan-American Copyright
Conventions. Published in the United States by Pantheon Books,
a division of Random House, Inc., New York, and simultaneously in
Canada by Random House of Canada Limited, Toronto.

ISBN: 0-679-40453-8

Random House Web Address: http://www.randomhouse.com/

*Book design by M. Kristen Bearse*

Printed in the United States of America

First Edition
2  4  6  8  9  7  5  3  1

# CONTENTS

~~~~~~

⠿

T W O

## SONG GAMES FROM DOMINICA AND ST. LUCIA          71

THREE
## Song Games from Anguilla and Nevis
## 129

VIII

# FOREWORD

~~~~~~

目

*by Alan Lomax*

There's a brown girl in the ring,
Tra la la la la,
There's a brown girl in the ring,
Tra la la la la la,
There's a brown girl in the ring,
Tra la la la la,
For she looks like a sugar and a plum,
      plum, plum . . .

THIS WAS THE REFRAIN OF the summer I spent in 1962 recording folk songs in many of the small islands of the West Indies as, one by
one, they moved away from British control and into independence. The
children sensed that something was in the air and—as only children can
do—summed up the whole situation in a song. This was their topical song
that summer, but they had many, many more—a potpourri of fragments
from all their many-sourced island traditions.

My work centered on a skein of small islands (called by some the
Lesser Antilles and by others the Windward and Leeward Islands) that
together with Trinidad and Tobago form the southeastern edge of the
Caribbean Sea. They were colonized and fought over first by Spaniards,
then by Dutch, French, and English, but after the indigenous native populations had been cruelly annihilated, they were mainly populated by Ibo,
Yoruba, Ashanti, and other peoples transported from West and Central
Africa. This complex history can still be felt as one moves from French to
English to Dutch to Spanish language zones; for no one who ever settled
in these islands ever wanted to leave their fertile soils, nourishing warm
climate, and lambent fish-filled seas.

In 1959, because I was to some extent an old West Indies hand, having done fieldwork in Haiti, the Bahamas, and those southern United States that form the northern edge of the Caribbean, the Rockefeller Foundation sent me to the Lesser Antilles with a fascinating goal in mind. At that time there was a possibility that these various island polities could be joined together with Jamaica to form a new democracy, the Federation of the West Indies. The enlightened presidents of both Jamaica and Trinidad were working hard to bring this idea to reality. My task as a folklorist was to look for the creative cultural commonalities among these many powers in support of their great dream of unity.

As in the past, I took a recording machine with me as my carte de visite and a way of documenting the things I found. Besides, I wanted to test the effect of playing back to the village singers the recordings I would make; I called the notion "cultural feedback." There were no pocket-portable speakers at that time, and I hauled onto the plane two huge loudspeakers that stood three feet high and required high-voltage power so as to display even adequately the stereo sound that I was testing out in my fieldwork.

My companions on the voyage were my then wife Toni, and later on, my daughter Anna. Wherever we recorded, we played back the music to its makers, filling mountain hamlets and village streets with the thunder of the speakers, while whole neighborhoods danced in delight. My Caribbean colleagues told me that in two or three places musical practices that were on the point of dying out were revived by that one act of sonorous support.

It was a mad voyage, planing and deplaning, hauling, heaving, unpacking, working always through the good offices of the University of the West Indies and its friends throughout the islands to establish quick and fruitful working relationships in all sorts of little villages that aren't on the big maps. Trinidad, Tobago, Martinique, Dominica, Guadeloupe, Anguilla, Nevis, Carriacou—this chain of magic places poured out their jeweled music to us in that long summer.

Back in Trinidad, the home port of the trip, I wrote my report for the Rockefeller Foundation, putting together the patterns that, as I saw them, provided a rich soil of unity for the future Federation. The most striking was this very unity. No matter what their language or dialect, the hundreds of Windward and Leeward Islanders we had met were stamped with a common Creole style. Whether their vocabularies are French-, Dutch-, or English-based, all are clearly related black transformations of West African linguistic structures.

What was true of speech was even more patently true of lifestyle and of music. In this world, music was based in rhythmic movement, whether dance, ritual, or work. At that time every task of life was still made easier and more effective by group work songs. Teams of sailors hauled the native-made sailboats into the water and raised their sails with chanteys. A group of singing Windward Islanders could put up a pleasant dwelling made of native wood and roofed with palm leaves in a day—a house that breathed cool air in the hottest weather, demanding no importations of cinder blocks or corrugated iron roofing.

Everywhere I found tidal pools and freshets of indigenous music and dance styles reflecting both the particular qualities of local life and the mainstream Creole performance style that plainly stemmed from West Africa. Africa was present in the polyrhythmic accompaniment of the music, whether played on sets of drums, created by hot multipart clapping, or sounded in the fife-and-drum bands of the northern islands or the stringed orchestras of central Trinidad and the classic jazz of Martinique.

Africa was present in the normal singing style, which was collective, the chorus overlapping its part with the leader so as to produce unexpected harmonies and hot licks, the melodies repetitious but each one forever setting some everyday phrase into a never-to-be-forgotten form. And each island had a treasure of such melodies, potentially unlimited because still growing. I believed that all of this music could become a national resource for a federated West Indies.

Among the richest veins were the children's songs encountered on every island. These songs were usually sung by clutches of young girls about to become young women, who sometimes allowed their young brothers to join in. The enunciation of these young singers who danced as they clapped and sang was hound's-tooth clean. In spite of the rapid pour of short notes and many syllables that characterized their peppery songs, every syllable was as clear as a drop of water on a palm leaf.

And as I listened, it seemed to me that these children had adopted the same performance strategy as the calypsonians of Trinidad, whose crystal enunciations reinforced their satirical pieces, which so often were aimed at bringing down their British lords and masters. And going back to my old song-game recordings in Britain, Bess Hawes and I found that the same emphasis upon crisp languaging was distinctively characteristic of British game songs. Nothing is so potent in Great Britain as a "good accent." It will open any door, as Shaw's *Pygmalion* shows us. The children of the West Indies had picked up this key for climbing the social ladder and were honing it to perfection as they sang.

And there is one other part of this pattern I wish especially to mention. I once asked a very old lady on the island of Carriacou what she felt when she sang the kissing games. She and her friends broke into squeals of old-lady laughter, and she actually ran off into the darkness, remembering perhaps what I take to be a main social purpose of these games for the girls—to teach them in a safe circle of play what they need to know for the passages of courtship soon to come.

All these things—including my still-to-be-published observations on the even more complex and numerous adult repertoires of the Lesser Antilles—went into my report to the Rockefeller Foundation and were sent on to Federation movers and shakers. Struggles for power between the politicians of the islands sank the scheme for federation long ago, but its essential dream, which many shared, may still not be vain.

My own subsequent studies of world performance styles show that the West Indies, in spite of underlying linguistic differences, constitutes perhaps the most culturally unified area of its geographic extent in the world. This is because the major population of every island had the same experience—transportation from Africa, enslavement by Europeans, and the subsequent development of a renewed and rich Creole African culture based in their hardworking and fête-filled lives.

Another believer in this dream of a new and unified democratic empire where Creole cultures could flower and people could dance and sing together across language lines was my longtime comrade and colleague J. D. Elder. Dr. Elder heard I was coming to Port of Spain on the Rockefeller mission. He met me at the plane, took me in hand, and introduced me to the incredible culture of Trinidad in two magic weeks. We have been working together ever since.

Among Dr. Elder's achievements as primary-school teacher and community development officer in his young days was to encourage the growth of the steel bands of Trinidad as an outlet for the restless youths of Port of Spain. He also helped develop the Best Village Folklore competition and still later the Tobago Heritage Festival movement on his home island of Tobago. He spent four years in Nigeria as a research professor at the University of Ibadan and dean of the Faculty of Social Sciences and Law at the University of Maiduguri, Nigeria. Upon his return to the Caribbean, he served as minister of culture for Tobago and as consultant for culture to the Ministry of Youth, Sport, Culture, and Creative Arts for the government of Trinidad and Tobago.

Dr. Elder has written widely on calypso, the steel band, the Yoruba religion in the old and new worlds, and Caribbean folktales. But his seminal work, *Song Games of Trinidad and Tobago,* has become a classic in international children's literature. Excerpts from his account, printed here, of growing up with singing games in his native island of Tobago take us straight into the heart, the very process, of cultural growth. We collaborated on this memoir in an amusing way. First, J. D. wrote the story in his fine Dickensian prose. We both felt it was a little stiff. Then he retold it on tape. Next I cut the two versions together into a lengthy autobiographical account, portions of which you may read in part five, "I Recall . . ." His vivid memories, as well as the actual voices of the children and adults who so generously recorded for this project some thirty years ago, bring our book alive and refresh us all with yet another demonstration of the unstoppable forces of human creativity.

*Dominica, 1959*

# ACKNOWLEDGMENTS

IN ACKNOWLEDGING THE SCORES of individuals who in their several ways contributed to and ensured the authenticity and cultural quality of the Trinidad and Tobago material in this book, I am regretfully apologetic for the fact that, because of their number, I have to be selective in my listing of names. I have first to acknowledge Professor Andrew A. Pearse, University College of the West Indies, St. Augustine, Trinidad, and Professor Prince Ferdinand, superintendent of education in Tobago.

To Dr. Eric E. Williams, prime minister of Trinidad and Tobago, I am very deeply indebted for recognizing the work I had been doing in the field of culture and, in 1962, adopting my field project and giving it official status. Two senior officials, Doddridge Alleyne and Eugenio Moore, were almost totally responsible for the successful development of the Cultural Project, especially its field and research aspects which created the National Folklore Archive.

To Alan Lomax, director of the Cantometrics Project at Columbia University, profound gratitude is due for including me in his extensive Folksong Research Project financed by the Rockefeller Foundation and supported by the University of the West Indies and the government of Trinidad and Tobago. This project gave me a most profound and intimate acquaintance with eastern Caribbean folklore, especially the traditional music of the East Indian and of the Hispanic ethnics that had entered the country from the Spanish Main in the early days of Spanish rule in Trinidad. The relationship set up between Lomax and myself during this project led to my introduction into the Cantometric system, which Professor Lomax and his collaborators were establishing as a new and exciting technique in the field of ethnomusicology in the United States.

I have finally to express my thanks to Archibald Chaharjarsingh and Harrington Jack, my two excellent and faithful field collectors, who really carried out the day-to-day collecting in the villages in Trinidad and Tobago. Associated with them are Pat Joseph, typist and oftentimes field-worker, and John Moreau, the excellent translator of French Creole who left Dominica and joined my research team in Trinidad.

Scores of villagers all over Trinidad and Tobago and in Grenada, Carriacou, and St. Lucia deserve my mention. Among them are Alfie Cadallo, an expert in Spanish traditional music; Cyrus Smith, a most wonderful tale teller of Grenadian birth; Ma Stoute, an expert in belé dance music, and her group from Blanchisseuse; Johnny Cooper, the great chanticleer of the Moruga Road "jubilees" (Trinidad spirituals); and the Colley family of Hindustan Village, Prince's Town, specialists in the Bongo dead-wake music. Outstanding among the village singers who worked with us was the late Papa Goon (Pedro Segundodolabaille), the master of décima and aguinaldo music at Lopinot in Trinidad. The name of Aurelia Moore, the singer of slave songs and sea chanteys from Charlotteville, Tobago, will ever remain in the history of the fieldwork which we carried out in Tobago folk music in the 1950s. Skeptical as all these villagers were at first about our intentions, they eventually became our firm supporters and admirers of our work in recording their tales and songs. To them—artists in their own right, all of them—I dedicate my input into this little book of folk music. May their children and successors enjoy the work of those who went before in making this work possible.

To my wife, Nevada, and my daughter, Patricia, for your love and support, I thank you.

J. D. ELDER, PH.D.
Petit Valley
Republic of Trinidad and Tobago
October 31, 1996

Those who collaborated with Alan Lomax in this book are many: among others, musicians Roswell Rudd, Alan Carey, and Nicholas Hawes; field assistants Anna Chairetakis and Antoinette Marchand; West Indianists Lambros Comitas, Winston Fleary, and Morton Marks; producer Gideon D'Arcangelo and researcher Marion Jacobson. The recording project of 1962 was graciously funded by the Rockefeller Foundation.

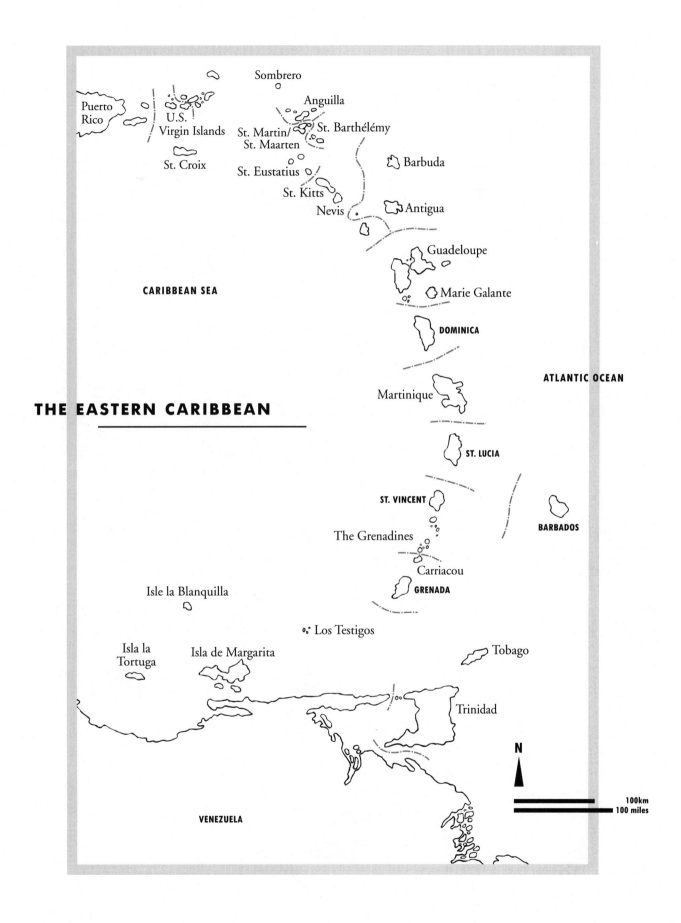

Sombrero

Puerto Rico

U.S. Virgin Islands

Anguilla

St. Martin/ St. Maarten

St. Barthélémy

St. Croix

St. Eustatius

Barbuda

St. Kitts

Nevis

Antigua

Guadeloupe

CARIBBEAN SEA

Marie Galante

DOMINICA

ATLANTIC OCEAN

Martinique

# THE EASTERN CARIBBEAN

ST. LUCIA

ST. VINCENT

BARBADOS

The Grenadines

Carriacou

GRENADA

Isle la Blanquilla

Los Testigos

Isla la Tortuga

Isla de Margarita

Tobago

Trinidad

N

100km
100 miles

VENEZUELA

PART ONE

# Song Games

# from

# Trinidad and Tobago

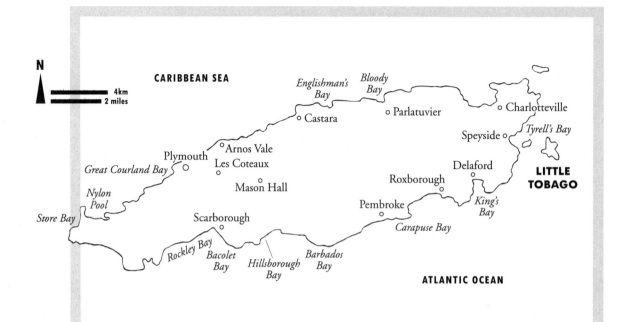

CARIBBEAN SEA

*Englishman's Bay*    *Bloody Bay*

○ Parlatuvier    ○ Charlotteville

○ Castara    Speyside ○    *Tyrell's Bay*

○ Arnos Vale    Delaford ○    **LITTLE TOBAGO**

Plymouth ○    Les Coteaux ○    Roxborough ○

*Great Courland Bay*    Mason Hall    *King's Bay*

*Nylon Pool*    Pembroke ○

*Store Bay*    Scarborough ○    *Carapuse Bay*

*Rockley Bay*    *Barbados Bay*

*Bacolet Bay*    *Hillsborough Bay*

**ATLANTIC OCEAN**

# TRINIDAD

## AND TOBAGO

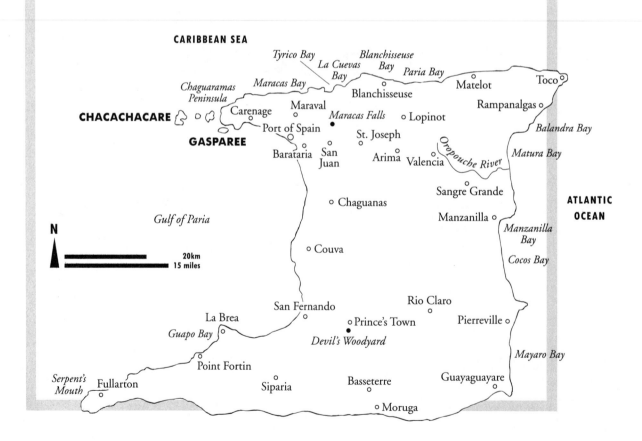

CARIBBEAN SEA

*Tyrico Bay*    *Blanchisseuse Bay*

*La Cuevas Bay*    *Paria Bay*

*Maracas Bay*    ○ Matelot    Toco ○

*Chaguaramas Peninsula*    Blanchisseuse ○    Rampanalgas ○

**CHACACHACARE**    Carenage ○    Maraval ○    *Maracas Falls* ●    ○ Lopinot    *Balandra Bay*

**GASPAREE**    Port of Spain ○    St. Joseph ○    *Matura Bay*

Barataria ○    San Juan ○    Arima ○    Valencia ○

*Oropouche River*

Sangre Grande ○    **ATLANTIC OCEAN**

○ Chaguanas    Manzanilla ○

*Gulf of Paria*    *Manzanilla Bay*

○ Couva    *Cocos Bay*

Rio Claro ○

San Fernando ○    Prince's Town ● ○    Pierreville ○

La Brea ○    *Devil's Woodyard*

*Guapo Bay*    *Mayaro Bay*

Point Fortin ○    Basseterre ○    Guayaguayare ○

*Serpent's Mouth*    Fullarton ○    Siparia ○

○ Moruga

# Trinidad and Tobago

**G**eologists believe that most of the islands of the Lesser Antilles originally rose up singly out of the ocean floor, some made of lava spewed out by great underwater volcanic explosions, some made of uplifted coral limestone.

Trinidad and Tobago, however, are broken-away pieces of the South American continent. Trinidad is not only the largest but the most southerly of all the Caribbean islands, lying opposite the delta of Venezuela's Orinoco River, only seven miles away. And once in Trinidad, you feel somehow inside a continent, for it is a maze of different environments—arid hills, jungle-covered plateaus, fertile valleys, mangrove swamps. One side of the island faces the Atlantic, and there huge breakers thunder onto the beaches. On the other, facing South America, the ocean is gentle and calm. Both Trinidad and Tobago are practically free of the storms, volcanic eruptions, and earthquakes that harass the more northerly islands.

But what excitement the people provide! Trinidad has one of the most ethnically variegated populations in the entire Caribbean, and each small separate geographical environment seems to have attracted its particular group of settlers, each with its own patois—Creole, Spanish, Hindu, French. Overall, 43 percent of the population is of African descent and 36 percent of East Indian, but there are significant groups of Lebanese, Chinese, Caribs, Syrians, and Europeans. The capital city, Port of Spain, is so complicated that it actually never sees itself except at Carnival, when all the ethnic neighborhoods fill the streets with street bands, drum choirs, and dancers in fabulous costumes.

This jostling, energetic, rampaging mixture of peoples has produced two musical inventions that have spread throughout the world—the calypso song and the steel drum. Calypso—the teasing song of social and personal comment, often initially improvised in public song contests—has been accepted joyfully throughout the Caribbean, and such diluted examples as "Rum and Coca-Cola" have become worldwide popular hits. The complex tuned drums, or "pans," that make up the Trinidadian steel band, originally constructed from the discarded fifty-gallon oil cans that litter Antillean shores, constitute what some musical scholars feel is the most original musical invention of the century. A full steel band has enormous musical scope; it can play Debussy or the hottest, newest calypso with equal authority.

**⠗**

Trinidad is shaped like a boot; Tobago, its "little sister" lying to the northeast, is long and slender. Columbus, who was the first European explorer to visit Trinidad and gave it its name, sighted Tobago but never landed. Later invading Spaniards apparently named Tobago after the Carib word *tabaco,* not referring to the plant but to the shape of the island, which they thought resembled the Carib Indian pipe.

Tobago, unlike Trinidad, is today almost entirely inhabited by people

*Trinidad, 1992*

of African descent. Its history is remarkably bloody, even for the Caribbean. Spanish, French, Dutch, and British fought over it for two centuries, attracted by its potential for sugar and rum production. In an attempt in 1704 by the big European powers to quell the fighting, Tobago was declared a neutral zone, but this only allowed pirates to use it as a base for shipping raids in the eastern Caribbean, leading to yet more fearsome invasions and bloody skirmishes.

By the 1800s the British had taken complete control, importing thousands of Africans into slavery, setting up a plantation economy, and eventually making Tobago a ward of neighboring Trinidad. Today, Trinidad and Tobago form a two-island independent nation, and Tobago has become a peaceable home for farmers and fishers. Many Trinidadians now visit Tobago to rest and enjoy its quiet pleasures: the gentle sloping beaches, the encircling coral reefs, and the tropical bird forests of this lovely island. Some people say that Defoe was thinking of Tobago when he wrote *Robinson Crusoe*.

# There's a Brown Girl
# in the Ring

Sung by a children's group at the San Juan Girls' Government School,
San Juan, Trinidad; also by a group of children at The Valley
Secondary School, The Valley, Anguilla.

All over the eastern Caribbean, the children sing this song.

## IN TRINIDAD

*There's a brown girl in the ring,*
*Tra la la la la,*
*There's a brown girl in the ring,*
*Tra la la la la la,*
*(There's a) Brown girl in the ring,*
*Tra la la la la,*
*For she looks like a sugar and a plum, plum,*
    *plum.*

*Show me your motion,*
*Tra la la la la,*
*Girl, show me your motion,*
*Tra la la la la la,*
*Show me your motion,*
*Tra la la la la,*
*For she looks like a sugar and a plum, plum,*
    *plum.*

*Hug and kiss your partner,*
*Tra la la la la,* etc.

Original key: E♭

♩ = 144

1. There's a brown girl in the ring, Tra - la - la - la - la, There's a brown girl in the ring, Tra - la - la - la - la - la, Brown girl in the ring, Tra - la - la - la - la, For she looks like a su - gar and a plum, plum, plum.

2. Show— me your mo - tion,
3. Hug and kiss your part - ner, Tra - la - la - la - la, Girl,

show— me your mo - tion,
hug and kiss your part - ner, Tra - la - la - la - la - la, 

Show— me your mo - tion,
Hug and kiss your part - ner,

Tra - la - la - la - la, For she looks like a su - gar and a plum, plum, plum.

---

**To play**   Players form a ring of clappers and singers facing the center, where a single child dances about during the first verse. During the second, she "makes her motion," which may consist of "winding" or any other dance step she elects. During the third verse she stands in front of a child in the ring and the two hug or dance together. The "partner" becomes the "brown girl" for the next run-through of the game, which continues till every child has had a turn at the center role.

Anguillan children play the game approximately the same way but to a variant of the Trinidadian tune and with more direction from the lead singer. "Crossing the ocean" means dancing back and forth across the ring; "work up your calabash" means to move belly and pelvis. In St. Kitts, children sing, "Now make up your cat backs," and the dancer arches her back like a cat. Other dance steps may be called for as desired.

**About the song**   "Brown Girl" has been reported as a favorite in Trinidad, Tobago, St. Kitts, Anguilla, and Jamaica, but not in the United States nor elsewhere in the English-speaking world. Apparently, it is a

*There's a brown girl in the ring,*
*Tra la la,*
*There's a brown girl in the ring,*
*Tra la la,*
*There's a brown girl in the ring,*
*Tra la la,*
*It's sweet like sugar and plum.*

*Now cross the ocean,* etc.

*Now work up your calabash,* etc.

*Now make your motion,* etc.

*Now the rest of your motion,* etc.

*Now run and kiss your partner,* etc.

genuinely original contribution by Caribbean children. The Trinidadian and Anguillan versions are included here as excellent examples of variation in traditional music; besides, both are fun to do and to sing.

Wherever and however played, this song game epitomizes the classic and central form of Caribbean ring play, in which a single dancer occupies the center of the circle, "shows her [or his] motion," and then selects a partner who shares the dance briefly and ultimately takes over the central role. Such dances serve in part as preparation for later courtship experiences; indeed, Caribbean parents encourage their children to participate in such games, to "hug and kiss" their partners and to demonstrate their physical skills in the art of "winding," a sinuous movement of the trunk, an act which might well be disapproved of if the child were not dancing. Thus dance becomes a theater in which children can rehearse adult behavior in a socially approved situation.

Original key: D♭

1. There's a brown girl in ___ the ring, Tra - la - la, There's a brown girl in ___ the ring,

Tra - la - la, There's a brown girl in ___ the ring, Tra - la - la, It's

sweet like su - gar and plum. Now ⎰ 2. cross ___ the o - cean, ⎱ Tra - la - la, Now
                                   ⎱ 3. work up your cal - a - bash, ⎰

⎰ cross ___ the o - cean, ⎱ Tra - la - la, Now ⎰ cross ___ the o - cean, ⎱
⎱ work up your cal - a - bash, ⎰                ⎱ work up your cal - a - bash, ⎰

Tra - la - la, It's sweet like su - gar and plum. ⎰ 3. Now
                                                   ⎱ 4.–6. Now

9

# ONE, TWO, THREE

Sung by a group of children in their early teens in Brick Kiln Village, Nevis;
also by pupils of the same age at El Socorro Central Government School,
Port of Spain, Trinidad.

The children of Trinidad and Nevis practice their counting skills to a lilting tune that takes them all the way from one to one hundred.

*One, two, three,*
*Four, five, six,*
*Seven, eight, nine, ten.*

*Eleven, twelve, thirteen,*
*Fourteen, fifteen, sixteen,*
*Seventeen, eighteen, nineteen,*
  *twenty.*

*One-and-twenty, two-and-twenty,*
*Three-and-four-and-five-and-six-and-twenty,*
*Twenty-seven, twenty-eight,*
*Twenty-nine,*
*Thirty.*
*One-and-thirty, two-and-thirty,*
*Three-and-four-and-five-and-six-and-thirty,*
  *[and so forth, up to one hundred]*

**To play** Couples stand in a circle with an extra player in the center. At the word "twenty-one," the center player "cuts into" one of the couples, taking the place of one of the two, leaving the other without a partner. The single player then cuts into another couple, and so on. In Trinidad the song gets steadily faster until the play dissolves into giggling by the term "one hundred"; the player left without a partner must start the next round.

**About the song** Like numbering songs from many parts of the world ("The Twelve Days of Christmas," "Children Go Where I Send Thee," "Green Grow the Rushes-O," et al.), "One, Two, Three" is metrically irregular. If a strong and steady one-beat clap is maintained throughout the song, the bar lines may be disregarded, and any child (or even any adult) can sing it easily. In fact, this is an easy practice piece to introduce a beginner into the subtleties of Afro-Caribbean rhythms.

Original key: F

♩ = 156+

♩ = clap hands

One, two, three, four, five, six, se - ven, eight, nine, ten. E - le - ven,

twelve, thir - teen, four - teen, fif - teen, six - teen, se - ven - teen, eigh - teen, nine - teen,

etc.

1. Twen - ty. One - and - twen - ty, two - and -
2. Thir - ty. One - and - thir - ty, two - and -

twen - ty, three - and - four - and - five - and - six - and - twen - ty, twen - ty -
thir - ty, etc.

se - ven,___ twen - ty eight, twen - ty - nine,

*Last time:

(shouted)

... nine - ty - eight, nine - ty - nine, one hun - dred!

The song was brought to Tobago around 1945 by a Charlotteville teacher who had worked in St. Vincent. It has not been widely found in Trinidad, but in Tobago, where rote learning is very popular in schools, it became a favorite, especially in moonlight play sessions in rural villages, where the children sometimes make it into a game.

# ZINGLITO

Sung by two young women in Lopinot, Trinidad.

This brief song with its lyrical melody is easily learned by rote in the original Creole and can be sung in solo or, as originally performed, by two voices in duet. There are no accompanying dance or game movements.

| | CREOLE | SINGABLE TRANSLATION |
|---|---|---|
| Voice A: | *Zinglito,* | *Zinglito,* |
| Voice B: | *Ti Malengé,* | *My little one,* |
| Voice A: | *Ki zafè sa?* | *What do you do?* |
| Voices A & B: | *Ti manmay nonm-la ka siyé bwa.* | *He's cutting wood out in the noonday sun.* |

### LITERAL TRANSLATION

*Zinglito, [probably a person's name]*
*Little Malengé, [probably a family or pet name]*
*What's going on here?*
*The man's little child is sawing wood.*

**ABOUT THE SONG**  Lopinot is a small mountain village that stands in the tropical rain forest at the head of the Arouca River in northern Trinidad. Lopinot men are famed throughout Trinidad for their stringed orchestras of handmade fiddles and cuatros (small ten-stringed lutes). Most support their families as timber workers in the nearby giant hardwood forests, and in the child's song "Zinglito" a little boy tries to copy his lumberman father, working like a man with his own small saw.

12

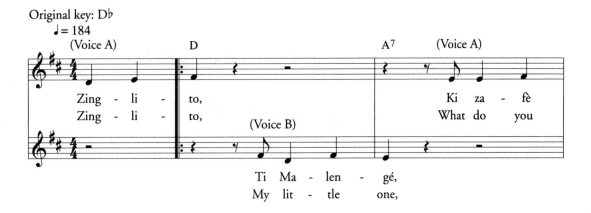

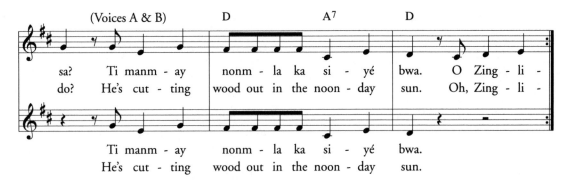

The town itself was founded and named for Count Lopinot, a Spanish royalist refugee who fled Santo Domingo for Trinidad in 1800 with one hundred slaves. This heritage is reflected in local custom, including a distinctive Creole patois. The various Creoles spoken in many forms on many islands in the Caribbean are now believed by linguists to be aspects of a newly created language, not a misheard or mispronounced French, Spanish, or Portuguese, although elements of all three languages may be present. Similarly, all the Creole dialects of the Caribbean world contain West African words and constructions.

The complexity of the overall situation is reflected in this book by the use of Standard English spelling for English song texts, French for French, and Creole orthography—which may vary from island to island—for songs in Creole. All of these are subject to the primary requirements of the melodies.

# Gypsy in the Moonlight

Sung by a group of children at the San Juan Girls' Government School,
San Juan, Trinidad.

Group:

*Gypsy in the moonlight,*
*Gypsy in the dew,*
*Gypsy never come back*
*Until the clock strike two.*

*Walk in, Gypsy, walk in,*
*Walk right in, I say,*
*Walk into my parlor*
*To hear my banjo play.*

Gypsy (solo):

*I don't love nobody*
*And nobody love me,*
*All I want is Sarah (Harold, Marva, etc.)*
*To come and dance with me.*

Group:

*Tra la la la la la,*
*Tra la la la la.*
*Tra la la la la la,*
*Tra la la la la.*

14

**TO PLAY** Players stand in a ring facing inward, singing and clapping. An extra player, "Gypsy," dances around the outside of the circle during verse 1, and inside during verse 2. She or he then remains in the ring, singing verse 3 in solo and choosing one of the ring players as a partner. During verse 4 they dance together, at the end of which Gypsy joins the circle, leaving the chosen player as the new Gypsy for another round of play.

Original key: E♭

Clap: etc.

Gyp - sy in the moon - light, Gyp - sy in the dew,

Gyp - sy nev - er come back un - til the clock strike two.

**ABOUT THE SONG** The second verse of "Gypsy in the Moon-light" rephrases the chorus of a minstrel song widely popular in the 1840s and '50s. It was variously titled "The History of the World" or "Walk in the Parlor" ("as sung by Charles White, the popular Ethiopian Serenader with tremendous applause—New York City, 1847"). Though a few additional lines have been reported from black sources in the United States, this lilting and danceable song game is actively played only by the children of Trinidad and Tobago. It seems evident that, in this form at least, it is their own original creation.

# COMING DOWN
# WITH A BUNCH OF ROSES

Sung by a children's group at the San Juan Girls' Government School,
San Juan, Trinidad; also by a group of girls at El Socorro Government School,
Port of Spain, Trinidad.

Group: *Annie, Annie,*
*Coming down with a*
*bunch of roses,*
*Coming down.*

Solo: *You walk in style,*
Group: *Coming down with a*
*bunch of roses,*
*Coming down.*

Solo: *You show me your dress, etc.*
*You show me your hat (watch,*
*hair, shoes, slip, friend), etc.*
*You dance the rhumba (limbo), etc.*

**TO PLAY** Several ways of dancing "Coming Down with a Bunch of Roses" have been reported in Trinidad and Tobago. In one, a single player dances down between the parallel lines of singing and clapping players, matching actions to the lead singer's directions, and then takes a new place at the end of the line. His opposite from the head of the line then follows and the game continues till all have soloed.

Alternatively, the end couple makes an arch by clasping hands across the lines; the lead couple dances down and under the arch, stops, and makes a new arch, allowing the original end couple to drop hands. The new head couple turns away from the arch, separates, and leads the files around and back down to the arch, where they join hands and lead the dancers under the arch and back up to position for a repetition with the new head and end couples.

**ABOUT THE SONG** The people of the Caribbean are widely thought to be among the finest small-boat sailors in the world. In the old days of sail, British, French, and American merchant ships vied to obtain Caribbean seamen for their crews. On board, Caribbean sailors

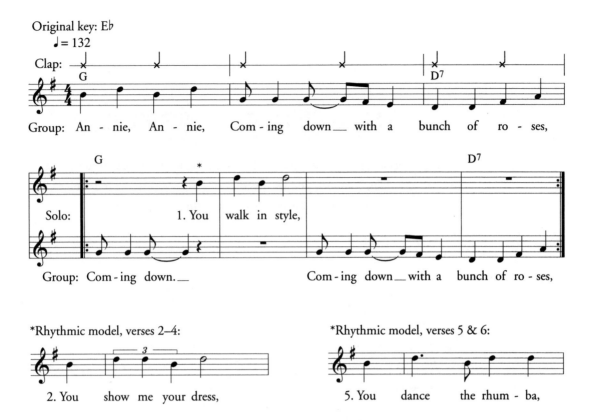

Original key: E♭
♩ = 132

Clap:

Group: An - nie, An - nie, Com - ing down___ with a bunch of ro - ses,

Solo: 1. You walk in style,

Group: Com - ing down.___ Com - ing down___ with a bunch of ro - ses,

*Rhythmic model, verses 2–4:

2. You show me your dress,

*Rhythmic model, verses 5 & 6:

5. You dance the rhum - ba,

not only learned Anglo-American chanteys but added many island-born sea songs to the international chantey repertory. Today sea chanteys are more widely sung in the Caribbean than in any other part of the world, for small sailing vessels still form a vital part of informal inter-island transport and several islands still have fishing fleets. It is thus quite possible that the children's song game "Coming Down with a Bunch of Roses" is a children's remembrance of the rare and beautiful British work chantey:

Go down, you blood red roses, go down,
Oh, you pinks and posies,
Go down, you blood red roses, go down.

Caribbean children dance "Coming Down with a Bunch of Roses" in parallel lines of partners facing each other, a popular British country dance formation described by Iona and Peter Opie in *The Singing Game* as "longways for as many as will." A widespread African-American children's game in the United States, variously titled "Willowbee," "Zudie-O," "This-A-Way Valerie," etc., is still another member of this venerable game family, along with such country dances as the "Virginia Reel" and "Sir Roger de Coverley."

17

# IN A FINE CASTLE

Sung by a group of adults and children in La Plaine, Dominica; also by two
women in Lopinot, Trinidad; and by a group of girls aged ten to fourteen at the
San Juan Girls' Government School, San Juan, Trinidad.

Some feeling for Caribbean singing style may be gained by attending to
the shifting musical accents (indicated by underlining) in this apparently
simple song.

| | |
|---|---|
| All children: | *In a fine castle,* |
| | *Do you hear my sisi-o?* |
| | *In a fine castle,* |
| | *Do you hear my sisi-o?* |
| | |
| Group I: | *Mine (Ours) is the prettiest,* |
| | *Do you hear my sisi-o?* |
| | *Mine is the prettiest,* |
| | *Do you hear my sisi-o?* |
| | |
| Group II: | *I (We) want one of them, etc.* |
| Group I: | *Which of them do you want? etc.* |
| Group II: | *I (We) want Antoni, etc.* |
| Group I: | *What will you give her? etc.* |

At this point a series of inappropriate gifts may be offered—rotten figs,
soursops, stuffed rats—all of which are refused, as this example shows:

| | |
|---|---|
| Group II: | *We'll give her a rotten fig, etc.* |
| Group I: | *That won't suit her, etc.* |

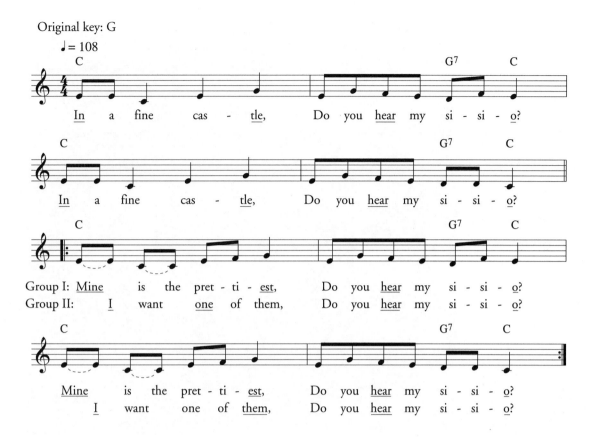

Original key: G

♩ = 108

In a fine cas - tle, Do you hear my si - si - o?

In a fine cas - tle, Do you hear my si - si - o?

Group I: Mine is the pret - ti - est, Do you hear my si - si - o?
Group II: I want one of them, Do you hear my si - si - o?

Mine is the pret - ti - est, Do you hear my si - si - o?
I want one of them, Do you hear my si - si - o?

---

The players then think up the finest gifts imaginable—motorcars, wedding rings, golden chains—all or one may be accepted:

> Group II: *I'll (We'll) give her a radiogram, etc.*
> Group I: *Well, Antoni,*
> *Go and take your radiogram. [Repeat the two lines.]*

TO PLAY  Several different formations are used:

1. In two facing lines Groups I and II march in turn toward the other during the first two lines of each verse and retreat during the last two. Or:

2. From a single circle, one child outside the ring chooses one player to join him during each repetition of the game until the whole circle has shifted over.

3. (As practiced in a Trinidad schoolyard.) In two circles side by side, each ring holds hands and swings them in time as they sing alternate verses to each other. During verse 3 (which is sung by Circle I) Circle II whispers ear-to-ear the name of the selected child. Similarly, while Circle I sings "What will you give her," Circle II decides the item to be offered (always something unpleasant for the first offer and something

*Trinidad, 1959*

pleasant for the second). During the verse "That won't suit her," the players in Circle I stamp their feet in rhythm. In the final verse the child selected leaves his own circle and goes to join the other. Circle II then starts the song again for a second repetition, and it becomes their turn to select a child from Circle I.

ABOUT THE GAME   This drama of courtship resembles the ancient British song game "Three Knights from Spain" (see "One Spaniard Came," p. 24) but demonstrates a Caribbean content and flavor. The British scholars of children's lore, Iona and Peter Opie, trace a marvelously complex route for the historical distribution of the parent game from the medieval courts of France and Italy to Great Britain during the nineteenth century, to the United States, to the Caribbean, and back to Great Britain during World War II via American Air Force and immigrant West Indian families. They quote a ten-year-old West Indian girl speaking in London in 1975: "We used to play that game a long time ago, about two years ago just amongst ourselves. . . . Nobody ever does see Sisi and I don't know who she is, unless she is somebody's sister. And I don't know where the game came from, it just arrived."

The game did indeed just arrive in many places around the world, ordinarily played to some variation of the generic, far-flung melody known in the United States as "Skip to My Lou." The wide international distribution of the game may account for the number of formations in which it is played. The Opies feel that the oldest is the double ring formation in which the two circles once represented rival castles.

# I HAVE A TREE
# IN MY RIGHT HAND

Sung by the Rose of Sharon Friendly Society Chorus, an adult chorus in
Blanchisseuse, St. George, Trinidad.

This charming song with its sweetly flowing melody is in a $\frac{5}{4}$ meter, believed by some to be necessarily "hard." The logic of the tune, however makes the "hard" easy indeed, and properly fearless young children can sing it without difficulty. The underlined syllables in the text may be helpful. It may also be sung in harmony (as shown in the music).

> *I have a tree <u>in</u> my right hand,*
> *I have a tree <u>in</u> my right hand,*
> *It bears ro<u>ses</u> in the month of May,*
> *It bears ro<u>ses</u> in the month of May.*
>
> *Get up, get <u>up</u>, my darling love,*
> *Get up, get <u>up</u>, my darling love,*
> *And kiss the <u>one</u> you love the best,*
> *And kiss the <u>one</u> you love the best.*

TO PLAY    Players stand in a circle with one outside who dances around the ring during verse 1, and inside during verse 2. Then this player chooses a successor, who is hugged and sent to the outside to begin the play again. The first player then rejoins the ring. In Tobago this game is played exclusively by girls.

ABOUT THE SONG    "I Have a Tree" has been collected frequently in Tobago and Trinidad but not elsewhere in the Caribbean. It is an almost verbatim translation into English of a medieval European Maytime round that has been found in Paris, Loiret, Poitou, and Provence. A characteristic text from France reads:

22

Original key: Bb

♩ = 84

1. I have a tree in my right hand, I have a tree in my right hand, it bears ro-
2. up, my dar-ling love, Get up, get up, my dar-ling love, And kiss the

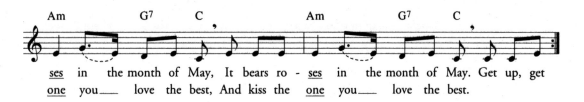

ses in the month of May, It bears ro-ses in the month of May. Get up, get
one you___ love the best, And kiss the one you___ love the best.

A la main droite j'ai un rosier
Qui fleurira
Au mois de Mai
Au mois de Mai
Qui fleurira.
    Entrez, entrez, charmante rose,
    Embrassez celle que vous voudrez,
    La rose ou bien le rosier.

Apparently, this song came to the Western Hemisphere at the time of new-world French settlement, for Canadian versions have been reported. And in the Trinidadian villages of Blanchisseuse and Lopinot, there are May festivals and fiestas with Maypole dancing and singing, and shrines to Pastora and Santa Rosa abound. Although the French settled Trinidad in 1783, the French text of this song seems to have been forgotten and it has been preserved only in English.

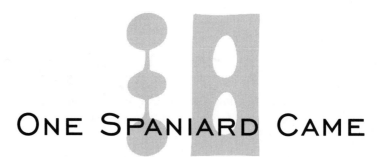

# ONE SPANIARD CAME

Sung by children aged fourteen at El Socorro Central Government School,
Port of Spain, Trinidad.

Spaniards were the first Europeans to occupy "La Trinidad," and Spanish is still spoken and sung in some parts of the island.

Solo:    *One Spaniard came from Port of Spain*
            *To come and marry your daughter Jane.*

Group:   *My daughter Jane, my daughter Jane,*
             *She is too young to be engaged.*

Solo:    *I'm going away, I'm going away,*
             *Perhaps I'll come another day.*

Group:   *Come back, come back, come back, come back,*
             *And choose the one you love the best.*

Solo:    *The fairest one, the dearest one,*
             *Is Mrs. (Susan); come along.*

             *Two Spaniards came, etc. [through entire song]*
             *Three Spaniards came, etc.*

TO PLAY  Players stand in a straight line facing a single player, the "Spaniard," who sings the first two lines of the song while moving toward the line of players. The players reply with the third and fourth lines. The Spaniard then sings the next couplet while moving back to his starting point. While the other players sing "Come back," the Spaniard goes for-

One Span-iard came from Port of Spain To come and mar-ry your daugh-ter Jane. My

daugh-ter Jane, my daugh-ter Jane, She is too young to be en-gaged.

The chorus phrase "Come back, come back," etc., is sung as follows:

Come back, come back, come back, come back, And choose the one, *etc.*

---

ward again and makes his choice. These two players then retire and decide on the name of the next child to be chosen. The game repeats until all have become Spaniards.

**ABOUT THE SONG** This game of European origin reflects the courtship customs of the pre-romantic era, when brides were chosen for reasons of state or family, as was the case in most cultures during most of human history. Recent research by Iona and Peter Opie shows that possibly the earliest versions of this game were played in Spain in the days of Don Quixote, citing an anonymous comedy printed in Barcelona in 1616 as well as a quotation from a work by Lope de Vega (b. 1562). A nineteenth-century Portuguese variation of the game, "A Condessa," is known today throughout Latin America. Many parallels in this song text, however, suggest that the Trinidadian version came to the island from Great Britain, although the first line (normally sung by British children "Here are three brothers just from Spain") has been smoothly altered by island children to name the capital city of Trinidad.

# JANE AND LOUISA

Sung by a group of children at the San Juan Girls' Government School,
San Juan, Trinidad; by two women in Lopinot, Trinidad; and by children aged
nine to eleven at the Barataria A.C. School, Barataria, Trinidad.

1.

*Jane and Louisa will soon come home,*
*Soon come home, soon come home.*
*Jane and Louisa will soon come home*
*Into this beautiful garden.*

2.

*My dear, will you 'low me to pick a rose,*
*Pick a rose, pick a rose.*
*My dear, will you 'low me to pick a rose*
*Into this beautiful garden.*

3.

*My dear, will you 'low me to waltz with you,*
*Waltz with you, waltz with you.*
*My dear, will you 'low me to waltz with you*
*Into this beautiful garden.*

**TO PLAY** Although the delicate melody and lyrics of "Jane and Louisa" make it highly enjoyable as a simple song, there are two ways the island children play it as a song game or dance.

1. *In ring-play formation:* "Jane" waltzes alone outside the circle during the first verse and inside during the second. During the third, she selects a "Louisa" from the circle and the two waltz together before the first Jane retires to the ring, leaving the chosen dancer to begin the game again. During the words "pick a rose" the dancer sometimes plucks gently at the dresses of the ring players as though she were picking flowers.

2. *In a longways set* (couples standing facing each other in widely spaced parallel rows): Two children stand side by side but at some distance from one end. During verse 1, this couple moves in rhythm toward and down the set, each facing the row on her side. During verse 2, they pick gently at the dresses of the players as they continue waltzing down. In the third verse, each waltzes with the nearest child until the last line, when the old

Original key: A

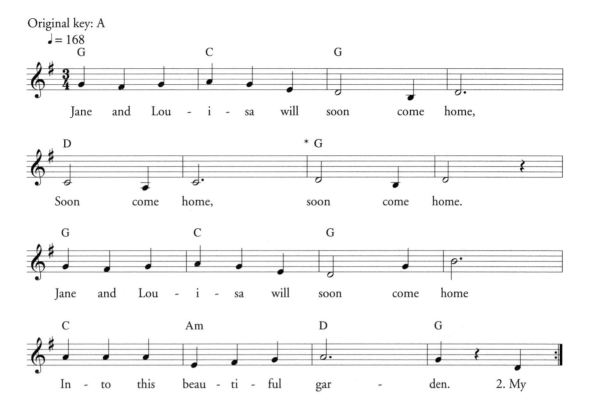

Jane and Lou - i - sa will soon come home,
Soon come home, soon come home.
Jane and Lou - i - sa will soon come home
In - to this beau - ti - ful gar - den. 2. My

*A variant of this phrase is:

Soon come home.

Jane and Louisa go to the end of the set and the new couple to the head position and the game begins again. This version appears to be the favorite in Trinidad.

ABOUT THE SONG   Although its waltz rhythm gives "Jane and Louisa" a vaguely European "feel," this song game has only been recorded in the Caribbean. It appears to be another cultural creation of the children of the islands—in all events, a prime favorite, being everywhere sung to the same melody and with almost identical words. The widespread emotional attachment to this song game suggests that it may on a deep level symbolize the main trauma of the West Indies—the out-migration of young and old that is so destructive to island culture. At the same time, this nostalgic song epitomizes the powerful feelings that link all overseas West Indians to their island homes.

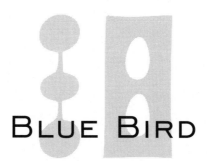

# BLUE BIRD

Sung by children aged ten to twelve at the San Juan Girls' Government School, San Juan, Trinidad.

Both Caribbean and American children sometimes alter the words of this old favorite to identify a child wearing a yellow shirt or a white dress as a yellow or a white bird.

*Blue bird, blue bird, through my window,*
*Blue bird, blue bird, through my window,*
*Blue bird, blue bird, through my window,*
*I am very, very tired.*

*So take a little bird and tap her on the shoulder,*
*Take a little bird and tap her on the shoulder,*
*Take a little bird and tap her on the shoulder,*
*I am very, very tired.*

**TO PLAY**  Children stand holding hands in a ring, their arms raised high to form arches. A single dancer, "Blue bird," trots in and out of the arches during the first verse; during the second, he takes his place behind one of the children and taps rhythmically on her shoulder. The child selected becomes the blue bird for the next round of play and begins leading the first player in and out the "windows." The shoulder tapping is repeated behind a third child, who in turn becomes the blue bird leading the other two children through the arches. The game continues until all the children are moved out of the circle formation into a long line.

**ABOUT THE SONG**  Though many assume this game is British in origin, the earliest printed versions of it are from the United States, where

Original key: C

♩= 84

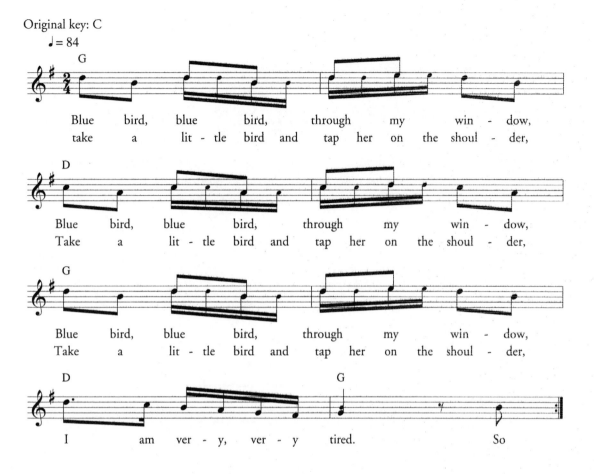

Blue bird, blue bird, through my win - dow,
take a lit - tle bird and tap her on the shoul - der,

Blue bird, blue bird, through my win - dow,
Take a lit - tle bird and tap her on the shoul - der,

Blue bird, blue bird, through my win - dow,
Take a lit - tle bird and tap her on the shoul - der,

I am ver - y, ver - y tired. So

it has long been a favorite among both white and black children. Iona and Peter Opie report that the game came to Great Britain from the United States during the first decades of the twentieth century. Connections between the United States and the West Indies for this song game are less clear; "Blue Bird" has turned up both in Trinidad and in Jamaica along with its more complex cousin "Round and Round the Village" (see p. 110).

# ROMAN SOLDIERS

Sung by a group of children at the San Juan Girls' Government School, San Juan, Trinidad; also by a group of girls aged fourteen at El Socorro Central Government School, Port of Spain, Trinidad.

In the United States a reworked edition of "Roman Soldiers" ends with both sides declaring themselves to be the United Nations. In the Caribbean, however, the mock battle is still unresolved, though there is never much fuss made about who wins. The fun appears to lie in the ferocious threats and the general mock free-for-all with which the game concludes.

Group I:     *Have you any bread and wine,*
             *For we are the Romans,*
             *Have you any bread and wine,*
             *For we are the Roman soldiers.*

Group II:    *Yes, we have some bread and wine,*
             *For we are the English,*
             *Yes, we have some bread and wine,*
             *For we are the English soldiers.*

Group I:     *Will you give us some of it,* etc.

Group II:    *We will give you none of it,* etc.

Group I:     *We will bring a policeman,* etc.

Group II:    *We ain't afraid (of) no policeman,* etc.

Group I:     *We will bring a big-foot man,* etc.

Group II:    *We ain't afraid (of) no big-foot man,* etc.

Original key: E♭

♩ = 126

Group I: Have you an-y bread and wine, For we are the Ro - mans,
Group II: Yes, we have some bread and wine, For we are the Eng - lish,

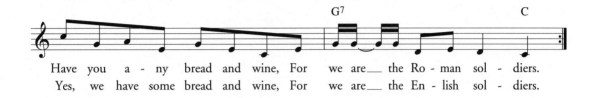

Have you a - ny bread and wine, For we are___ the Ro - man sol - diers.
Yes, we have some bread and wine, For we are___ the En - lish sol - diers.

Group I:   *We will bring a sore-foot man,* etc.

Group II:  *We ain't afraid (of) no sore-foot man,* etc.

Group I:   *We will bring a jigger-foot man,* etc.

Group II:  *We ain't afraid (of) no jigger-foot man,* etc.

Group I:   *Are you ready for a fight,* etc.

Group II:  *Yes, we're ready for a fight,* etc.

TO PLAY    Players stand in two facing straight lines, an equal number of "English" on one side and "Romans" on the other. The appropriate side sings each verse, marching forward with ferocious gestures during the first two lines and retreating to position during the last two. The last verse signals a mock battle in which each player of the opposing pairs tries to pull the other across the center back to his own side.

ABOUT THE GAME    Through its celebration of the conquest of Britain by Roman legions, this widespread British children's game points up the conservatism often found in children's folklore. Indeed, its popularity may seem outlandish until one remembers that the British, having learned their lessons from the Romans all too well, eventually established the second "world" imperium. Such apparently childish and fortuitous folkloric survivals suggest there may indeed be things to be learned from the often odd and unbelievable antiquities enshrined in local tradition.

# SANDY GIRL

Sung by a group of children at the San Juan Girls' Government School,
San Juan, Trinidad.

*There was a little sandy girl*
*Sitting on a stone,*
*Crying, weeping,*
*All the days alone.*

*Rise up, sandy girl,*
*And wipe your tears away,*
*And kiss the one you love the best,*
*And then run away.*

TO PLAY   Children stand in a circle, with the "little sandy girl" sitting or stooping in the center. As the players sing their instructions, the center player stands up, wipes her eyes, chooses a player from the ring, and the two run outside the singing circle together. When play resumes, the first "sandy girl" takes a place in the circle, while the child chosen goes into the center of the circle to become "sandy girl" for the next round of the game. Eventually, every child should have had a turn at the center role.

ABOUT THE SONG   Though its melodic line is more lyrical and its actions less feisty, "Sandy Girl" is generally thought to be a version of the older and more widespread "Little Sally Water" (see p. 140). In *The Singing Game* the Opies print a "Sandy Girl" with a text almost identical with the one given here and describe it as a nineteenth-century party game widespread in Scotland and the north of England, where it is sung to the tune of still another British jollification, "The Best Bed's a Feather Bed":

Original key: F♯

♩. = 120

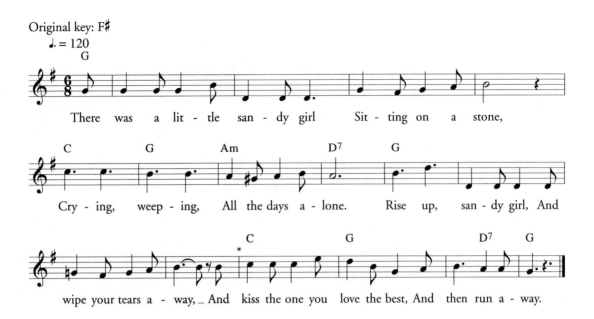

There was a lit - tle san - dy girl Sit - ting on a stone,

Cry - ing, weep - ing, All the days a - lone. Rise up, san - dy girl, And

wipe your tears a - way, — And kiss the one you love the best, And then run a - way.

* Frequently sung:

kiss the one you love the best, And

The best bed's a feather bed,
The best bed of all;
The best bed in our house
Is clean pease straw.

Pease straw is dirty,
And will dirty all my gown;
But never mind, my bonny lass,
Just lay the cushion down.

This same lilting tune has followed "Sandy Girl" through many Caribbean islands, particularly Jamaica, Trinidad, and Tobago.

# SALLY GO ROUND THE MOON

Sung by children aged fourteen at El Socorro Central Government School,
Port of Spain, Trinidad.

*Sally go round the moon,*
*Sally go round the sun,*
*Sally go round the chimney top*
*One Sunday afternoon.*
*Whoops!*

**TO PLAY** In Trinidad, children stand in a circle holding hands. They dance to the right until the word "Whoops!" when each one kicks forward as high as possible. They all then try to balance on one leg, keeping the other high in the air until the song and dance are begun again and the circle reverses to the left. The challenge of the game is not to fall down.

**ABOUT THE SONG** This prophetic cosmological fantasy, now made real as women astronauts launch into space,* has been sung and danced by British children since the nineteenth century at least, as well as by children all over the United States. In its earliest described form "Sally Go Round the Moon" is a sedate British game for the littlest children, in which they join hands and circle to the right, reversing to the left as the song is repeated. In the north of England each child takes a number as the circle is formed; they leave off the "Whoops!" but on the word "afternoon" one player at a time in numerical order turns outward as the circling continues; the game is played at top speed and "when

*In 1983, astronaut Sally Ride was the first American woman to go into outer space.

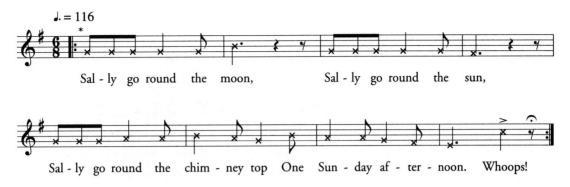

Sal - ly go round the moon, Sal - ly go round the sun,

Sal - ly go round the chim - ney top One Sun - day af - ter - noon. Whoops!

*Here, and in several other songs, clapping notes ( ♩ ) instead of standard notes are used in the music to indicate that the song has no singable pitches and is chanted rather than sung.

you've all been outwards, you turn back inwards when you're singing it again."

Trinidadian children, with whom this game is very popular, include the "Whoops!" and turn the dance into an acrobatic challenge—or a prediction of what was in store for the airborne cosmonaut Sallys of the twentieth century.

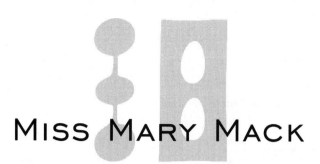

# MISS MARY MACK

Sung and played by a group of girls aged fourteen at El Socorro Central Government School, Port of Spain, Trinidad.

This classic rhyme has a marvelous swing. Thousands of English-speaking children in the Caribbean and elsewhere have clapped, swung, skipped, and danced to it as, no doubt, will thousands more to come.

*Miss Mary Mack, Mack, Mack,*
*All dressed in black, black, black,*
*With silver buttons, buttons, buttons,*
*Upon her back, back, back.*
*She asked her mother, mother, mother,*
*For fifty cents, cents, cents,*
*To see the elephant, elephant, elephant,*
*Jump over the fence, fence, fence.*

*It jumped so high, high, high,*
*It started to fly, fly, fly,*
*It was so funny, funny, funny,*
*Like bread and honey, honey, honey.*
*And that's the end, end, end,*
*Of Mary Mack, Mack, Mack,*
*All dressed in black, black, black.*

The rhyme may continue, if desired, with the next line "With silver buttons," et seq., so that play need never end.

TO PLAY Trinidadian children clap to this rhyme, facing partners, either as pairs or in parallel lines. Unlike those clapping games in which a steady clap is maintained throughout, Trinidadian children clap here only on the repeated words at the end of each line, using a series of three movements repeated in order. This pattern continues throughout the song.

1. On "Mack, Mack, Mack," partners clap hands straight across three times (right hand to partner's left; left to partner's right).

2. On "black, black, black," the same clap is used except that between each clap each player crosses her wrists on her own chest before reaching forward to clap again.

Original key: A
♩ = 204–276

Miss Ma - ry Mack, Mack,— Mack, All dressed in
black, black,— black, With sil - ver but - tons, but-tons, but-tons,— Up - on her
back, back,— back. She asked her mo - ther, mo-ther, mo-ther,— For fif - ty
cents, cents,— cents, To see the el - e - phant, el-e-phant, el - e - phant, Jump o - ver the
fence, fence,— fence. It jumped so high, high,— high, *etc.*

---

3. On "buttons, buttons, buttons," each slaps his own knees with both palms three times.

**ABOUT THE SONG** The rhyme "Miss Mary Mack" is everywhere different and everywhere the same. From Great Britain to Georgia to Trinidad, this chant (used variously for jumping rope, marching, and clapping play) consists of a series of wandering couplets combined and recombined in hundreds of different patterns; the initial four lines are almost the only ones to remain unvaried. The universal popularity of this perfect song and its endless variations provide the most convincing possible evidence of the ineradicable strength, the sheer inevitability, of oral tradition.

# Some Like It Hot, Some Like It Cold

Sung by a group of children aged nine to eleven at the Barataria A.C. School, Barataria, Trinidad; also by a group of older women in Brick Kiln Village, Nevis.

| Group (singing): | Group (singing and clapping): |
|---|---|
| *One finger, one finger, keep moving,* | *Some like it hot, some like it cold,* |
| *One finger, one finger, keep moving,* | *Some like it in the pot nine days old.* |
| *One finger, one finger, keep moving,* | *Sweet porridge hot, sweet porridge cold,* |
| *You know, you know, you know.* | *Sweet porridge in the pot nine days old.* |

*Two fingers, two fingers, keep moving,* etc.

*Some like it hot, some like it cold,* etc.

*Four fingers, four fingers, keep moving,* etc.

*Eight fingers, eight fingers, keep moving,* etc.

*All fingers, all fingers, keep moving,* etc.

TO PLAY    Children stand in a circle, hands free for clapping. While the first verse is sung, the center player holds her right hand high, the index finger pointed upward, and dances inside the ring. During the chorus, beginning "Some like it hot," the ring players begin a steady two-four clap while the center child puts her arms akimbo at the waist and jigs sideways to the new beat. During the last two lines, beginning "Sweet porridge hot," the ring players continue clapping while the center player dances over to choose another player, who is brought into the center as well.

As the song continues with "Two fingers . . . ," the two children dance with their right-hand index fingers held high; now there are "two fingers" moving. During the following chorus, the two center players each then

♩. = 60   D                              A⁷                                    D

One fin-ger, one fin-ger, keep mov-ing, One fin-ger, one fin-ger, keep mov-ing, One

                                         G          D      A⁷        D

fin-ger, one fin-ger, keep mov-ing, You know,__ you know,__ you know.

♩. = ♩ (♩ = 120)

Clap:                                                                    etc.

D

1. Some__ like__ it hot,        some__ like__ it cold,
2. Sweet__ por - ridge hot.  etc.

                              A⁷                D

some__ like__ it in the pot,  nine days old.

---

choose another child from the ring, resulting in "four fingers"; and later
"eight fingers." J. D. Elder reports that children tell him, in an interesting
example of juvenile logic, that the eight must never pick sixteen, because
there are only ten fingers to a child. Therefore, at the last repetition of the
song, all the children ("all fingers") join in to end the round of play.

ABOUT THE SONG   The old rhyme "Pease Porridge Hot," widely
known in Great Britain and the United States as a clapping game, jump-
rope rhyme, or simple nursery recitation, has undergone some interesting
changes in the Antilles. A new first section ("One finger, one finger") has
been added, its tune an offshoot of the French song "Malbrough s'en Va-
t-en Guerre," generally sung in the United States as "The Bear Went over
the Mountain" and in England as "For He's a Jolly Good Fellow." This
ubiquitous melody was also known in medieval Spain, and may well have
reached the Caribbean from southern rather than northern Europe.

Adult Trinidadians seem to know nothing of the song's European
origin and simply claim that it came down to them from the "older
heads," their ancestors, as indeed it probably did. This is a game that is
played by adults and children alike; children play it in the school yard
while adults enjoy performing it at dead-wakes and other occasions of
traditional music and dance.

# RING A RING O' ROSES

Sung by children aged five and six at the Barataria A.C. School,
Barataria, Trinidad.

*Ring a ring o' roses,*
*A pocket full o' posies,*
*Rise Sally, rise Sally,*
*All fall down.*

**TO PLAY**   Children stand in a circle holding hands. During the singing of the first three lines of the song, they dance around in the circle. At the word "down," all stoop, still holding hands, and the game is repeated until exhaustion sets in.

**ABOUT THE SONG**   This ancient activity—probably the first singing game any English-speaking child learns—has defied attempts by scholars to settle upon its origin or its meaning. It is widespread in various forms throughout northern Europe, its most common version being the standard English stanza:

Ring a ring o' roses,
Pocket full o' posies;
A tissue, a tissue,
All fall down.

Historians have suggested that the rhyme stems from the time of the Black Death, citing the custom of wearing posies to ward off the disease, the imitation of sneezing in the third line ("a tissue, a tissue") and the final instruction to "all fall down," or die. Others feel the game is even more ancient and that the third line is speaking of laughing rather than sneez-

♩ = 120

Ring  a  ring  o'  ro  -  ses,  A  pock - et  full  o'  po  -  sies,

Rise  Sal - ly,  rise  Sal - ly,  All  fall  down.

ing, citing the Teutonic myth that "gifted children have the power to laugh roses as Treyja wept gold." Trinidadian children have cut through the many attempts at interpretation of this game by substituting "Rise, Sally" (as in "Little Sally Water") in the controversial third line. But in every English-speaking land the world around, "Ring a Ring o' Roses" is now and has been for untold generations the favorite game for the very littlest children, a joyous introduction into the magical world of song and dance.

# POP GOES THE WEASEL

Sung by a group of children aged fourteen at El Sorocco General
Government School, Port of Spain, Trinidad.

*Ev'ry night when I go home,*
*The monkey's on my table.*
*Take a stick and knock him off,*
*Pop! goes the weasel.*

TO PLAY   Players stand in a circle made up of groups of three. In each group two children join hands to encircle the third child, while in the middle of the circle of groups there is an extra child, a center player. During the singing of the song, in each group of three, the two holding hands dance around the third whom they are encircling. At the word "Pop!" each of the encircled players leaves his group and rushes to enter a new group; at the same time, the extra child in the center tries to do the same thing. The player who fails to find a new group becomes the new center player.

ABOUT THE SONG   "Pop Goes the Weasel" is an old British music-hall song of somewhat mysterious origins. Some commentators point out that in British slang the term "pop" means to pawn an object and that a "weasel" is an archaic term for a shoemaker's tool. Though the song may thus at one time have made a kind of occupational sense, in the heyday of its popularity—the mid nineteenth century—its stream of nonsensical verses caused one W. R. Mandale to compose a comic version in which he stated:

I'm still as wise as e'er I was,
As full's an empty pea-shell,

42

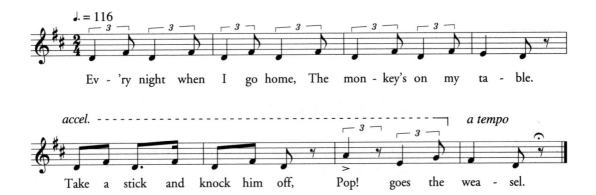

♩. = 116

Ev - 'ry night when I go home, The mon - key's on my ta - ble.

*accel.* - - - - - - - - - - - - - - - - - - - - - - - - - - - - - - *a tempo*

Take a stick and knock him off, Pop! goes the wea - sel.

> In as far as the true history goes
> Of 'Pop goes the weasel'!

Twentieth-century commentators would agree. But old rhymes often appear in new circumstances, and old and new meanings can clash. It appears from various Trinidadian versions of "Pop Goes the Weasel" that the minor character of the monkey is foremost on the singers' minds. In Trinidad people are sensitive about being called monkeys. There is also the East Indian monkey-god about whom Trinidadians of African descent make jokes. As in other traditional songs in this volume (for example, "Anana-O," p. 164), folk poetry may well touch upon contemporary, not only ancient, events and issues.

# LONDON BRIDGE

Sung by a group of children aged fourteen at El Socorro Central Government School, Port of Spain, Trinidad; also by children at The Valley Secondary School, The Valley, Anguilla.

Throughout the English-speaking world, "London Bridge" is demonstrably one of the oldest song games still in active play.

*London Bridge is broken down,*
*Broken down, broken down,*
*London Bridge is broken down,*
*My fair lady.*

*London Bridge is half way up,* etc.

*London Bridge is whole way up,* etc.

*And this is the one who stole my chain,* etc.

*Right round to prison you must go,* etc.

TO PLAY   Two children stand facing each other with arms at their sides, making, as it is put by Trinidadians, a "guard of honor." The rest of the players stand in a file, one behind the other, ready to pass between the two guards. During the first verse the file marches between the "guards of honor," returning to pass through again, a circular action that continues throughout the song. During the second verse each guard raises one hand to clasp across the players' heads, forming an arch (or half an arch, as the children apparently see it). During the next verse they raise both hands to complete the double arch. At the end of this verse they bring their arms down to capture the child then passing through.

At "Right round to prison" the two guards move away with their captive and ask that child to choose one of two things (perhaps something to eat), each having been secretly chosen by one of the guards as his

44

Original key: A

♩ = 132

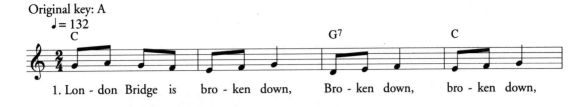

1. Lon - don Bridge is bro - ken down, Bro - ken down, bro - ken down,

Lon - don Bridge is bro - ken down, My fair la - dy.

2. . . . half way up, *etc.*
3. . . . whole way up, *etc.*

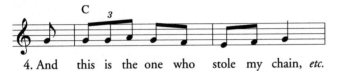

4. And this is the one who stole my chain, *etc.*

---

or her play name. The three return to the original formation, the captured child standing behind the guard whose name was chosen. The game repeats until all children are standing behind one or the other guard; the side with the most players is then declared winner, or there may be a tug-of-war between the two lines.

ABOUT THE SONG    In the script of a play published in London in 1659, a character reports dancing "the building of London Bridge" in her youth, though the earliest appearance in print of the song was not until 1744 in *Tommy Thumb's Pretty Song Book*. Some commentators link the origin of the game with the building of the original wooden bridge across the Thames in 994. Others find it more likely a remnant of the ancient rite of sacrificing a prisoner to the river gods before building a bridge.

In any case, the game "London Bridge" was combined very early on with another game involving arches, "Hark the Robbers Passing By," in which the actions were the same but the lyrics concerned capturing a robber ("the one that stole my chain") and marching him away to prison. Caribbean children play both "London Bridge," "Hark the Robbers Passing By," and various combinations of the two, as in the version printed here. In all of its various forms, it is a very popular game and has been recorded in Trinidad, Anguilla, Tobago, Dominica, Martinique, and Grenada. The other Antilles undoubtedly know it as well.

45

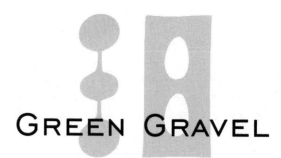

# GREEN GRAVEL

Sung by a thirteen-year-old girl at the San Juan Girls' Government School,
San Juan, Trinidad.

*Green gravel, green gravel, a bow [pronounced "bough"] shall be,*
*And a bow shall be and a kiss to you.*
*Will you get up and look at your hands and face,*
*And a bow to me and a kiss to you.*

**ABOUT THE SONG**   Although "Green Gravel" is one of the oldest
British children's games, and probably at one time referred to ancient
funerary ceremonies, this young Trinidadian girl simply sang it as she
might have any other love song. It is included because of the charm of
the melodic line, the antiquity of the original game, and its demonstration
of an important feature of Afro-Caribbean singing style—the imposition
of a two-line litany phrasing, characteristic of West Africa, upon a four-
line European strophic verse.

The melody is actually a bit difficult to sing in the proper Caribbean
two-line phrasing with only two breaths. Singers may require extra time
for breathing at the ends of lines two and four; in that case they must
either allow the meter to become irregular by taking an extra beat or two,
or allow a full measure of rest, thus sticking to the two-beat meter. The
first strategy would more accurately reflect Caribbean style.

While journeying around the English-speaking world, both the text and
the melody of "Green Gravel" have been altered in a great variety of ways.
Most versions, however, continue to center around the classic funeral song
game as first reported by Alice Bertha Gomme, the celebrated nineteenth-
century scholar of children's lore. There is general agreement that the
words "green gravel" originally referred to freshly turned earth.

Original key: E

Green grav - el, green grav - el, a bow shall be, And a

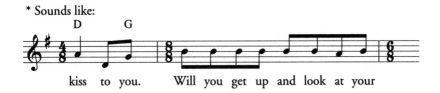

bow shall be and a kiss to you. Will you get up and look at your

hands and face, And a bow to me and a kiss to you. Green

* Sounds like:

kiss to you. Will you get up and look at your

# Sammy Dead-O

Sung by a group of girls at the San Juan Girls' Government School,
San Juan, Trinidad.

This is simply an eminently singable song with no accompanying movement except for a steady four-beat clap.

Group I:        *Sammy plant piece o' corn down the gully.*
Group II:            *(Mm-hmm)*
(alternation    *And it grow till it kill poor Sammy.*
continues)          *(Mm-hmm)*
                *Sammy dead, Sammy dead, Sammy dead-o.*
                    *(Mm-hmm)*
                *Sammy dead, Sammy dead, Sammy dead-o.*
                    *(Mm-hmm)*

                *'Twas a grudge when them branch broke on Sammy.*
                    *(Mm-hmm)*
                *'Twas a grudge when them branch broke on Sammy.*
                    *(Mm-hmm)*
                *Sammy dead, Sammy dead, Sammy dead-o.*
                    *(Mm-hmm)*
                *Sammy dead, Sammy dead, Sammy dead-o.*
                    *(Mm-hmm)*

ABOUT THE SONG   A topical song, "Sammy Dead-O" refers to an incident that occurred near the town of Manchester, Jamaica. A thriving young planter, Sammy, grew a thriving crop of corn that unaccountably died before the harvest. The local folks said that Sammy must have been "obeahed" (cursed) by jealous-hearted neighbors, and a song was com-

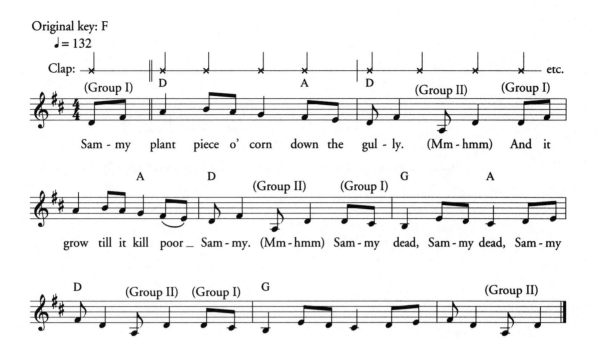

Original key: F

♩ = 132

Clap: etc.

(Group I)  D  A  D  (Group II)  (Group I)

Sam - my  plant  piece o' corn  down the  gul - ly.  (Mm - hmm)  And it

A  D  (Group II)  (Group I)  G  A

grow  till it  kill  poor __ Sam - my.  (Mm - hmm)  Sam - my  dead,  Sam - my dead,  Sam - my

D  (Group II)  (Group I)  G  (Group II)

dead - o.  (Mm - hmm)  Sam - my  dead,  Sam - my dead,  Sam - my  dead - o.  (Mm - hmm)

posed memorializing the event. In Trinidad, "Sammy" has become a stereotyped figure who often runs into trouble and is described as "bad-luckied" even when he engages in quite legitimate work, like planting a field of corn.

J. D. Elder believes that "Sammy Dead-O" originated in the island of Jamaica, where the first published version appeared in 1952. Its text demonstrates several linguistic features of Caribbean Creole. "Sammy dead" means "Sammy is dead" or "Sammy has died." Like U.S. Black English, Caribbean Creole often omits the auxiliary verb, a feature of many African grammatical structures that should be understood in that light rather than as "bad English." The term "piece" also has a specific Creole usage; it denotes a plot or field of any size whatever, no matter what the crop.

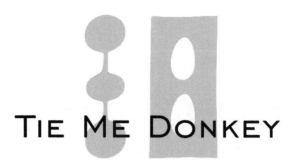

# TIE ME DONKEY

Chanted by a mixed group of children at the Barataria Eighth Street School, Barataria, Trinidad.

This chant was recorded in a performance of remarkable rhythmic precision by a group of five- and six-year-olds, who were thoroughly enjoying the challenge of group rhythmic recitation as well as the onomatopoetic effect of braying in the string of repeated "don-key, don-key, don-key's."

1.
*Daddy Dick, he had an ass,*
*He ride on Chicky Chaka.*
*He take a whip and make him go,*
*But he cannot go no faster.*

2.
*So come along, my darling,*
*Come along, my true love.*
*Just clear the way and let me pass,*
*I'm going over the mountain.*

3.
*I tie me donkey on top o' the hill,*
*And if he ain't dead, he dey.*
    *[Repeat couplet three times.]*

4.
*So donkey, donkey, donkey, donkey, donkey,*
*Tie me donkey down dey.*
    *[Repeat couplet three times.]*

5.
*I tie me donkey on top o' the hill,*
*And if he ain't dead, he dey.*

**TO PLAY** J. D. Elder reports that the chant is occasionally acted out, with gestures of the arms for "Come along, my darling," and later with players pretending to ride, holding the reins and galloping about, hitting themselves with imaginary whips as they say, "So donkey, donkey, donkey," etc.

**ABOUT THE SONG** The donkey is the most common beast of burden on many islands of the Caribbean; it is sturdy and needs less grazing

♩ = 216

Dad - dy Dick, he had an ass,__ He ride on Chick - y Cha - ka.__ He

take a whip__ and make him go,__ But he can - not go__ no fast - er.__ So

come a - long,__ my dar - ling,__ Come a - long,__ my true love.__ Just

clear the way__ and let me pass,__ I'm go - ing o - ver the moun - tain.__ I

tie me don - key on top o' the hill, And if he ain't__ dead, he dey, I dey. So

don - key, don - key, don - key, don - key, don - key, Tie me don - key down dey.

dey. I tie me don - key on top o' the hill, And if he ain't__ dead, he dey.

land than larger draft animals. Possession of a donkey is often a sign of relative wealth in rural areas, and the importance of owning a donkey is celebrated in numerous songs such as the calypso "Hold 'Em Joe—Me Donkey Want Water," popular on the island of Trinidad and elsewhere.

51

# RING DIAMOND

Sung by the Rose of Sharon Friendly Society Chorus, Blanchisseuse, St. George, Trinidad; also by an adult group led by Cyrus Smith in Green Hill Village, Diego Martin, Trinidad; a variant sung by a group of women in Brick Kiln Village, Nevis. This game, often included in adult play at dead-wakes in Trinidad villages, has also been recorded by a group of women in Woodford Hill, Dominica.

The "diamond in the ring" is a single child in the middle of a circle of clapping players, and "Diamond" should dance the role with all the brilliance and flash that he—or she—possibly can.

| | |
|---|---|
| Solo: | *Ring o ring o ring me diamond,* |
| Group: | *Hey, ring diamond.* |
| (alternation continues) | *Ring o ring o ring me diamond,* |
| | *Hey, ring diamond.* |

*Diamond in the ring already,*
  *Hey, ring diamond.*
*Diamond in the ring already,*
  *Hey, ring diamond.*

*Took me girl to buy calico,* etc.

*Come on, tell me who your lover,* etc.

*Diamond say he love (Mary),* etc.

*Hug and kiss and buss up, let me see,* etc.

TO PLAY (Trinidad version)  Players, one of whom is the song leader, stand in a clapping, singing ring. The center player, "Diamond," dances in the middle of the ring until the line "Come on, tell me who your lover" is sung, when she or he dances over to the song leader and whispers a name.

Original key: Db

♩ = 96

When the name is disclosed by the song leader in the next verse, the chosen child dances into the center of the ring with Diamond. After a hug and a kiss, the old Diamond leaves the center and joins the ring and the game repeats with the new Diamond.

This same song game appears in many delightful variations throughout the Caribbean, such as this from Nevis in which the play action, accompanied by group singing, follows the direction suggested by the words:

*Oh, ring-a-diamond,*
*Oh, ring-a-diamond,*
*Oh, ring-a-diamond,*
*Oh, ring-a-diamond.*

*Show me the one that you hugged up last night,*
*Show me the one that you hugged up last night,*
*Show me the one that you hugged up last night,*
*Oh, ring-a-diamond.*

*Ring-a-ring-a-ring-a-diamond,* etc.

*Show me a motion to your feeling,* etc.

*Say you love and I share more kiss now,* etc.

*Close them in the ring, a ring-a-diamond,* etc.

*Jenny in the ring, a ring-a-diamond,* etc.

**ABOUT THE SONG** Elegant and poetic speech is highly valued throughout the Caribbean, so it is no surprise that this song game, which centers on an attractive bit of wordplay, should be a favorite throughout the Lesser Antilles. The form is that of a British courtship game, but the poetic imagery is directly Caribbean.

Charm emerges in song through the interplay between the melody implicit in the text and the explicit melody of the tune. Africans with a deep background in tone languages seem to have more facility in discovering these nuggets of English-language melody than their white confreres. Thus new-world song making is replete with catchy African-American refrains that are totally pleasurable to sing: Swing low, sweet chariot . . . Let my people go . . . But he done her wrong . . . Coming down with a bunch of roses, coming down . . . Hey, ring diamond.

1. Oh, ring - a - dia - mond, Oh, ring - a - dia - mond,

Oh, ring - a - dia - mond, Oh, ring - a - dia - mond. __

2. Show me the one __ that you hugged up last __ night. *etc.*

3. Ring - a - ring - a - ring - a - dia - mond, *etc.*

4. Show me a mo - tion to your feel - ing, *etc.*

5. Say you love __ and I share more kiss __ now, *etc.*

6. Close them in the ring, a ring - a - dia - mond, *etc.*
7. Jen - ny in the ring, a ring - a - dia - mond, *etc.*

# MAMSELLE MARIE, MARRY THE GIRL ONE TIME

Sung by two groups of adults, one in Rampanalgas, Trinidad,
and one in Blanchisseuse, St. George, Trinidad.

This blithe song game mimes both courtship and marriage. J. D. Elder, who has seen it in both Trinidad and Tobago, reports that at one time it was considered too "adult" for children's play. The topic, however, proved so interesting to Antillean children that they evolved the following version in which all untoward connotations are carefully edited out, and now both generations play the game.

| | |
|---|---|
| Group: | *Mamselle Marie, woy yoy yoy, Mamselle Marie* |
| Solo: | *Marry the girl one time,* |
| Group: | *Mamselle Marie, woy yoy yoy, Mamselle Marie* |
| Solo: | *Give her the wedding ring,* |
| Group: | *Mamselle Marie, woy yoy yoy, Mamselle Marie* |
| (alternation | |
| continues) | *Look she ain't married yet,* etc. |
| | *Dance in the saga t'ing,* etc. |
| | *Dance in the bogan walk,* etc. |
| | *Dance in a la Grecian,* etc. |

"Bogan walk" and "a la Grecian" are names of local dance steps, now passed out of memory. M. P. Aladdin reports that "the saga t'ing" is a dance step in which the dancer raises the right shoulder as high as possible, while the right foot goes up on the toe; repeat on the left side and alternate in rhythm.

TO PLAY This song game takes place inside a circle of clapping singers, one of whom acts as the song leader. One player with a handker-

Original key: F

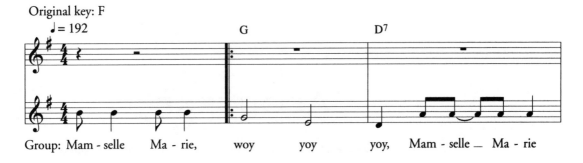

Group: Mam - selle Ma - rie, woy yoy yoy, Mam - selle __ Ma - rie

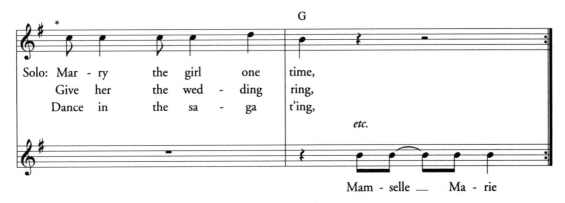

Solo: Mar - ry the girl one time,
Give her the wed - ding ring,
Dance in the sa - ga t'ing,

*etc.*

Mam - selle __ Ma - rie

* Solo variation:

Look she ain't mar - ried yet,

chief dances alone inside the ring until she has selected the boy she wants to "marry" her, before whom she drops the handkerchief. He picks it up and dances with the girl until the song leader covers the heads of the two with a large towel. When the song leader next sings "Marry the girl one time," the boy is expected to kiss the girl under the towel, which is then removed and the two dance again together and return to the circle. The song leader then chooses another "Mamselle Marie" and play—which may be varied to allow a boy to take the lead—begins again.

**ABOUT THE SONG** Dr. Elder writes: "In the folk community, feelings run high in condemnation of a man who does not marry a girl who is deserving . . . and pressure is usually brought to bear on him to marry the girl 'one time,' a Creole expression for 'at once' or 'immediately.' " In Tobago the song is sung "Mizay Marie," from the Creole word meaning "miserable" or "poor and destitute." In both versions it is quite clear where the community's sympathies lie.

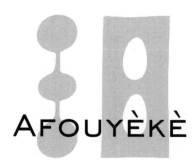

# AFOUYÈKÈ

Sung by the Rose of Sharon Friendly Society Chorus in Blanchisseuse,
St. George, Trinidad.

| | CREOLE | SINGABLE TRANSLATION |
|---|---|---|
| Solo: | *Afouyèkè* | *Afouyèkè* |
| | *Dou man-, dou manman* | *Oh, my sweet mama* |
| Group: | *Afouyèkè* | *Afouyèkè* |
| Solo: | *Ròch larivié gonmbo* | *Slippery river stones* |
| Group: | *Afouyèkè* | *Afouyèkè* |
| (alternation continues) | *Hach ka haché bwa* | *Axes cutting wood* |
| | *Afouyèkè* | *Afouyèkè* |
| | *Maché laronn-la* | *Come into the game* |
| | *Afouyèkè* | *Afouyèkè* |
| | *Ouvè laronn-la* | *Open up the game* |
| | *Afouyèkè* | *Afouyèkè* |
| | *Dansé laronn-la* | *Dance into the game* |
| | *Afouyèkè* | *Afouyèkè* |
| | *Yèkè pou mwen ouè-ou* | *Twist so I can see* |
| | *Afouyèkè* | *Afouyèkè* |
| | *O dou manman* | *Oh, sweet mama* |
| | *Afouyèkè* | *Afouyèkè* |
| | *Dou-dou manman* | *Sweet, sweet mama* |
| | *Afouyèkè* | *Afouyèkè* |

TO PLAY   This is not a true game, just a circle with partners dancing in the middle; as they tire, they rejoin the circle and others take their place. The dancers improvise their movements in response to the soloist's lead lines, each one different, each one joyous, inside the supportive circle, underneath the Caribbean night sky.

Original key: C

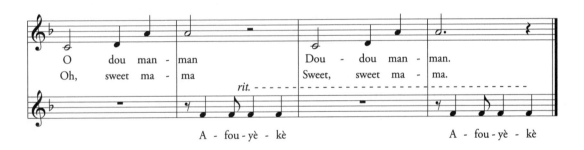

**ABOUT THE SONG** The Rose of Sharon singers of Trinidad are bilingual; though most of their songs are in English, this adult dance song is in the Creole language. The singable English translation given here is not as poetic as the Creole text but approximates its literal meaning. This song demonstrates well the characteristic two-phrase litany of West Africa: the second phrase, "Afouyèkè" (probably an African word), being repeated over and over by the group, the lead singer's brief, improvised poetic phrases being thrown in in no particular order. This is a very frequent dance accompaniment style in the Lesser Antilles.

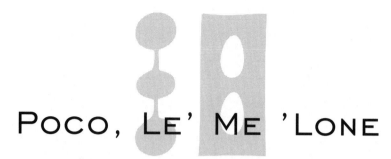

# Poco, Le' Me 'Lone

Sung by a group of children aged about fourteen in Cape Yard,
Pembroke, Tobago.

*Poco, le' me 'lone, le' me 'lone,*
*Me no marry yet, le' me 'lone.*
*Poco, le' me 'lone, le' me 'lone,*
*Me no marry yet, le' me 'lone.*
>    *When me marry, o bell go ring,*
>    *When me marry, o shell go blow.*
*Poco, le' me 'lone, etc.*

**TO PLAY** This can be danced out within a ring of singing, clapping children or sung without action as a simple song. Like many Caribbean melodies, it entices the singers on and on for "just one more time." These Tobagonian children used a vocal style called "overlap," in which an answering part actually begins *before* the first part has quite finished. Two groups sing in alternation, one line each; on the sixth line the group singing holds the word "blow" under the first few words of "Poco, le' me 'lone." This is not only a pleasing musical effect in this particular song; such a use of overlapping alternation is an important characteristic of African and African-American musical style.

**ABOUT THE SONG** "Poco" is a local name for a pestiferous sand flea found in some seasons on Caribbean beaches. This same song game, however, is sometimes sung about "Bobo"—a prominent character in Caribbean folktales, usually portrayed as large, bumbling, and a bit dim-witted. Whether specifying Poco or Bobo, the sentiments of the song seem clear: the lady in question is enjoying her single state and does not want to get married yet, at least not to Poco or Bobo. Caribbean weddings

Original key: A♭
♩ = 120

Clap: etc.

Po - co, le' __ me 'lone, le' me 'lone, Me no mar - ry yet, le' me 'lone.

When me mar - ry, o bell go ring, When me mar - ry, o shell go blow. __

__ Po - co, le' __ me 'lone, le' me 'lone, Me no mar - ry yet, le' me 'lone.

are celebrated by the European tradition of ringing bells and by the African tradition of blowing horns, the latter made from large conch shells that can be picked up on the beaches of the Antilles.

# MISS LUCY HAS SOME
# FINE YOUNG LADIES

Sung by a group of children in Cape Yard, Pembroke, Tobago;
also by a group aged seven to ten at the Bourge Mulatresse R.C. School,
Lower Santa Cruz, Trinidad.

*Miss Lucy has some fine young ladies,*
*Fine young ladies, fine young ladies,*
*Miss Lucy has some fine young ladies,*
*Tra la la la la la.*

*And ev'ry night is a sitting on a sofa,*
*Sitting on a sofa, sitting on a sofa,*
*And ev'ry night is a sitting on a sofa,*
*Tra la la la la la.*

*And he bring he culture to fool my daughter,* etc.

*Just take her home and marry her,* etc.

**TO PLAY** Although "Miss Lucy" can be enjoyed simply as a song, Trinidadian boys and girls occasionally act it out as well. Standing in parallel lines facing partners, the girls first mime what "fine young ladies" they are. During the second verse they stoop down whenever the word "sitting" occurs and pretend to smooth their skirts under them. During the third verse, the boys imitate playing a guitar, and during the last verse the partners join hands across, swinging them back and forth, or else dance in couples.

**ABOUT THE SONG** This song seems native to Tobago, having been collected there as early as 1954. It is popular also in Trinidad, but no parallel has been found elsewhere. In Tobago, "Miss Lucy," along with

1. Miss Lu - cy has some fine young la - dies, Fine young la - dies, fine young la - Miss (dies),

Lu - cy has some fine young la - dies, Tra - la - la - la - la - la.

2. And ev - 'ry night is a sit - ting on a so - fa, *etc.*

3. And he bring he cul - ture to fool my daugh - ter, *etc.*

4. Just take her home and mar - ry ___ her, *etc.*

her young ladies, sits elegantly on a sofa courted by a tasteful suitor. In Trinidad, "Miss Lucy" is occasionally "Miss Mary," who has "some fine young daughters," and the suitor in the third verse brings "his guitar" to fool one of them. Whether culture or guitar, the actual instrument of seduction is likely a cuatro, a ten-stringed instrument widely played throughout the Caribbean.

# Mister Ram Goat-O

Sung by a group of pupils at the San Juan Girls' Government School,
San Juan, Trinidad.

In African-American tales, animals are often addressed formally, and with respect, as Brother, King, Mister, Aunt, and so forth.

> *Mister Ram Goat-O!*
>> *Bam-ban-dy-a*
> *Mister Ram Goat-O!*
>> *Bam-ban-dy-a*
> *Can you lend me a razor?*
>> *Bam-ban-dy-a*
> *It's to shave off my long beard.*
>> *Bam-ban-dy-a*

**TO PLAY**  No associated dance was recorded. This song can be sung solo, as a duet between two groups, or, following the original recording, in straightforward antiphony, African-style call-and-response, between a song leader and a group.

**ABOUT THE SONG**  In the Antilles, storytelling is a highly developed art form involving songs and, often, dances and mimes in which the audience joins, some so fully dramatized that a full cast may be required to perform them. Perhaps the most important time for storytelling is during the wakes for the dead, when the whole community gathers to sit up with the family of the deceased. But any evening after sundown may also be an occasion for the neighborhoods to gather together to listen to old stories, many punctuated by a little song or two. It is certainly quite possible that "Mister Ram Goat-O" is a song that formerly enlivened a story now forgotten.

64

Original key: Eb

♩ = 96  Clap:

Solo: Mis - ter Ram Goat - O! Mis - ter

Group: Bam - ban - dy - a

etc.

Ram Goat - O! Can you lend me a ra - zor?

Bam - ban - dy - a

It's to shave off my long beard.

Bam - ban - dy - a     Bam - ban - dy - a

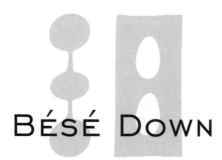

# BÉSÉ DOWN

Sung by a group of children aged nine to eleven at the Barataria A.C. School,
Barataria, Trinidad.

This song game is a great favorite among Trinidadian children. It has a particularly enjoyable tune and makes a delightful game, worthy of the affection Trinidadian children obviously feel for it.

Group:    *Lauran, Lauran, bésé down,*
          *Lauran, Lauran, bésé down.*
              *We no dry like a bambam,*
              *Bésé down,*
              *We no neeray, neeray,*
              *Bésé down,*
              *We no dry like a bambam,*
              *Bésé down.*

Lauran:   *Red rose, red rose, bésé down,*
Group:    *Red rose, red rose, bésé down.*
              *We no dry like a bambam,*
              *Bésé down,* etc.

Lauran:   *Green rose, green rose, bésé down,*
Group:    *Green rose, green rose, bésé down,* etc.

TO PLAY   Children stand in a ring with one child (Lauran) in the center. Each child making up the circle has claimed a colored rose as a name (Red rose, Blue rose, Pink rose). Lauran bows down ("bésé down") as the first verse is sung, either by kneeling or winding her waist in a downward-upward motion. At the beginning of the second verse she calls on another

♩ = 120

C    F    C    F
Laur - an, Laur - an, bé - sé down,— Laur - an, Laur - an,

C    F    C    F
bé - sé down.—We no dry like a bam - bam, Bé - sé down,—We no nee - ray, nee - ray,

C    F    G⁷    C
Bé - sé down,— We no dry like a bam - bam, Bé - sé down.—

---

child to join her ("Red rose, red rose, bésé down") and the two bow down together. They then decide which rose they will call on for the third repetition; then all three agree on the fourth, and so on. When all the children are inside the ring, they sing, "All rose, all rose, bésé down."

**ABOUT THE SONG**    On the island of Jamaica children play a game called "Bessie Down" in which "Bessie" is instructed to walk, jump, etc. It seems likely, however, that the term "bésé" is a creolization of the French word "baisser," meaning "to bow," though there is some punning possible with the French term "baiser," meaning "to kiss." "Bambam" means "pumpkin," and in Trinidad they sometimes sing, "For the sake of the pumpkin, bésé down." But no one has yet offered an explanation for the word "neeray."

# SI SI MARIA

Sung by a group of adults in Blanchisseuse, St. George, Trinidad;
"If You See Maria" was sung by a group of adults in Woodford Hill, Dominica.

This best-loved and most exciting bongo drum dance is frequently performed at dead-wakes. "Tamboulé" means to beat the drum.

Group:    *Si si Maria, Maria, Maria,*
              *Si si Maria, Maria, Maria.*
              *Tamboulé lé lé lé lé lé,*
              *Tamboulé-é————,*
Solo:       *One boy, one girl,*
Group:    *Tamboulé lé lé lé lé lé,*
              *Tamboulé-é————,*
Solo:       *In the turkey trot,*
Group:    *Si si Maria, Maria, Maria,* etc.

The refrain ("Si si Maria") may occur at any point and the solo lines appear in no special order.

Solo:   *Lé lé a la twist*          *Lé lé (dance) the twist*
       *Lé lé ba yo*             *Lé lé for them*
       *Lé lé mon oue*          *Lé lé for me to see*
       *A la Grecian*           *In the Grecian way*
       *In determine walk*      *[A dance step]*
       *A la bogan walk*       *[A dance step]*
       *In the saga t'ing*       *[A dance step: shoulders*
                                 *raised alternately]*

A Dominican variation of this tune is sung by two alternating groups, the singers switching cheerfully from English ("One boy, one girl") to

Creole ("Yon fi, yon ga'çon"), which means the same thing, in reverse order. Dominicans speak more than one language and often use them interchangeably.

Group I:    *If you see Maria, Maria Safaya,*
            *If you see Maria, Maria Safaya,*
            *Tamboulé lé-é———, tamboulé.*
Group II:   *One boy, one girl.*
Group I:    *Tamboulé lé-é———, tamboulé.*
Group II:   *Yon fi, yon ga'çon.*
Group I:    *Tamboulé lé-é———, tamboulé.*
            *If you see Maria, Maria Safaya,* etc.

**TO PLAY** In the center of a ring of clapping singers, one boy and one girl dance to the bongo. As one dancer tires, he or she goes out and another from the ring takes the center, but there must always be "one boy, one girl." In Trinidad the group holds the last note of the refrain word "Tamboulé-é-é" under the solo lines.

*The clapping scheme here indicates one rhythmic accompaniment above the clap line ( ♩ ) and another rhythmic accompaniment below it ( 𝄾 ).

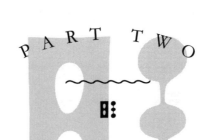

PART TWO

# SONG GAMES

## FROM

## DOMINICA AND ST. LUCIA

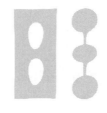

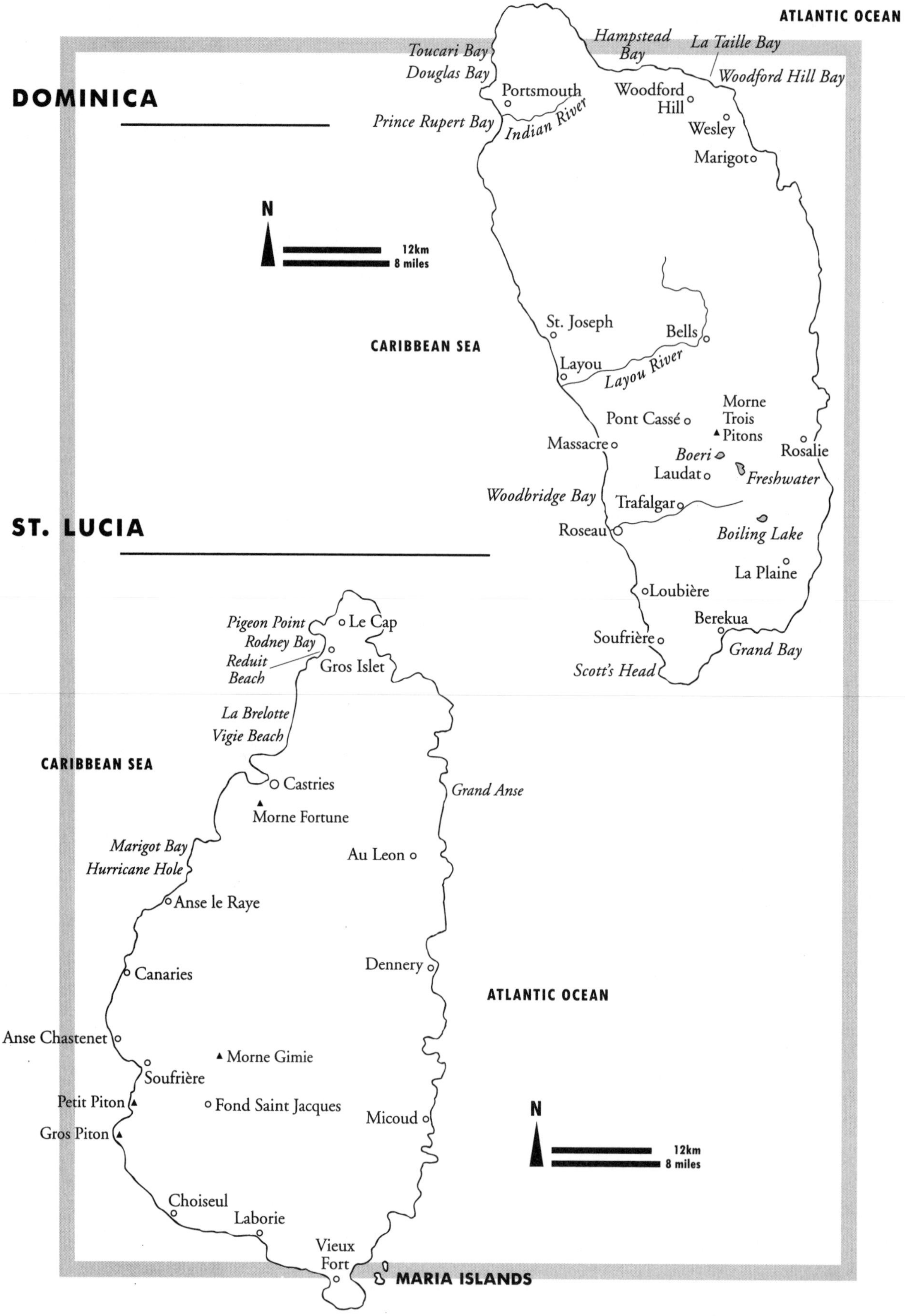

**DOMINICA**

ATLANTIC OCEAN

*Toucari Bay*
*Douglas Bay*
*Hampstead Bay*
*La Taille Bay*
*Woodford Hill Bay*

Portsmouth
Woodford Hill
*Prince Rupert Bay*
*Indian River*
Wesley
Marigot

N
12km
8 miles

CARIBBEAN SEA

St. Joseph
Bells
Layou
*Layou River*

Pont Cassé
Morne Trois Pitons
Massacre
*Boeri*
Rosalie
Laudat
*Freshwater*
*Woodbridge Bay*
Trafalgar
Roseau
*Boiling Lake*
La Plaine
Loubière
Berekua
Soufrière
*Grand Bay*
*Scott's Head*

**ST. LUCIA**

*Pigeon Point*
Le Cap
*Rodney Bay*
*Reduit Beach*
Gros Islet

*La Brelotte*
*Vigie Beach*

CARIBBEAN SEA

Castries
Morne Fortune
*Grand Anse*

*Marigot Bay*
*Hurricane Hole*
Au Leon
Anse le Raye

Canaries
Dennery

ATLANTIC OCEAN

Anse Chastenet
Morne Gimie
Soufrière
Petit Piton
Fond Saint Jacques
Micoud
Gros Piton

N
12km
8 miles

Choiseul
Laborie
Vieux Fort
**MARIA ISLANDS**

# DOMINICA AND
# ST. LUCIA

**B**oth Dominica and St. Lucia are tall islands. Intense volcanic eruptions thrust them up high out of the boiling Caribbean seas thousands of years ago. Dominica in particular seems almost all towering mountains, sharp ridges, deep valleys, laced with waterfalls. It is said that when Queen Isabella asked Columbus to describe the new island he had noted on his 1493 voyage, he took a piece of parchment paper and crumpled it, throwing it down on the table with all its sharp spikes and complicated folds. There's Dominica, he said.

The Carib Indians already in possession of the island had their own name for their home, Waitikubuli—"Tall Is Her Body"—and they defended their land against Spanish, French, and British trespassers with such vigor that in 1660 the British and French signed a neutrality treaty agreeing to leave the island in the possession of the Caribs. During the following century the treaty fell into disuse, and serious fighting between French and British colonists broke out before the island was finally ceded to Britain.

Today, Dominica is an independent republic within the British Commonwealth. Most of its citizens are of African descent, but it is also home to the last remnants of the Carib people, most of them still living in the interior rain forest where they get the logs for their famous dugout canoes. In the central, still not completely explored jungle wilderness of Dominica more than 139 species of birds have been identified—bananaquits, hummingbirds, flycatchers, parrots—and amazing insects like the blacksmith beetle, so huge and cumbrous that it clanks when it moves. On the dark sand beaches, Dominican men and women assemble casually now and then to make a little music and tell stories. Dominicans are great storytellers.

And so are their cousins, the St. Lucians, living to the south on another tall island, this one shaped, some say, like a teardrop. And the history of St. Lucia has sometimes taken the same mournful contour. The Arawak Indians were the first to settle there in prehistoric times but were conquered by migrating Caribs around A.D. 800. Though Columbus himself missed sighting St. Lucia, later exploring vessels did not make that mistake and began frequent raids. Only fierce and determined Carib resistance postponed European occupation until the eighteenth century; it is said that the Caribs drove off the earliest British invasions with red pepper smoke, a technique they had developed for capturing parrots. During the following 150 years, a dingdong struggle between the French and the British consumed the small island, the national flag changing fourteen times before the Treaty of Paris finally awarded St. Lucia to the British. By then, some were calling the island the "Helen of the West Indies," for the battles to win her were as fearsome as the fabled Trojan Wars.

Today, St. Lucia is an independent country within the Commonwealth, its peaceful banana, coconut, and cocoa plantations providing most of its revenue, along with fishing and tourism. But its lengthy con-

*St. Lucia, 1959*

tact with French culture is still evident in the local architecture, music, and language. Since some 85 percent of the island's population is African in origin, the resulting mix of British, French, Carib, and African languages has produced an especially rich Creole as well as a yeasty repertory of local songs and stories. Indeed, the poet and playwright Derek Walcott, who won the Nobel Prize for Literature in 1992, was born on St. Lucia and still maintains close ties with his creative home, the still-beautiful "Helen of the West Indies."

# Down to the Carpet

Sung by a group of schoolchildren in La Plaine, Dominica; also by an adult man in solo, accompanying himself with hand clapping, in Marigot, Dominica.

This children's comment on courtship and marriage also includes examples of the Caribbean game of "accenting the wrong syllables" (as the old joke goes).

> *Down to the carpet you must go,*
> *Like a blackbird in the air.*
> *Oh, rise and stand up on your knees,*
> *And choose the one you love the best.*
> *Oh, when you marry, you tell me so,*
> *First a boy, second a girl,*
> *Ten days after, ten days old,*
> *Kiss, kiss and say goodbye.*

TO PLAY    The Dominican children of La Plaine sang this easy but rhythmically supple melody without any accompanying action, but experienced ring players could easily improvise appropriate actions according to the standard pattern (see "There's a Brown Girl in the Ring," p. 6, "Gypsy in the Moonlight," p. 14, et al.).

In Jamaica the mysterious first two lines are sometimes sung this way:

On the carpet you must be
Happy as the grass-bird on the tree.

And in play, children sometimes use "Down to the Carpet" as a kind of second act for "Little Sally Water" (see p. 140). After Little Sally chooses her partner, "Down to the Carpet" is sung at a much speedier tempo

Original key: B♭

♩ = 192

Down to the car-pet___ you must go,___ Like a black-bird___ in the air. Oh,

rise and stand up___ on your knees, And choose the one you love___ the best. Oh,

when you mar-ry, you tell me so,___ First a boy, se-cond a girl,

Ten days af-ter, ten___ days old,___ Kiss, kiss and say good-bye.___

while the two children dance in the center of the ring. At the last line, "Kiss, kiss and say goodbye," the original Little Sally joins the ring, leaving the center player to repeat the game as the new Little Sally.

**ABOUT THE SONG** This eight-line stanza is a "wandering verse," found in at least two other well-known English-language song games: "King William Is King George's Son" and "Pretty Little Girl of Mine," both frequently reported in the United States and Great Britain. In the Caribbean, however, the verse has been turned into an independent song game, far more compact than the originals, and turning up frequently in both Jamaica and Dominica.

# MOSQUITO ONE

Chanted and clapped by a group in Massacre, Dominica.

*Mosquito one, <u>mosquito</u> two,*
*<u>Mosquito</u> jump in the old man's shoe.*
*Ten times ten, Dominicker hen,*
*The old man fell and he got up again.*

*My mother say not to play*
*With the Gypsies in the wood.*
*If I do, she will say*
*Naughty girls will disobey,*
*Disobey, disobey,*
*Naughty girls will disobey.*

*My father say not to play*
*With the heroes in the wood.*
*If I do, he will say*
*Naughty boys will disobey,*
*Disobey, disobey,*
*Naughty boys will disobey.*

*Mistress Brown teaches us*
*How to spell and arithmetic.*
*This is how the world goes round:*
*January, February, March, April, May, June,*
*July, August, September, October,*
*November, December!*

*Dominica, 1959*

TO PLAY   This somewhat surreal rhyme is accompanied here by a clap pattern that follows the words and rests between poetic lines. It can be chanted by a pair of children facing each other and clapping their own and their partners' hands alternately, or by a group in a ring clapping first their own hands and then those of the children standing to either side, as follows (O = clap own hands; P = clap partner's hands):

| (1) | 2 | 3 | (4) | (1) | 2 | 3 | (4) |
|-----|-----|-----|-----|-----|-----|-----|-----|
| rest | O | P | rest | rest | O | P | rest |
| Mos- | qui-to | one | | mos- | qui-to | two | |

| (1) | 2 | 3 | 4 | 1 | 2 | 3 | (4) |
|-----|-----|-----|-----|-----|-----|-----|-----|
| rest | O | P | O | P | O | P | rest |
| Mos- | qui-to | jump | in the | old | man's | shoe | |

| (1) | 2 | 3 | (4) | (1) | 2 | 3 | (4) |
|-----|-----|-----|-----|-----|-----|-----|-----|
| rest | O | P | rest | rest | O | P | rest |
| Ten | times | ten | | Do-mi-nick-er | hen | | |

| | 1 | 2 | 3 | 4 | 1 | 2 | 3 | (4) |
|-----|-----|-----|-----|-----|-----|-----|-----|-----|
| rest | O | P | O | P | O | P | O | rest |
| The | old | man | fell | and he | got | up a- | gain | |

Try first reciting the verse over an established regular count of 1-2-3-4 (tapping with a pencil or a foot). When that is easy, add the clapping pattern; its strong and weak beats will add to the syncopation.

ABOUT THE SONG   This clapping rhyme is a pastiche of wandering verses known to British, Australian, and American children, who have inserted them into numerous counting-out rhymes, jump-rope rhymes, and clapping games. The "Dominicker hen" of the early lines may be a corruption of the Latin word "Domine" ("Lord"), which W. W. Newell, the eminent scholar of American child lore, reports in many European counting-out rhymes. More likely it stems from "Dominique," the name of a type of fowl with barred black-and-white plumage. Dominican children may have found this ancient term especially delightful.

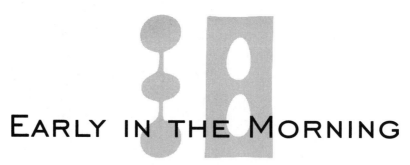

# EARLY IN THE MORNING

Sung by a group of children in La Plaine, Dominica.

*Ear-r-r-r-ly in the morning when the cock*
*begantocrow,*
*Ev'rybody take a cock before they go.*
*Pay two pounds ten before you go,*
*Pay two pounds ten before you go.*

**TO PLAY** This brief melody, so reminiscent of "The Peanut Vendor," is great fun to sing, full of spunk and hot rhythm and, like so many Dominican tunes, it always asks to be sung "just one more time." Any of the claps described in other songs ("Somet'ing Make Me Laugh Ha, Ha, Ha," "Miss Mary Mack," etc.) can be used, either between couples or in a circle, as described in "Mosquito One." Or, like these children in La Plaine, you can have a lot of fun just singing it, letting the circular melody take you on and on and round and round.

**ABOUT THE SONG** The history of popular music is full of periods when "Latin American" music came into vogue—Trinidadian calypso during the 1940s, Brazilian bossa nova in the early '60s, Jamaican reggae in the late '70s. These sudden "discoveries" of local musical systems that were there all the time always result in the reworking of traditional folk songs for commercial purposes. Sometimes the folk reverse this process and rework commercial hits for their own uses; it is not always clear which process has been at work in a given case.

The melody of "Early in the Morning" strongly resembles the popular "Peanut Vendor," a song said to have been composed by a Cuban musician, Moises Simons, who copyrighted it in the United States in 1928.

Original key: Db

♩ = 108

Clap (simple offbeat):

Early in the morning when the cock began to crow,

Ev - 'ry bod - y take a cock be - fore they go.

Pay two pounds ten be - fore you go.

Dominican children have either created their own song to Simons's tune, or Simons may have heard their tune and set his own words to it. The text is of little help in identifying or even dating the song. Pounds, shillings, and pence persisted in the British West Indies until quite recently, and guinea pieces are still prized heirlooms among country people. The crowing of a cock has been the universal indicator of the time in rural areas since the domestication of fowl.

# TRA LA LA VOUM-BÉ

Sung by a group of children in La Plaine, Dominica.

CREOLE

*Ophélia, Julien bò lariviè,*
*Ophélia koupé yon milé.*
*Afòs Julien kontan sa,*
*I hélé, "Mété an pann-a!"*
　　*Tra la la voum-bé [three times]*
　*Voum-bé, voum-bé,*
　*Voum-bé-o*

LITERAL TRANSLATION

*Ophélia, Julien by the river,*
*Ophélia cut a mullet.*
*Julien was so pleased about it,*
*He shouted, "Put it in the pan!"*
　　*Tra la la voum-bé, etc.*

SINGABLE
TRANSLATION

*Ophélia and Julien stay*
*Beside the river all the day,*
*Catching mullets for the pot,*
*They make their dinner good and hot.*
　　*Tra la la voum-bé, etc.*

**TO PLAY** Though these Dominican children cross-clap occasionally and briefly in a sort of casual "shave and a haircut" pattern with this tune, it is usually just sung. In Toco, Trinidad, a police corporal recalls his mother's verse:

See the fishes in the sea,
Papa ketch them three by three,
Mama fry dem in her pot,
And we eat dem nice and hot.
　　Te-ra-ra boom-de-hey!

**ABOUT THE SONG** This song is clearly related to "Ta-ra-ra Boom-der-e," copyrighted by Henry J. Sayers, a theatrical press agent for an 1891

Original key: E♭

♩ = 208

Clap:

D

O - phé - lia, Ju - lien bò la - riviè, _ O - phé - lia kou - pé yon mi - lé. _
O - phé - li - a and Ju - lien stay _ Be - side the ri - ver all the day, _

A⁷                                    D

A - fòs Ju - lien kon - tan sa, _ I hé - lé, "Mé - té an pann - a!" _
Catch - ing mul - lets for the pot, _ They make their din - ner good and hot. _

Tra la la voum - bé, _ Tra la la voum - bé, _

A⁷                                    D

Tra la la voum - bé, _ Voum - bé, voum - bé, voum - bé - o. _

etc.

---

musical, *Tuxedo.* The star of this production, Lottie Collins, "made it a riot in England by singing the first part of the tune ultrademurely and then going into a kicking chorus with what was undoubtedly the jazziest effect of 1891." The tune became instantly popular and parodies sprang up far and wide in the United States and Great Britain alike.

Mr. Sayers is said to have first heard the song in a St. Louis cabaret run by a black woman, Babe Connors; the text was too bawdy to print, and Sayers therefore kept only the tune and the nonsense chorus and wrote new verses. The era of the "gay nineties" in the United States was a period when Mississippi River steamboats spread African-American music from one end of the river to the other, so it is reasonable to suggest that an earlier "Ta-ra-ra Boom-der-e" may have come into New Orleans from the Caribbean. We will probably never know for certain.

The tune has the ring of a West Indian song game, but the Creole text is enigmatic, dealing with Caribbean river fishing in which adults and children sweep the river bottoms with coconut palm fronds, drawing the mullet into the shallows where the fishermen chop at the floundering fish with machetes. The mullet is a delicious small black freshwater fish; possibly this is why Ophélia and Julien are so excited by the day's catch.

# BONJOUR, MA COUSINE

Sung by a group of children in La Plaine, Dominica.

This song is in French, not Creole. It ends on the fifth rather than the first note of the scale, making it seem as though the song has no end at all, so that singers tend to repeat the tune. Apparently, this is all right with Caribbean children, who, like their age mates in all climes, have a sense of timelessness and enjoy experimenting with infinity.

### FRENCH

*Bonjour, ma cousine,*
*Bonjour, mon cousin germain.*
*On m'a dit que vous m'aimez;*
*Ce n'est pas la vérité.*
*O, je n'm'en soucie guère,*
*O, je n'm'en soucie guère.*
*Passez par ici et moi pas là.*

### LITERAL TRANSLATION

*Hello, my cousin,*
*Hello, my first cousin.*
*They say you love me;*
*That's not true.*
*Oh, I hardly care about it,*
*Oh, I hardly care about it.*
*You come by here and I won't*
*be around.*

### SINGABLE TRANSLATION

*Hello, cousin darling,*
*Hello, cousin darling.*
*They say you're in love with me;*
*I say that it cannot be.*
*Oh, I don't care about it all,*
*Oh, I don't care about it all.*
*And I won't be home if you should call.*

Original key: E♭

♩ = 208

Bon - jour, ma cou - si - ne, ___ Bon - jour, mon cou -
Hel - lo, cou - sin dar - ling, ___ Hel - lo, cou - sin

sin ger - main. ___ On m'a dit que vous m'ai - mez; ___ Ce n'est pas la
dar - ling. ___ They say you're in love with me; ___ I say that it

vér - i - té. ___ O, je n'm'en sou - cie guè - re, ___ O, je n'm'en sou - cie
can - not be. ___ Oh, I don't care a - bout it all, ___ Oh, I don't care a -

guè - re, ___ Pas - sez par i - ci et moi pas là.
bout it all. ___ And I won't be at home if you should call.

---

**To play**  The Dominican children who recorded "Bonjour, Ma Cousine" simply sang it as a song. It has been reported to J. D. Elder that in Haiti this song is sometimes played as a kissing game, probably along the lines of the ring play so frequently described in these pages.

**About the song**  In the Caribbean it is considered rude not to greet every passerby, and the term "cousin" is frequent in such salutations. The term "cousin germain," however, refers to a true blood relationship, specifically to cousins descended from two brothers or two sisters.

# SIKOLA OLA VANNI

Sung by a group of children in La Plaine, Dominica.

"Sikola ola vanni" means "chocolate and vanilla" in Creole. The Creole verse lines are just as easy to enunciate as the refrain line, and as mouth-filling.

CREOLE    *Ay nou ka lélé kako, bai-la,*
     *Sikola ola vanni.*
   *Le baton lélé en Koubari,*
     *Sikola ola vanni.*
   *Yun, dé, trois, la vanni,*
     *Sikola ola vanni.*
   *Ay nou ka lélé kako, bai-la,* etc.

SINGABLE TRANSLATION    *We're stirring cocoa beneath a tree,*
     *Sikola ola vanni.*
   *The stirring stick is in Koubari,*
     *Sikola ola vanni.*
   *One, two, three, vanilla,*
     *Sikola ola vanni.*
   *We're stirring cocoa beneath a tree,* etc.

88

TO PLAY   "Sikola ola Vanni" is sung to accompany the "winding" action (moving hips in a circular motion) so frequent in Caribbean children's play. Most typically, the dance takes place inside a ring of clapping, singing children. The song itself, with its circular Dominican melody, has an elegant symbolic fit with the vigorous action of stirring up cocoa.

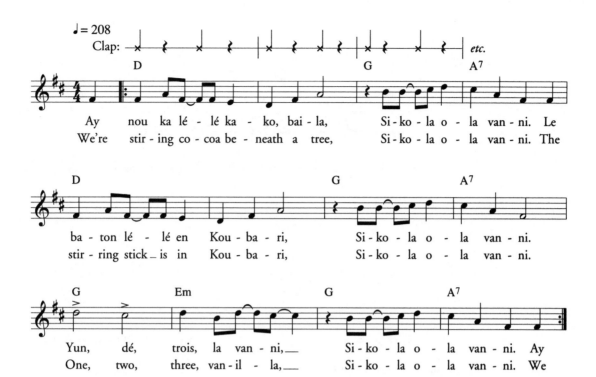

**ABOUT THE SONG** Though the major Dominican export crops are bananas and citrus fruits, both coffee and cocoa are also grown there, and one of the largest local cocoa plantations is Koubari, referred to in this Dominican children's dancing song. The cocoa (or "cocoa tea") of the Caribbean is often spiced with cinnamon, nutmeg, vanilla, and coconut milk.

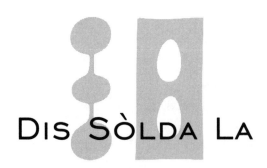

# Dis Sòlda La

Sung by a group of children in La Plaine, Dominica.

| CREOLE | | LITERAL TRANSLATION |
|---|---|---|
| Group I: | *Dis sòlda la,* | *Ten soldiers there,* |
| Group II: | *Wo yo yoy* | *Wo yo yoy* |
| | *Son-a pa-ka maché.* | *The sound isn't traveling.* |
| | *Wo yo yoy* | *Wo yo yoy* |
| | *Dis sòlda la,* | *Ten soldiers there,* |
| | *Wo yo yoy* | *Wo yoy yoy* |
| | *Son-a sé aeroplan.* | *Sound like an aeroplane.* |
| | *Wo yo yoy* | *Wo yo yoy* |

### SINGABLE TRANSLATION

*Ten soldiers there,*
*Wo yo yoy*
*Can't hardly hear them sing.*
*Wo yo yoy*
*Ten soldiers there,*
*Wo yo yòy*
*Sound like an aeroplane.*
*Wo yo yoy*

90

**TO PLAY** Dominican children sometimes divide into two groups to sing "Dis Sòlda La" as a song—half singing the poetic lines, the other half answering with the "Wo yo yoy's." On the playground the game could be enacted with opposing lines facing each other and marching back and forth as in "Roman Soldiers."

---

**ABOUT THE SONG** From the sixteenth century onward, the Caribbean islands have been settings for war and struggle; soldiers, redcoats, and warriors are common figures in traditional song and story. Thus many of the Caribbean song games, like those of British children, center on battles between rival groups (see "Roman Soldiers," p. 30). These battle games of childhood, as well as other forms of socially approved combat such as kalinda (stick fights; see "Meet Me on the Road," p. 168), song competitions, and word battles, serve to ritualize conflict into play.

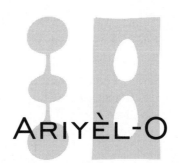

# ARIYÈL-O

Sung by a group of adults and children in La Plaine, Dominica.

"Ariyèl-O" is an especially striking example of the expertise of traditional song makers. Both the melody and the Creole words are elegantly designed to simulate the effect of the chiming of the noonday bells. The English translation is singable, but misses the effect of the repeated "ban-m's" in the original poetic text, and readers are urged to try this charming song as it should be sung: in the Creole language.

| CREOLE | LITERAL TRANSLATION |
|---|---|
| Group I: *Ariyèl-O, ban-m bagay mwen,*<br>*Ban-m bi-tin mwen,*<br>*Midi ka sonnin.* | *Ariyèl-O, give me my thing,*<br>*Give it back to me,*<br>*Midday is ringing.* |
| Group II: *Ariyèl-O, ban-m bagay mwen,*<br>*Ban-m bi-tin mwen,*<br>*Midi ka sonnin.* | *Ariyèl-O, give me my thing,*<br>*Give it back to me,*<br>*Midday is ringing.* |

SINGABLE TRANSLATION

*Ariyèl-O, hand it over,*
*Midday bells say*
*Give it up right now.*
*Ariyèl-O, hand it over,*
*Midday bells say*
*Give it up right now.*

TO PLAY   Though this song was described as a ring play by the singers, no specific directions were given. Probably there would be a singing circle

Group I:  A - ri - yèl - O,  ban-m ba - gay mwen,  Ban-m bi - tin mwen,  Mi - di ka son - nin.
A - ri - yèl - O,  hand it  o - ver,  Mid - day bells say  Give it up right now.

Group II: A - ri - yèl - O,  ban-m ba - gay mwen,  Ban-m bi - tin mwen,  Mi - di ka son - nin.
A - ri - yèl - O,  hand it  o - ver,  Mid - day bells say  Give it up right now.

---

within which one child (or one couple) after another dance through one repetition of the tune. However, this song was originally recorded by singers who had divided into two groups, the first singing the first three lines, the second the last three. This suggests another familiar Caribbean game formation: two lines of players facing each other, advancing and retreating as they sing. As a final suggestion, the third and sixth lines of the melody harmonize if both are sung at the same time.

ABOUT THE SONG  In the Caribbean the working man often comes home to eat his lunch in the company of his wife (perhaps the Ariyèl of this song) before the midday bell reminds him he must hurry back to his work.

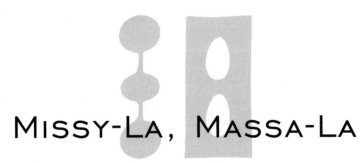

# Missy-La, Massa-La

Sung by a group of women in Au Leon, St. Lucia.

*Missy-la, massa-la,*
*Missy lost her gold ring, go'way.*
*Missy-la, massa-la,*
*Missy lost her gold ring.*
  *I got to find 'em, find 'em, find 'em, find 'em,*
  *Find 'em, let me see, la la la la,*
  *Find 'em, find 'em, find 'em, find 'em,*
  *Find 'em, let me see.*

**TO PLAY** During the song a circle of children, standing very close together with their hands behind their backs, pass from hand to hand some small object such as a ring on a cord, moving as little as possible. Meanwhile a single player in the center tries to guess whose hands the ring is in. Sometimes the center player is blindfolded; if so, she brings her hands down along the children's shoulders and feels in their hands to discover if the ring is there. Or the singers can change volume to indicate the proximity of the ring to the seeker—singing more softly when the seeker is close, louder when far away, adding another element of fun.

**ABOUT THE SONG** Versions of this game are played throughout the English-speaking world as "Who's Got the Button?" "Thimble," "Fox, Fox, Who's Got the Box," "Hold Fast My Gold Ring," et al. The song "Missy-La, Massa-La," however, is particular to the Caribbean; J. D. Elder suggests this version of the worldwide game may have originated among the gold prospectors of Guyana—that modern El Dorado where the streams give up gold and diamonds to those courageous enough to

Original key: B♭

Mis - sy-la, ___ mas - sa-la, ___ Mis - sy lost ___ her gold ring, go 'way.

Mis - sy-la, ___ mas - sa-la, ___ Mis - sy lost ___ her gold ring. I got to

find 'em, find 'em, find 'em, find 'em, Find 'em, let me see ___ la, la, la, la,

Find 'em, find 'em, find 'em, find 'em, Find 'em, let me see. ___

* Variation:

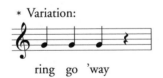

ring go 'way

venture into the jungles and up the wild rivers. For many Caribbean folk a gold ring is not so much an item of decorative jewelry as it is a symbol of status and community prestige. To lose a gold ring is a near-tragedy and even magic may be employed to "find 'em."

# LINDI MWEN LARIVIÈ

Sung by a group of adults in Anse la Raye, St. Lucia.

This lament of a hardworking Caribbean woman is an example of the close ties between adult and child song.

| CREOLE | SINGABLE TRANSLATION |
|---|---|
| *Lindi mwen lariviè,* | *Monday I wash my clothes,* |
| *Madi mwen la blanni,* | *Tuesday I bleach each one,* |
| *Mèkrédi mwen ka rinsé,* | *Wednesday I rinse them clean,* |
| *Jédi mwen k'anpézé,* | *Thursday the starching's done,* |
| *Vendrédi mwen ka pasé,* | *Friday is my ironing day,* |
| *Samdi a la kai ouè,* | *Saturday, we'll have to see,* |
| *Dimanch matin vini,* | *When Sunday morning comes,* |
| *Dou mwen pa sa ouè mwen.* | *My love won't come to me.* |

TO PLAY   This is simply a song; however, it could be turned into a singing game in which the movements of washing, ironing, and so on are acted out by the singers.

ABOUT THE SONG   Here is an ironic comment on the woes of a lady who carefully follows the precepts of her childhood only to be disappointed at the end of the week's work. She vents her disappointment in the stepwise, up-and-down-the-scale progression so typical of French-based melodies. Most English-speaking grown-ups will recall similar youthful song games, such as "This Is the Way We Wash Our Clothes."

Original key: E♭

Lin - di mwen la - ri - viè,     Ma - di mwen la blan - ni,     Mè -
Mon - day I wash my clothes,     Tues - day I bleach each one, ___

kré - di mwen ka rin - sé,     Jé - di mwen k'an - pé - zé,
Wednes - day I rinse them clean,     Thurs - day the starch - ing's done,

Ven - dré - di mwen ka pa - sé,     Sam - di a la kai ouè,
Fri - day is my iron - ing day,     Sat - ur - day, we'll have to see,

Di - manch ma - tin vi - ni,     Dou mwen pa sa ouè mwen.
When Sun - day morn - ing comes,     My love won't come to me.

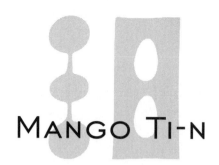

# MANGO TI-N

Sung by a group of adults in Au Leon, St. Lucia.

## CREOLE

Solo:     *Mango ti-n, la Babad ka brilé*
Group:        *Say-wa [pronounced "Sah-ee-wah"]*
Solo:     *Mango ti-n, la Babad ka brilé*
Group:        *Say-wa*
(alternation   *Ki li dou ki li si-ou-ka di mwen*
continues)      *Say-wa*

           *K'ay tchinbé-i nan tèt pou nou ouè*
             *Say-wa*
           *K'ay tchinbé-i nan kou pou nou ouè*
             *Say-wa*
           *K'ay tchinbé-i nan rin pou nou ouè*
             *Say-wa*
           *K'ay ba-i toua ti kou a la dousè,*
             *Say-wa*
           *K'ay ba-i toua ti kou a la dousè*
             *Say-wa*

## SINGABLE TRANSLATION

*Mangotine, Barbados is afire,*
    *Say-wa*
*Mangotine, Barbados is afire.*
    *Say-wa*
*Is it sour or sweet, don't you know?*
    *Say-wa*

Original key: D

♩ = 108

**Solo:** 1. Man - go ti-n, la Ba - bad ka bri - lé  Man - go - lé
Man - go - tine, Bar - ba - dos is a - fire,  Man - go - -fire.

**Group:**
—  Sa - y - wa  Sa - y - wa

2. Ki li dou ki li si-ou - ka di mwen  ki li mwen
Is it so - ur or sweet, don't you know?  Is it know?

3. K'ay tchin - bé-i nan (tèt) pou nou ouè  K'ay tchin - ouè
Now you hold her (head) in your hands.  Now you hands.

4. K'ay ba - i toua ti kou a la dou - sè  K'ay ba - sè
Now you give her three ea - sy lit - tle knocks.  Now you knocks.

**Clap:**  *etc.*

*Now you hold her head in your hands.*
    *Say-wa*
*Now you hold her neck in your hands.*
    *Say-wa*
*Now you hold her waist in your hands.*
    *Say-wa*
*Now you give her three easy little knocks.*
    *Say-wa*

TO PLAY  Singers and clappers stand in a circle. Two dancers dance inside, following the directions of the lead singer, who can improvise freely, singing the lead lines in any order desired and with any number of repetitions. Ordinarily, each lead line is repeated at least once. And when the line "Mango ti-n, la Babad ka brilé" is sung, the dancers should retire into the circle as another pair comes inside.

This dance song is in a two-phrase pattern in which the lead singer dips into a stock of poetic lines, directing the actions of the dancers. Overlapping the solo voice, the group sings the response "Say-wa" over and over in African-style litany; the musical transcription shows this

*St. Lucia, 1959*

mutually supportive pattern clearly. (It might be fun for a group to try singing this song without any overlap whatever, cutting the ends of the lines off short, which would be the European way of singing it, to experience the difference for themselves.) In place of a drum choir, a few singers clap the downbeat and others cross-clap, providing polyrhythm for some really hot dancing.

**ABOUT THE SONG** The title of this delightful but enigmatic song may refer to a little mango fruit ("ti" meaning "small" in Creole), or perhaps it is a local variation of "Mangotine," a girl's name, or of "mangosteen," a Caribbean type of cherry. The first explanation is more likely, as St. Lucia grows a good-sized mango crop, much of which is exported to Barbados, where mangos do not grow.

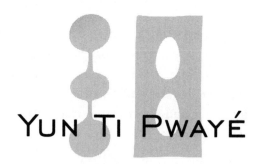

# Yun Ti Pwayé

Sung by a group of women in Au Leon, St. Lucia.

The ladies of St. Lucia sing "Yun Ti Pwayé" ("Little Cedar Tree") in the forceful and vigorous vocal style to be found all over the West Indies. They use no harmony and their voices are strong, harsh, and vibrant with energy.

| CREOLE | SINGABLE TRANSLATION |
|---|---|
| *Mwen teni yun ti pwayé,* | *Once I had a cedar tree,* |
| *I té chagé flè,* | *Blossoms all around,* |
| *Yun ti vent vini,* | *Then a breeze came by,* |
| *Qui jèté tout atè.* | *Threw them all to the ground.* |

### REFRAIN

| Solo (shouting): | *O bon ti kaliko,* |
|---|---|
| Group (shouting): | *Kaliko!* |
| Solo (shouting): | *O bon ti kaliko,* |
| Group (shouting): | *Kaliko!* |

**TO PLAY**  A single child dances in the center of the clapping ring throughout the verse, which is sung by all. During the refrain, which is shouted rather than sung, the dancer mimes the action of the gusts of wind that blow the flowers off the tree. A new dancer takes the center for the next repetition of the song.

**ABOUT THE SONG**  The Creole verse is undoubtedly French in origin, and the melody goes up and down the major scale in typical

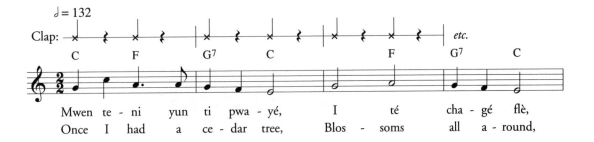

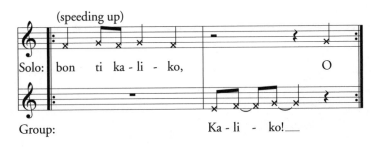

French stairstepping fashion. The refrain takes the song out of Europe and into Afro-America, the accent switching back and forth in fine Caribbean style—"O bon ti ka-li-ko, ka-li-ko."

The word "kaliko" seems to be a St. Lucian variation on the Creole term "zabriko," which means "apricot." In Haiti, where the song is also known, the refrain goes "Zakoliko, zabriko." It is possible also that this song concerns a "pear tree" ("poirier" in French); however, there is a widespread tropical plant known as "pwayé" or "cedar tree" that bears many inconspicuous small flowers.

# Ay Zabèl-O

Sung by a group of adults in Anse la Raye, St. Lucia.

For children everywhere, sometimes the world is not all sunshine.

CREOLE

Group:     *Ay Zabèl-O*
Solo:          *Manman-ou mò lan lopital,*
                  *Jodi sa fet.*

Group:     *Ay Zabèl-O*
Solo:          *Manman-ou mò lan lopital,*
                  *Ou pa konnèt.*

(alternation  *Ay Zabèl-O*
continues)    *I mò, i mò, i mò, i mò,*
                  *A ya yay.*

              *Ay Zabèl-O*
              *I ka mandé si lyin kalbas-la,*
              *Ka brilé?*

              *Ay Zabèl-O*
              *Zabèl-O, Zabèl-O,*
              *A ya yay.*

Original key: F#

♩ = 120

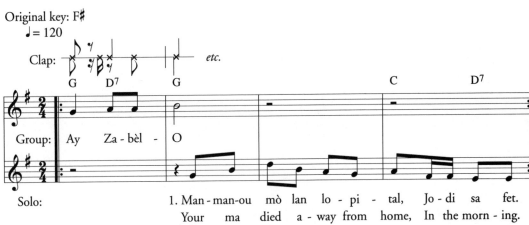

Clap: *etc.*

G    D⁷    G          C    D⁷

Group: Ay    Za - bèl - O

Solo:

1. Man - man - ou  mò lan lo - pi - tal,  Jo - di sa fet.
   Your    ma   died a - way from home,  In the morn - ing.

2. Man - man - ou  mò lan lo - pi - tal,  Ou pa kon - nèt.
   Your    ma   died, you did - n't  know When it hap - pened.

3. I   mò,    i   mò,   i   mò,   i   mò,  A   ya  yay.
   Now  she's  gone, she's  gone, she's  gone for - e - ver.

4. I   ka   man - dé  si  lyin  kal - bas - la,  Ka bri - lé?
   Do  you   feel  the sting - ing  cal - a - bash a - burn - ing?

5. Za - bèl - O,    Za - bèl - O,   A   ya  yay.
   Za - bèl - O,    Za - bèl - O,   For - e - ver.

---

SINGABLE TRANSLATION

*Ay Zabèl-O*
> *Your ma died away from home,*
> *In the morning.*

*Ay Zabèl-O*
> *Your ma died, you didn't know*
> *When it happened.*

*Ay Zabèl-O*
   *Now she's gone, she's gone, she's gone*
   *Forever.*

*Ay Zabèl-O*
   *Do you feel the stinging*
   *Calabash a-burning?*

*Ay Zabèl-O*
   *Zabèl-O, Zabèl-O,*
   *Forever.*

TO PLAY   This passionate song can be led by a single voice with a responding chorus, or two choruses can overlap the parts. The English translation is somewhat free in order to make it singable. The verses may be sung in any order.

ABOUT THE SONG   "Ay Zabèl-O" depicts a neglectful daughter and the shame and disgrace showered upon such a girl for allowing her mother to die unattended in the hospital. Caribbean folk society emphasizes the mutuality of the bond between parents and children, and songs pointing to hard truths are often taught and supervised by adults. Young people can be expected to postpone marriage, if need be, to stay home and "mind" their old parents until they have, in effect, repaid them for their sacrifices in their children's behalf.

The reference in the song's text to the calabash is based on the ancient belief that the dead can return to chastise the living for wrongdoing. The calabash (*Crescentia cujete*) is a common tropical plant whose twigs are used as switches by Caribbean parents to punish their children. Zabèl (Isabelle) is being warned by the singers of the anguish she will feel because of her coldheartedness.

*St. Lucia, 1959*

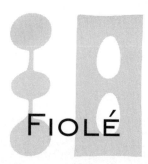

# FIOLÉ

Sung by a group of women in Au Leon, St. Lucia.

This song, sung with wild power by the ladies of St. Lucia, stems from the poverty, unemployment, and overpopulation that force so many West Indians to leave their lovely islands.

| CREOLE | SINGABLE TRANSLATION |
|---|---|
| *Fiolé-é, femme, fiolé,* | *Fiolé-é, femme, fiolé,* |
| *Pas ni femme ankò,* | *Women gone away,* |
| *Fiolé-é, femme, fiolé,* | *Fiolé-é, femme, fiolé,* |
| *Femme, femme, femme,* | *Gone, gone, gone,* |
| *Fiolé-é, femme, fiolé,* | *Fiolé-é, femme, fiolé* |
| *Femme alé Kayinn.* | *Way off in Cayenne [French Guiana].* |
| *Fiolé-é, femme, fiolé,* | *Fiolé-é, femme, fiolé,* |
| *Femme ay byen levé,* | *All the finest girls,* |
| *Fiolé-é, femme, fiolé,* | *Fiolé-é, femme, fiolé,* |
| *Femme alé Babad,* | *Way off in Babad [Barbados],* |
| *Fiolé-é, femme, fiolé,* | *Fiolé-é, femme, fiolé,* |
| *Femme alé Kayinn.* | *Way off in Cayenne.* |
| *Fiolé-é, femme, fiolé,* | *Fiolé-é, femme, fiolé,* |
| *Pas ni femme ankò,* | *Women gone away,* |
| *Fiolé-é, femme, fiolé,* | *Fiolé-é, femme, fiolé,* |
| *Woy, woy, woy!* | *Gone, gone, gone!* |
| *Fiolé-é, femme, fiolé,* | *Fiolé-é, femme, fiolé,* |
| *Pas ni femme ankò, etc.* | *Women gone away, etc.* |

TO SING  Additional lines include "Femme ay Langlitè" ("Women gone to Britain") and " Tout femme ay Englan' " ("All the women are in England"). The anguish that lies back of these decisions to leave home

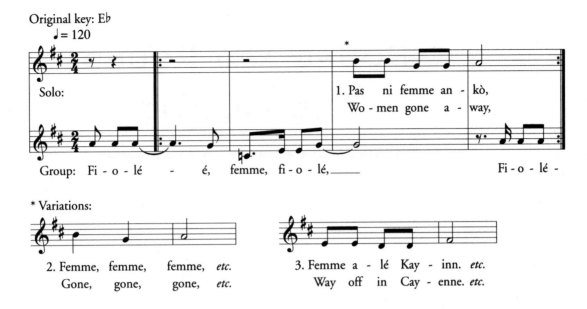

Solo:

1. Pas ni femme an - kò,
Wo - men gone a - way,

Group: Fi - o - lé - é, femme, fi - o - lé,_____ Fi - o - lé -

\* Variations:

2. Femme, femme, femme, *etc.*
Gone, gone, gone, *etc.*

3. Femme a - lé Kay - inn. *etc.*
Way off in Cay - enne. *etc.*

---

and loved ones, perhaps forever, is vividly expressed in this supreme
example of what the overlapping vocal style of Africa does for singers.
This is not a straightforward call followed by a simple response. Instead,
the immediate, passionate reply of the group of singers creates all sorts
of syncopations, hot licks, and strange harmonies as it spills its messages
*through* the repeated first phrase.

**ABOUT THE SONG**  In bad times Caribbean men emigrate first in
search of steady jobs. In the worst of times, the women must leave as well
and look for work as domestics or as hucksters of fruit and vegetables in
the markets of the larger islands.

The word "fiolé" (pronounced "fee-o-lay") may be a proper name;
indeed, there was a fabled Haitian legislator named Fignole whose popularity was so great that many songs were circulated about him. (A possibly
apocryphal good deed of Fignole's memorialized in Haitian song concerns a hospital visit when he observed the wealthy patients in beds while
the poor lay on mats on the floor. Fignole quietly reversed the situation
and was ever after revered.)

In certain games "fiolé" means to play evasive tactics, to be unduly on
the defensive. In nearby Suriname (Dutch Guiana) a tiny invasive insect
and the spirit that takes its shape, both known as "fiofio," can cause a
condition of "festering soul" that can result in illness, even death. Finally,
the title of this song may actually be "Fi yo lay," a Creole phrase meaning
literally "Girls they want."

"Fiolé" may mean one or all of these things. The power of poetry,
and thus, in part, of song, derives from its ambiguity, which allows a
single phrase to encompass several meanings.

# ROUND AND ROUND THE VILLAGE

Sung by a group of schoolchildren in La Plaine, Dominica.

*Round and round the village, village,*
*Round and round the village, village,*
*Round and round the village*
*As you have done before.*

*Oh, in and out the window, window,*
*In and out the window, window,*
*In and out the window*
*As you have done before.*

*Oh, stand and face your lover, lover,*
*Stand and face your lover, lover,*
*Stand and face your lover*
*As you have done before.*

*Oh, kiss her before you leave her, leave her,*
*Kiss her before you leave her, leave her,*
*Kiss her before you leave her*
*As you have done before.*

**TO PLAY** The "village" is a circle of children holding hands, with one player outside the ring. During the first verse the single player dances around the circle. The ring players then hold their clasped hands high in "arches" that the single player ducks under during the second verse, going "in and out the windows." In the third verse the center player reaches a desired partner, and the two dance together during the fourth

Original key: F

1. Round and round the vil - lage, vil - lage, Round and round the vil - lage, vil - lage,

Round and round the vil - lage As you have done be - fore. 2. Oh,

* 4th verse rhythmic model:

4. Oh, kiss her be - fore you leave her, leave her,

---

verse of the song. When the game is repeated, the first center player joins the circle while the chosen partner goes outside the ring to dance "round and round the village" and the play goes on.

ABOUT THE GAME  Many scholars believe this British game derives from the ancient custom of staging ceremonial parades to mark off the boundaries of the village (common property) from the surrounding lands (generally owned by individual landholders). This custom has been commemorated in the form of a game by children all over the English-speaking world. It is particularly popular in the United States, where it is usually sung as "We're Marching Round the Levee."

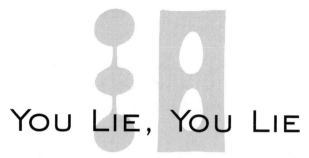

# YOU LIE, YOU LIE

**Sung by a group of children in Massacre, Dominica.**

The Dominican children who recorded this prancing, teasing song sang it with enormous energy, getting faster and faster, spinning and reeling, with that explosive African energy which burst into the new world over two centuries ago.

Boy: *Look at a fine, fine girl,*
Girl:     *You lie, you lie,*
Boy: *Look at she up and down,*
Girl:     *You lie, you lie,*
Boy: *Look at she wish no mind,*
Girl:     *You lie, you lie,*
Boy: *Oh, let me know,*
Girl:     *You lie, you lie.*

Girl:     *If I meet you tonight,*
        *I buck up your head tonight,*
Boy: *And I wish you a kiss tonight,*
        *Oh, let me know,*
Girl:     *You lie, you lie. [Repeat from beginning.]*

112

**TO PLAY** In Jamaica, "You Lie, You Lie" is a ring game in which a girl in the ring is chased by a boy and "beaten" with a knotted handkerchief until she escapes by breaking through the surrounding circle of children. In Dominica the children simply sang it, sometimes all together, sometimes in familiar African call-and-response style, while they danced about, whirling round and round until they bumped into the microphone and

Original key: A

♩ = 208+

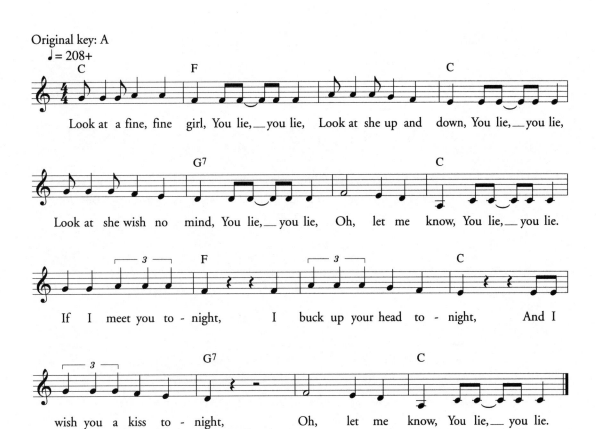

Look at a fine, fine girl, You lie, — you lie, Look at she up and down, You lie, — you lie,

Look at she wish no mind, You lie, — you lie, Oh, let me know, You lie, — you lie.

If I meet you to - night, I buck up your head to - night, And I

wish you a kiss to - night, Oh, let me know, You lie, — you lie.

collapsed in giggles. Part of the fun seemed to be to try to keep singing perfectly together at extremely high speeds.

**ABOUT THE SONG** "You Lie, You Lie" is another of the Dominican circular tunes that never seem to stop. Projecting the song as a dialogue (the work of the editors) is an attempt to make a kind of "sense" out of a text that is otherwise not only elusive but allusive in the African tradition of public teasing. A possibly related song has been reported from Jamaica.

# WENT TO THE MARKET

Sung by a group of children at the San Juan Girls' Government School,
San Juan, Trinidad; and by a group of adults in Woodford Hill, Dominica.

Two versions of this jazzy melody—another of the nonsensical teasing
songs so beloved throughout the Caribbean—are included here.

DOMINICA    *Went to the market to buy brown paper,*
            *Magazine and me and you,*
            *Magazine and a Queen of Sheba,*
            *Magazine and me and you.*
                *O landé, Angelina,*
                *Angelina, Angelina,*
                *O landé, Angelina,*
                *Rick, chick kala, rick chick chick,*
                *Zapap!*

TRINIDAD    *Went to Jamaica to buy brown paper,*
            *Magazine and me and you,*
            *Magazine and a Queen of Sheba,*
            *Magazine and me and you.*
                *O landé, woup si nan-nan,*
                *O landé, woup si nan-nan,*
                *O landé, woup si nan-nan,*
                *O landé, woup si nan-nan, etc. [may be*
                    *repeated ad infinitum]*

TO PLAY    Either version makes an excellent melody for dancing in the
Caribbean pattern—single dancers or couples, taking turns—inside a ring
of clappers and singers.

Original key: E

♩ = 192

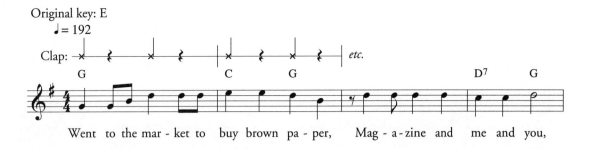

Went to the mar-ket to buy brown pa-per, Mag-a-zine and me and you,

Mag-a-zine and a Queen of She-ba, Mag-a-zine and me and you.

O lan-dé, An-ge-li-na, An-ge-li-na, An-ge-li-na,

O lan-dé, An-ge-li-na, Rick, chick ka-la, rick chick chick, Za-pap!

ABOUT THE SONG   The circular Trinidad version is a parody of the Dominican song game that was brought to Trinidad by children during the 1960 Federation. Both texts are obscure; various words may be embedded in them—"Hollandais" (a person from Holland); "Woupsin" (which means a hunchback); "Sinanan" or "Nanan" (common East Indian surnames). "Queen of Sheba" is a derisive phrase referring to a "highty-tighty woman," a woman who gives herself airs.

*Dominica, 1959*

Original key: E♭

♩ = 132

Clap:

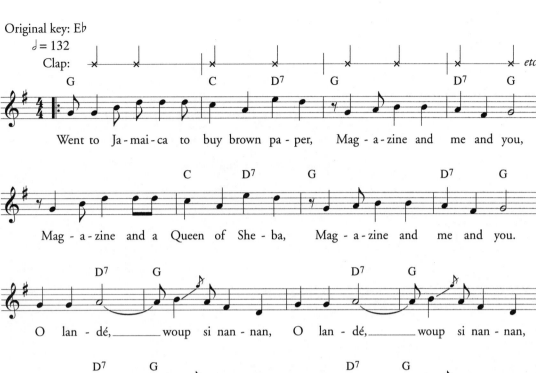

Went to Ja-mai-ca to buy brown pa-per, Mag-a-zine and me and you,

Mag-a-zine and a Queen of She-ba, Mag-a-zine and me and you.

O lan-dé, _____ woup si nan-nan, O lan-dé, _____ woup si nan-nan,

O lan-dé, _____ woup si nan-nan, O lan-dé, _____ woup si nan-nan.

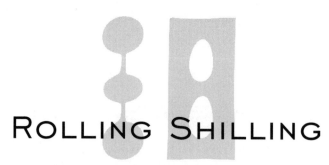

# ROLLING SHILLING

Sung by a group of adults in Woodford Hill, Dominica.

*A white man give me a shilling,*
*A shilling to buy a corset,*
*A corset to keep up me body,*
*Pre<u>vent</u> me from <u>rolling</u> shilling.*

*Rol<u>ling</u> shilling, <u>rolling</u> shilling,*
*Rol<u>ling</u> shilling, <u>rolling</u> shilling,*
*Rol<u>ling</u> shilling, <u>rolling</u> shilling,*
*Rol<u>ling</u> shilling, <u>rolling</u> shilling,*

*A white man give me a shilling,* etc.

**TO PLAY** This is simply a song and a fine dance tune. Like so many other Dominican songs, it has no end but leads the singer back to the beginning again, tempting one always to sing it just one more time. Note, too, the hot syncopated effect produced by the shift in stress between "<u>roll</u>ing" and "roll<u>ing</u>"—another example of the African approach to expressive behavior, in which change and variation is the rule. In speech and song the Caribbean practice of skillfully shifting accents at one time gave the black man playful control over the language of his masters. Sometimes he accented so many "wrong" syllables as to make it impossible for whites to understand him.

**ABOUT THE SONG** The shilling was once a common British coin and, as such, traveled through the British colonies of the seventeenth and eighteenth centuries. In the Caribbean it was at one time made in a square

shape; perhaps this song celebrates the fact that the newfangled round shilling could indeed roll. There is probably also an allusion to the fickleness of women in this song as there is in the various "silver dollar" songs of the United States.

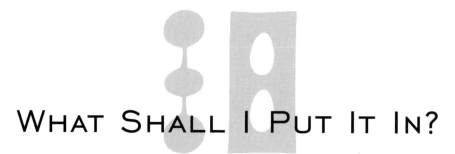

# WHAT SHALL I PUT IT IN?

Sung by a group of children in Woodford Hill, Dominica.

*What shall I put it in?*
*In a piece of paper.*
*Paper is not good enough,*
*So use a silver waiter [tray].*

*Take that lady [player's name sometimes inserted]*
    *to your side,*
*Do your courting ev'ry night,*
*Take somebody for your wife*
*And turn them to the altar.*

TO PLAY   The children recorded in Dominica simply sang this song to a variation of the tune of "Yankee Doodle," accompanying themselves with cross-clapping. The instructions for standard ring play (see "There's a Brown Girl in the Ring," p. 6) can easily be adapted if more active play is wanted.

ABOUT THE GAME   In most published collections this song game is titled "Uncle John," and it was played as a kissing game at adult play parties throughout Great Britain and the midwestern United States. One of the thousands of young American girls who played it (in her case, in Minnesota during the 1870s) was Laura Ingalls Wilder, the future author of the famous "Little House" series of children's books.* British scholars

*"What Shall I Put It In?" is mentioned in chapter 21 of Wilder's *On the Banks of Plum Creek*.

have speculated that the game is a faint echo of a "love history" from the Middle Ages, concerning an imprisoned knight saved from death by the daughter of the king who has confined him.

# Van-La

Sung by a group of children in Massacre, Dominica; also by a group of adults in La Plaine, Dominica.

In one of their favorite song games, the children of Dominica sing about the winds of Layou and St. Joseph, two villages along the western shore of the island. They fancy themselves attacking the wind, sticking it full of holes, breaking it up with sharp, thrusting movements. This song game, especially fancied by little boys, goes faster and faster and the children's voices grow more and more shrill as they battle with the wind.

*Van-la vanté,*
  *O van,*
*Van Layou-la,*
  *O van,*
*Van-la Sin Jo,*
  *O van.*

*Nou kay pitché-i, nou kay pitché-i,*
  *O van,*
*Nou kay pitché-i, nou kay pitché-i,*
  *O van, etc. [repeated indefinitely ad lib., faster and faster]*

The original Creole words of the last section simply say, "We're going to stick, we're going to stick, O wind." A free English translation might be sung as follows:

*Wind is blowing,*
  *O wind,*
*Out of Layou,*
  *O wind,*
*Out of Saint Joe,*
  *O wind.*

*We're gonna stick, we're gonna kick,*
  *O wind.*

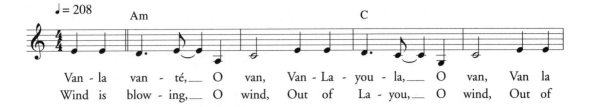

*We're gonna rock, we're gonna sock,*
    *O wind.*
*We're gonna fight, we're gonna bite,*
    *O wind.*
*We're gonna pound it all around,*
    *O wind.*
*We're gonna whack it on the back,*
    *O wind, etc. [as long as one's*
       *imagination holds out]*

**TO PLAY** Dominican children dance this game inside the usual ring, getting faster and faster as the play goes on. Like most African-American dancers, they make strong use of the pelvic area in this dance, thrusting their hips out sharply as they do battle with the buffeting winds.

**ABOUT THE SONG** Island fishermen, who supply much of the protein in the Caribbean diet, fish offshore in homemade dugout canoes, often powered only by sail or oars, vulnerable to winds and seas. Moreover, the inhabitants of these little islands are all familiar with the devastation of tropical gales, living as they do from hurricane to hurricane with perhaps a volcanic eruption thrown in for good measure. In the late summer and early autumn storm season, the blue Caribbean can turn black and destructive while cyclonic winds devastate the green plantations of the islands. The wind is an ever-present topic of conversation among both children and adults.

# Mwen Lévé Lindi Bon Matin

Sung by a group of children in Massacre, Dominica.

| CREOLE | SINGABLE TRANSLATION |
|---|---|
| *Mwen lévé lindi bon matin,* | *I wake up early Monday morning,* |
| *Mwen ka désann atè Rozo,* | *I go down into Roseau town,* |
| *Mwen ka mandé pou Lokadi,* | *I'm looking for that Lokadi.* |
| *Yo ka di mwen Lokadi dèyè* | *They tell me Lokadi's behind* |
| *    kontouè.* | *    the counter.* |
| | |
| *Ay sala sala loumbé, loumbé,* | *O this way, this way, loumbé, loumbé,* |
| *Sala sala loumbé, loumbé,* | *This way, this way, loumbé, loumbé,* |
| *Sala sala loumbé, loumbé,* | *This way, this way, loumbé, loumbé,* |
| *Loumbé a kay Rozo.* | *Loumbé all through Roseau.* |

TO PLAY   The Dominican children who sang this complex song with such authority were also dancing at the same time. Their performance presents a challenge to the skill and talent of all the children who may hear it. The English words are actually singable, though the translation is lumbering compared to the graceful lilt of the original Creole poetry.

No attempt has been made to simplify the musical transcription of this song. Other songs in this book have been evened out a trifle here and there in the interests of easy learning; this one is presented with its irregularities in order to show both the rhythmic virtuosity of Caribbean children and the extraordinary complexity of African and African-American phrasing.

ABOUT THE SONG   The meaning of this remarkable song is obscure. The term "Lokadi" could be the name of a girl (perhaps a ver-

124

♩ = 120

Mwen lé - vé lin - di   bon ma - tin,  Mwen   ka dé - sann a - tè____ Ro - zo,  Mwen

ka man - dé pou Lo - ___ ka - di,  Yo   ka di mwen Lo - ka - di dè - yè kon - touè.

Ay___ sa - la  sa - la    loum - bé,  loum - bé,    Sa - la  sa - la loum - bé,  loum - bé,

Sa - la  sa - la loum - bé,  loum - bé,    Loum - bé a  kay    Ro - zo.

sion of the French "Léocadie") or the name of an illness (epilepsy, or
"the fits," is known in Haiti as "malkadi"). Roseau is the capital city of
Dominica.

# ÉLIZA KONGO

Sung by a group of adults in Woodford Hill, Dominica; also by a group of children in Massacre, Dominica.

### CREOLE

| | |
|---|---|
| Group I: | *Nou ka mouté anro-a ché lapé* |
| Group II: | *Éliza Kongo* |
| Group I: | *Mwen ka mouté anro-a ché lapé* |
| Group II: | *Éliza Kongo* |
| (alternation | *Ay jou-joup, jou-joup, jou-joup nou ka mandé* |
| continues) | *Éliza Kongo* |

*Ay pawé-ou, pawé-ou, pawé-ou mwen ka vini*
   *Éliza Kongo*
*Ay meté-ou, meté-ou, meté-ou nou ka vini*
   *Éliza Kongo*
*Ay soukwé-ou, soukwé-ou, soukwé-ou, nou ka vini*
   *Éliza Kongo*

### SINGABLE TRANSLATION

*We're climbing upward, looking for peace,*
   *Éliza Congo*
*We're climbing upward, looking for peace,*
   *Éliza Congo*
*Oh jou-joup, jou-joup, jou-joup, I'm asking you,*
   *Éliza Congo*
*Oh get set, get set, get set, I'm coming now,*
   *Éliza Congo*
*Oh get up, get up, get up, we're on our way,*
   *Éliza Congo*
*Oh jump up, jump up, jump up, we're on the way.*
   *Éliza Congo*

**TO PLAY**  A singing, clapping group stands in a circle as single dancers or couples exhibit their virtuosity in the center of the ring. The song lines are sung with considerable freedom, the first two lines by Group I being relatively stable while the remaining lines are sung ad lib. The song can be led by a single voice or a series of voices in turn.

**ABOUT THE SONG**  "Éliza Kongo" is rooted in Dominican history. Many families in the neighborhood of Neg' Maron Mountain, near Bells and Jaco Heights where the runaway slaves went to hide, have African names. There are families there named "Africa," and there is a family named "Congo," linking them with the central part of Africa that supplied a large proportion of the tribal peoples brought to the Americas. One translation suggests that the song tells about an attempt to patch up a quarrel between Éliza Kongo and her friend, but in the children's version, at least, "the devil put a prickle in it"—put an obstacle in the way. The Creole term "lapé" might be translated, as here, as "peace" ("la paix" in French) or possibly quite differently as "le pays"—a French word for "homeland" or "birthright."

Grown-ups sing and dance to this exciting melody at dead-wakes while their children practice adult skills by singing the same song after school in the context of ring play. Like much folk poetry, this thrilling song with its extra-hot melody has more than one connotation and more than one meaning.

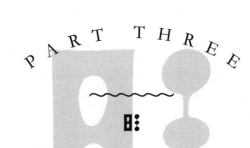

PART THREE

# SONG GAMES

# FROM

# ANGUILLA AND NEVIS

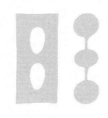

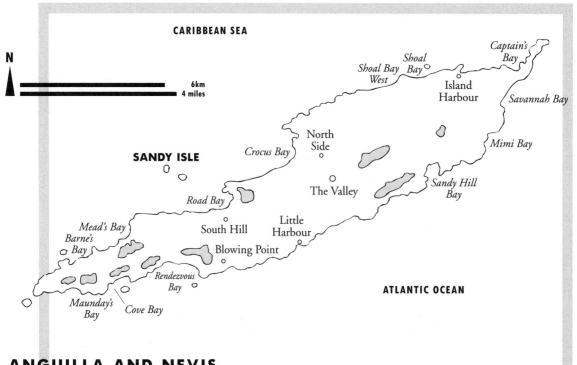

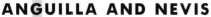

## ANGUILLA AND NEVIS

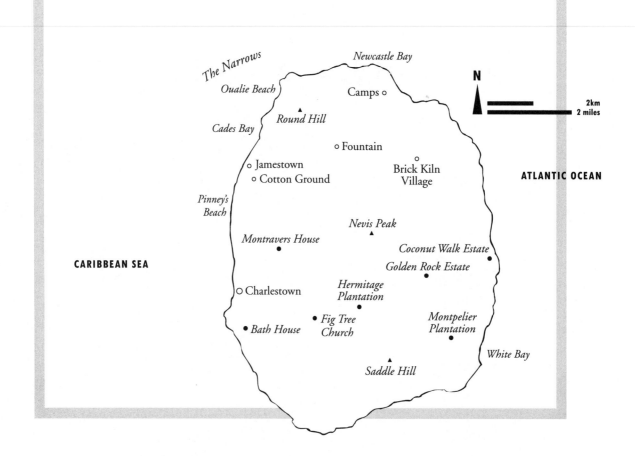

# ANGUILLA AND NEVIS

nguilla and Nevis lie to the north, in that section of the Lesser Antilles chain called the Leeward Islands; indeed, Anguilla is the most northerly of all. It is lean and flat; early Spanish explorers named it Anguilla, which means "the eel," because of its slender length. The terrain of Anguilla is arid and scrubby, though masses of seabirds populate its salt ponds, and its numerous and lengthy sparkling beaches are spectacular.

Amerindians settled Anguilla thirty-five hundred years ago. Over time it became a major center for the early Arawak Indians, until they were driven out by invading Caribs. European settlement did not begin until the mid seventeenth century, when Great Britain sent in a colony. But the dry climate of Anguilla was found to be hostile to growing sugar cane, the money crop of the slavery era. Smaller yields of cotton, salt, and tobacco could be produced with imported labor, of course; still, the plantation system never took hold in Anguilla and thus the proportion of islanders of African descent is much smaller than elsewhere in the Caribbean. Along the eastern coast there is even a significant number of people descended from Irish colonists, whose ancient birthright still sounds in their speech. But at night out in the country the African-American cane-fife-and-drum bands still play sometimes for dancing, and in the small harbors the men work on their fishing boats and perhaps sing the old British chanteys.

Nevis, by contrast, is a dumpling of an island, almost completely circular, with a single towering forested mountain, Mount Nevis, in its center. Columbus christened the island "Nevis" (a reworking of "nieves," which means "snow") because of the clouds that so frequently hide its single mountaintop. Today green vervet monkeys still live wild on the remoter parts of Mount Nevis, and every sunset the pale pinkish Caribbean egrets fly past its dark green slopes, headed for their roosts near the beaches.

The British saw Nevis as an agricultural site and imported thousands of Africans as laborers under the system of chattel slavery. Sugar cane and sea-island cotton thrived for a time, and Nevis became a depot for the slave trade throughout the Leewards, producing a short-lived but dramatic prosperity then unmatched elsewhere in the Caribbean. Lord Horatio Nelson found his first love in a Nevisian great house, courted, and married her; Alexander Hamilton was born and spent his childhood on Nevis. Today the old stone sugar mills are empty and abandoned, the great estate houses crumbling or turned into guest houses. Ninety-five percent of the people of Nevis are of African descent.

In 1967, Great Britain elected to combine Anguilla, St. Kitts, and Nevis into a single nation under British protection. Apparently, they had not consulted enough of the islanders as to their approval of the scheme, because the Anguillans in particular rose up, armed themselves, and announced themselves to be in a state of rebellion, some referring to their action as the "mouse that roared" and "the eel that squealed." Two years of unsuccessful negotiation followed, culminating with an "invasion" by British troops, which was welcomed with flowers and song by the Anguillans, who were possibly simply pleased to have somebody paying serious attention to their situation. (Local wags referred to the British military campaign as "the Bay of Piglets.") Nevisians also objected strenuously to the tri-federation idea and it was eventually abandoned. In 1983, however, after serious local negotiations, Nevis and St. Kitts did join together as a federated state within the British Commonwealth. Anguilla elected to remain independent, a part of Great Britain with a governor appointed by the queen.

*Anguilla, 1959*

# HERE WE GO LOO-BY LOO

Recorded by Alan Lomax from children of The Valley Secondary School,
The Valley, Anguilla; also recorded as "Mary Go Loo Go Loo"
by J. D. Elder (1970) from pupils aged nine to eleven at the
Barataria A.C. School, Barataria, Trinidad.

Chorus:    *Here we go loo-by loo,*
                 *Here we go loo-by lie,*
                 *Here we go loo-by loo,*
                 *All on a Saturday night. Oh!*

Verse:      *Put your left foot in,*
                 *Put your left foot out,*
                 *Shake it a little, a little,*
                 *And turn yourself about. Oh!*

The song continues, alternating verse and chorus with "right foot," "left hand," "right hand," "left heel," "right heel," and "whole self" substituted for the "left foot" of the verse above.

TO PLAY   Players form a circle. During the chorus they join hands and swing them back and forth, or the ring may revolve at a walking pace. During the verses, hands are dropped, the part of the body named is extended into the ring, drawn out again, and shaken "a little, a little"; then each child turns around in place. In the final verse the children put their "whole selves" into the ring by moving in and out, thus contracting and expanding the formation. During the "shake it" part of the last verse, the children "wind," in the common Caribbean dance movement of hip rotation.

Anguillan and Trinidadian children ordinarily introduce rhythmic variations into this widely known melody, casually switching between two- and three-count phrasing. A solid one-beat clap makes simple the rhythmic subtleties that Caribbean children have worked into this well-loved piece of hilarity.

Original key: D

♩= 132

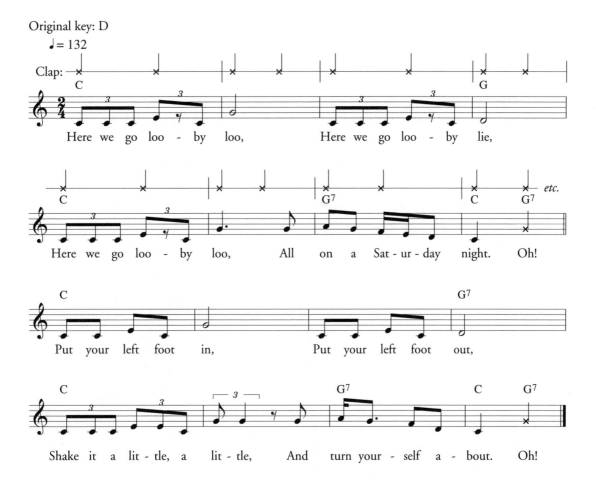

Clap:

Here we go loo - by loo, Here we go loo - by lie,

Here we go loo - by loo, All on a Sat - ur - day night. Oh!

Put your left foot in, Put your left foot out,

Shake it a lit - tle, a lit - tle, And turn your - self a - bout. Oh!

ABOUT THE GAME   Children in every English-speaking country appear to know this song game, and it has been found all over Europe as well. A trace in print occurs as early as the mid eighteenth century: "IN and OUT and TURN ABOUT... and so they DANCE LOOBY round about, to the tune of *John Bob'd in and John Bob'd out*," as a London political broadside dated 1745 put it. The Opies feel that "Loo-by Loo" and "Hokey-Pokey" are intertwined in a single European-based game family.

# DROP, PETER, DROP

The Anguillan version was recorded from a group of children at The Valley Secondary School, The Valley, Anguilla, and also by a group of adults at North Side, The Valley, Anguilla; the Trinidadian version was sung by children at the San Juan Girls' Government School, San Juan, Trinidad.

Two versions of this Caribbean children's reworking of "Drop the Handkerchief" are included here. The game is played the same way on both islands.

ANGUILLA

*I lost my gloves on Saturday night,*
*And found them Sunday morning,*
*Sunday morning, Sunday morning.*
*Drop, Peter, drop.*
*Drop, Peter, drop.*
*Drop, Peter, drop.*
*[Repeated until chase is over.]*

TRINIDAD

*I lost my gloves on Saturday night*
*And found them Sunday morning.*
*So I drop, Peter, drop, boy,*
*Peter wouldn't drop, boy,*
*Drop, drop, drop.*
*[The singers then fall silent until*
*the chase is over.]*

TO PLAY    Players stand in a circle with one player ("Peter") outside; he carries a knotted handkerchief or rope of plaited towels (a "pessie") and trots around the outside of the ring during the singing. When the word "drop" first occurs, Peter drops the pessie behind the back of a player, who must pick it up and chase Peter around the outside of the ring, trying to tag him with it. If Peter gets back to the vacant space before being tagged, the chaser becomes the new "Peter" and play goes on. If not, Peter must try again in a new repetition of the game. A local variation requires the two children to run in opposite directions around the outside of the ring. There is no tagging in this version; the one who gets back to the vacant space first is free, and the other child becomes the new "Peter."

ABOUT THE GAME    "Drop the Handkerchief" is a widespread favorite, known throughout the English-speaking world. "Drop, Peter,

I lost my gloves on Sat - ur - day night, And found them Sun - day

\* (Repeat as needed.)

morn - ing, Sun - day morn - ing, Sun - day morn - ing. Drop Pe - ter, drop.

\* In an adult version, this two-part refrain was sung:

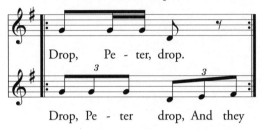

Drop, Pe - ter, drop.

Drop, Pe - ter drop, And they

Original key: F

Clap:

I lost my gloves on Sat - ur - day night, And found them Sun - day

*etc.*

morn - ing, So I drop, Pe - ter, drop, boy, Pe - ter would - n't drop, boy, Drop, drop, drop.

Drop" seems to be an original West Indian variant of this ancient pas-
time. The object lost (dropped) is sometimes a letter, sometimes a handkerchief, sometimes gloves. The theme of loss is a constant, however, and
may account for the frequent appearance of this game of childhood in
adult wake-house ceremonies, as a poetic metaphor of death.

# WHO STOLE THE COOKIE
# FROM THE COOKIE JAR?

Sung by a group of children in Brick Kiln Village, Nevis.

Group:    *Who stole the cookie from the cookie jar?*
           *Number One stole the cookie from the cookie jar.*
Solo #1:  *Who me?*
Group:    *Yes you!*
Solo #1:  *Can't be!*
Group:    *Then who?*
Solo #1:  *Number (Eight) stole the cookie from the cookie jar.*
Solo #8:  *Who me?*
Group:    *Yes you!*
Solo #8:  *Can't be!*
Group:    *Then who?*
Solo #8:  *Number (Three) stole the cookie,* etc.

TO PLAY   Each child assigns himself a number in sequence (one, two, three, four, etc.) by which he or she is known throughout the game. The players then stand in a circle and clap to a steady, even $\frac{4}{4}$ beat, clapping hands with the players on either side of them on the downbeat, clapping their own hands together on the upbeat.

All players together ask "Who stole the cookie . . . ?" and then accuse Number One to get the game started. Number One then begins the ritual exchange, first denying, then eliciting a response from another player by calling out a number at random. The object of the game is to name each of the group's members as the culprit without calling any number twice, all the while keeping to a steady rhythm both in the clapping and the recitation. If someone is caught unaware, speaks out of rhythm, or calls a number a second time, he or she is out of the game. Normally, though,

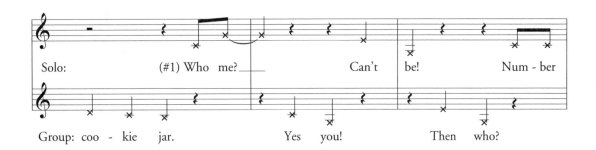

Group: Who stole the coo-kie from the coo-kie jar? Num-ber One stole the coo-kie from the

Solo: (#1) Who me? ___ Can't be! Num-ber

Group: coo - kie jar. Yes you! Then who?

Solo: (Ten) stole the coo-kie from the coo-kie jar. (#10) Who me? Can't be! Num-ber

Group: Yes you! Then who?

Clap: = adjacent performers clap each other's hands
= each performer claps own hands

---

when somebody "misses" in this way, the play breaks up in laughter and then resumes as before.

Quick wit, a nimble tongue, and skill in verbal repartee are highly valued assets throughout Caribbean society. This answer game fosters all these skills in children, requiring presence of mind, concentration, and the ability to "speak right up."

ABOUT THE GAME  This amusing play is related to a widespread family of similar games known throughout Europe—"King Plaster Palacey," "The Priest of the Parish," "The Parson Hath Lost His Cloak," as well as German, Spanish, and Greek variations. Apparently, the "Cookie Jar" version originated in the United States, spreading from there to the British Isles and the Caribbean.

# LITTLE SALLY WATER

Sung by a group of children led by Anita Wilkens, aged fourteen,
in Brick Kiln Village, Nevis.

Singing:

*Little Sally Water,*
*Sitting in a saucer,*
*Crying and weeping for someone to come.*
*Rise, Sally, rise, Sa-la-ly,*
*Wipe your weeping eyes, Sa-la-ly,*
*Turn to the East, Sa-la-ly,*
*Turn to the West, Sa-la-ly,*
*Turn to the very one that Sally loves the best.*

Chanting:

*Put your hands on your hips,*
*Let your backbone shake,*
*Shake it to the East,*
*Shake it to the West,*
*Shake it to the very one that*
*Sally loves the best.*

**TO PLAY**  No matter where or how it turns up, "Little Sally" is a special favorite. It has been used for jump-rope and clapping games, but most commonly for the classic ring game, in which a group of children stand in a circle with "Little Sally" in the center. As the children sing, Sally acts out the words, getting up from her stooped position, wiping her cheeks, spinning first to the right ("Turn to the East") and to the left ("Turn to the West") and then to face the child she selects as a partner. The two then put their hands on their hips and "shake their backbones" in the familiar Caribbean "winding" motion. The child chosen then takes Sally's place in the center and the game continues. Like all ring games, this should continue until every child has had a chance to be Little Sally.

140

**ABOUT THE SONG**  When the popular Trinidadian singer King Radio made a calypso hit of this song in the 1950s, he was using the most popular of all African-American children's song games, played all over the southern United States and the West Indies. The forces of variation at work in child lore have renamed her "Little Sally Walker" in the United

Original key: E♭

♩ = 132

Lit - tle Sal - ly Wa - ter, Sit - ting in a sau - cer,

Cry - ing and weep - ing for some - one to come.

Rise, Sal - ly, rise, Sa - la - ly, Wipe your weep - ing eyes, Sa - la - ly,

Turn to the East, Sa - la - ly, Turn to the West, Sa - la - ly,

Turn to the ve - ry one that Sal - ly loves the best.

Freely, very rubato:

Put your hands on your hips, Let your back - bone shake,

Shake_____ it to the East, Shake_____ it to the West,

Shake_____ it to the ve - ry one that Sal - ly loves the best.

States and "Little Sandy Girl" in Trinidad. But this heroine of black girl-hood in the new world has her roots in ancient British lore. Once it was the custom for British brides to step over a saucer of water on the way to their weddings; thus "Little Sally Water" may, in its original form, be a sur-vival of early European beliefs about water and purification rituals. The Caribbean version, however, suggests Sally is simply weeping with impa-tience for "one that she loves best" and is prepared to welcome him by letting her backbone shake or slip to every point on the compass.

# WALKING UP THE GREEN GRASS

Sung by a group of women in Brick Kiln Village, Nevis.

Group I:        *I'm walking up the green grass,*
                *Green grass, green grass,*
                *I'm walking up the green grass*
                *This dusty, dusty day.*

Group II:       *And what're you walking here for,*
                *Here for, here for,*
                *What're you walking here for*
                *This dusty, dusty day?*

Group I:        *I'm walking here to marry, etc.*

Group II:       *An' who're you going to marry? etc.*

(alternation    *I'm going to marry Lyna, etc.*
continues)
                *An' how're you goin' to get her? etc.*

                *I walk up the doorway, etc.*

                *An how're you goin' to get her? etc.*

                *I climb up the chimney (chim-ba-lee), etc.*

                *My clothes are wet and dirty, etc.*

                *My clothes are white as snow, etc.*

Original key: A♭
♩. = 104

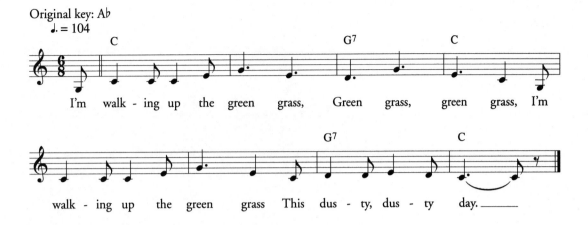

I'm walk-ing up the green grass, Green grass, green grass, I'm walk-ing up the green grass This dus-ty, dus-ty day.____

In verse 9, some of the women sing:

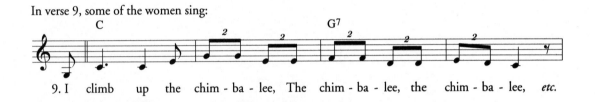

9. I climb up the chim-ba-lee, The chim-ba-lee, the chim-ba-lee, *etc.*

TO PLAY   The ladies of Nevis simply sang this as a song, one group answering the other. It could easily be played out, though, using parallel facing lines marching toward and away from each other as in "Roman Soldiers" (see p. 30), or the directions for "One Spaniard Came" (see p. 24) or "In a Fine Castle" (see p. 18) could be adapted.

ABOUT THE GAME   These Nevisian ladies sing a curious mixture of two standard and widely popular British game songs—"Green Grass" and "Three Dukes A-Riding"—the first stanza and the refrain suggesting the former, the later verses and the melody, the latter. Both are games of choosing partners, the common theme of so many children's pastimes both in the Caribbean and Great Britain. There is evidence that versions of both games were played in medieval courts, and many historians believe that they reflect the ancient custom of taking brides by capture in old Europe.

# How Green You Are

Recorded from a group of children led by Anita Wilkens, aged fourteen, in Brick Kiln Village, Nevis.

*How green you are, how green you are,*
*How green you are, how green.*
*How green you are, how green you are,*
*How green you are, how green.*

*How silly you are,* etc.

*How stupid you are,* etc.

**To PLAY**   Players, sitting or standing in a circle, "hide" very conspicuously a small object on the head or clothes of one player. During this time a single child, the searcher, stands in the center with eyes closed. When the song begins, the searcher begins the hunt. The loudness or softness of the singing indicates nearness to or distance from the object. The player on whom the object is found is next in the circle.

**To SING**   The children of Nevis Island have fun with the old British tune "Auld Lang Syne" by speeding it up so that they can sing it in just two long breaths. This transforms the song from a typical European four-phrase verse or strophe, where you breathe at the end of every line, into a two-phrase litany form that is more characteristic of West African singing style. Either way, it's a funny song.

*To experiment with cross-clapping:* Gather several friends who will clap with you in unison, a plain

    c      c      c      c
ONE and TWO and ONE and TWO and . . .

while learning to sing a simple tune such as "How Green You Are" really well. Then, leaving at least one solid on-beat clapper at work, try adding

Original key: E

1. How   green you are, how   green you are, How   green you are, how   green.   How

green   you are, how   green   you are, How   green you are, how   green.   How

2. sil-ly   you are, how   sil-ly you are, How   *etc.*

*Periodic variation on clapping:

etc.

---

the variation shown in the music (ONE and TWO AND ONE and TWO AND) and top it all off with

ONE and two AND one and TWO and ONE and
two AND one and TWO and . . .

Just clap it at first. You will discover, when you get around to singing the tune again, that the cross-clap actually fits the words quite nicely.

**ABOUT THE SONG**   "Auld Lang Syne" was not an original composition of Robert Burns; like many another good folklorist and poet, Burns collected and edited the version that has since become the standard. A parody, "We're Here Because We're Here, Because We're Here, Because We're Here," is widely sung in U.S. summer camps.

# Man o' War in the Harbor

Sung by a group of children at The Valley Secondary School,
The Valley, Anguilla.

*Man o' war, man o' war,*
*Man o' war in the harbor,*
*Man o' war in the harbor,*
*You go and never coom back.*

*T.S.O., T.S.O.,*
*If you le' me T.S.O.,*
*If you le' me T.S.O.,*
*I'll go and never coom back.*

**TO PLAY**   This was recorded as a simple song but can be performed as a ring play in which a central dancer, on the last line of the second verse, chooses another to take the center role.

**ABOUT THE SONG**   Overall, this jolly song refers to the blood-drenched early history of the Caribbean islands, for three centuries ravaged by piracy and by naval warfare between the rival colonial powers of Europe. The appearance of any armed naval vessel could mean invasion, looting, or forced recruitment of the local young men, who, once they signed on the "man o' war," might never be heard of again. The islanders must often have wished that the men-of-war ships would "go and never coom back." No likely explanation for the mysterious "T.S.O." has yet been advanced.

Original key: C♯

Man o' war, man o' war, Man o'__ war__ in the har - bor,

Man o'__ war__ in the har - bor,__ You go and ne - ver coom__ back.__

T. S. O., T. S.__ O.,__ If you le' me T. S.__ O.,__

If you le' me T. S.__ O.,__ I'll go and ne - ver coom__ back.__

*Actual scoring for measures 3-6, indicating subtle rhythmic complexity:

Man o'__ war__ in the har - bor, Man o'__ war__ in the har - bor,__ You

# AUNTIE NANNY, T'READ THE NEEDLE

Sung by a group of children at The Valley Secondary School,
The Valley, Anguilla; also by children in Brick Kiln Village, Nevis.

In Anguilla:

| | |
|---|---|
| A (speaking): | *Man o' war, man o' war!* |
| Z (speaking): | *Hello!* |
| A (speaking): | *What you have for me today?* |
| Z (speaking): | *Bread and cheese!* |
| A (speaking): | *Come on to Nanny!* |
| Group (singing): | *Auntie Nanny, t'read the needle,* |
| | *Long, long, long.* |
| | *Auntie Nanny, t'read the needle,* |
| | *Long, long, long. [Song is repeated until* |
| | *part 1 has been completed.]* |

| | |
|---|---|
| A (speaking): | *Man o' war, man o' war!* |
| Z (speaking): | *Hello!* |
| A (speaking): | *What you have for me today?* |
| Z (speaking): | *Bread and cheese!* |
| A (speaking): | *Loose the needle!* |
| Solo (singing): | *Lucy, me Lucy,* |
| Group (singing): | *Long, long Lucy,* |
| Solo (singing): | *Lucy, me Lucy,* |
| Group (singing): | *Long, long Lucy. [Song is repeated until* |
| | *part 2 has been completed.]* |

TO PLAY   In both Anguilla and Nevis, this game is played by various groups of children in various ways. Here is one of the possibilities:

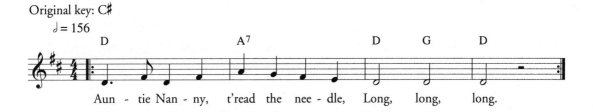

Original key: C#

♩ = 156

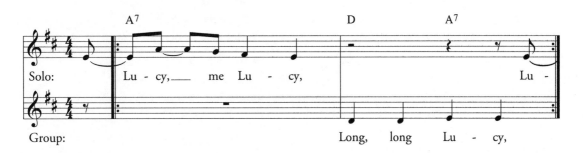

---

*Part 1* (during the singing of "Auntie Nanny"): Two children stand facing each other, holding hands, their arms in a high arch (as in "London Bridge"), while the other children walk through the arch in a long file. Sometimes several pairs of players form arches and the file winds, serpentine fashion, from one to the other.

Or all the children stand in a single line holding hands. Player A is at one end, player Z at the other. During the singing of "Auntie Nanny," player A turns under the arch made by her own arm and that of player B, then leads through the next arch made by the arms of players B and C, then of C and D, then of D and E, and so on in gradually larger looping "stitches." No one lets go of hands; the line simply follows along. This is a more complex movement than the one described above, but fun to do and pretty to watch.

*Part 2* (during the singing of "Lucy, me Lucy" or "Loose me, Johnny"): Here either of the first movements described may be repeated, or, from the line position, holding hands, player A may start out leading the line in a continuing circle around player Z, who should stand still. This action will eventually wind the players up into a large ball of children, from which they can only be "loosed" by player A's reversing the action and skipping back the other way, all players still holding hands.

A second possibility is for the whole line, including player Z, to follow A, who leads them into making a circle but, instead of closing the circle, keeps on leading inside of it, forming a large loose concentric spiral formation. When player A has reached as close to the center as practical, he or she again reverses and leads the line back out again so that the coil of children is winding and unwinding at the same time. Again, this is a more difficult movement but a great deal of fun to do. (The difference between the two ways of doing part 2 is that in the first, player A remains on the outside of the coil; in the second, A reaches its center before reversing.)

The children of Nevis sing the song differently:

| | |
|---|---|
| A (speaking): | *Man o' war, man o' war!* |
| Z (speaking): | *What cha calling me for?* |
| A (speaking): | *Piece of hot bread and butter!* |
| Z (speaking): | *Put it in my mouth and spit it out!* |
| Group (singing): | *Auntie Nanny, t'read the needle,* |
| | *T'read, t'read, t'read the needle.* |
| | *Auntie Nanny, t'read the needle,* |
| | *T'read, t'read, t'read the needle.* |
| | *[Song is repeated until part 1* |
| | *has been completed.]* |
| | |
| Group (singing): | *Loose me, Johnny, loose me,* |
| | *Loose me, Johnny, loose me,* |
| | *Loose me, Johnny, loose me,* |
| | *Let me go where my mama send me.* |
| | *[Song is repeated until part 2* |
| | *has been completed.]* |

**ABOUT THE GAME**  This West Indian remake of a European game, also popular in the United States, features the dance movement referred to in British game play as "threading the needle," which is associated with festivals of springtime, being sometimes only danced on Shrove Tuesday, sometimes on Easter Monday. Among African-American children in both the United States and the Caribbean, "threading the needle" also occurs within the framework of a traditional dialogue.

The Opies group the various needle games with the many variations on "London Bridge" and write: "These games once moved like living embroidery across the continent of Europe; the chains of dancers were the bright-colored threads, the captives trapped by falling arms were the somber emblems of mortality. 'Threading the needle' must be the happiest and most ingenious way ever invented of possessing a town or encircling a village. In the Middle Ages it was thought an entertainment worthy of Heaven, for in Fra Angelico's 'Last Judgment,' c.1420, ... angels and saints can be seen dancing ... together, the pair at one end making an arch with their arms for the other end of the line to file through."

♩ = 156

Aun - tie Nan - ny,  t'read  the nee - dle,  T'read,  t'read,  t'read  the nee - dle.

Loose  me,  John - ny,  loose  me, __  Loose  me,  John - ny,  loose  me, __

Loose  me,  John - ny,  loose  me, __  Let  me  go  where  my  ma - ma  send  me. __

*Sounds like:

loose    me, __  Let  me

# ANNIE, LE' GO ME FOWL

Recorded by Alan Lomax from a group of children at
The Valley Secondary School, The Valley, Anguilla.

*Annie, le' go me fowl,*
*Annie, le' go me fowl,*
*First she catch it, then she sell it,*
*Annie, le' go me fowl.*
    *Tee nan-ny, nan-ny, nan-ny, nan-ny.*

*Country people, go home,*
*Country people, go home,*
*Don't you hear the steel band playing?*
*Country people, go home.*
*[Repeat from "Tee nan-ny . . ."]*

**TO PLAY** Anguillan children skip rope to this song. Whereas in the United States both black and white children usually turn their ropes to a steadily continuing beat, Caribbean rope turners, like Caribbean child clappers, like to follow the musical phrases. In this song one can hear the rope pausing on the rests at the end of the first, second, and fourth poetic lines.

| 1 | 2 | 3 | 4 |
|---|---|---|---|
| *rope* | *rope* | *rope* | *(pause)* |
| Annie, | le' go me | fowl, | |
| *rope* | *rope* | *rope* | *(pause)* |
| Annie, | le' go me | fowl, | |
| *rope* | *rope* | *rope* | *rope* |
| First she | catch it, | then she | sell it, |
| *rope* | *rope* | *rope* | *(pause)* |
| Annie, | le' go me | fowl. | |

**ABOUT THE SONG** This local rope-skipping rhyme is a lively poetic composition that combines a number of popular topics including chicken snatching (always of great interest in farming communities) as well as some acid political comments on outlanders and the exciting new music of the steel bands.

Original key: E♭

The invention of the steel band by the people of Trinidad in the twentieth century is one of the most remarkable African-American cultural innovations. Earlier, Trinidadian blacks had defied British ordinances against playing drums in public places by forming orchestras of roughly tuned strips of bamboo or scraps of metal that could simply be discarded when the police appeared. In the 1940s these street bands gave birth to orchestras composed of steel drums, or "pans," made out of the heads of discarded oil barrels.

Musicologists believe the steel drum represents the first completely original acoustical principle in instrument making since the piano; electronic instruments came later. Today the steel band has become *the* typical Caribbean ensemble, and symphonic steel bands from Trinidad tour the world performing the classics as well as the hot dance music of their own island. And throughout the West Indies small children weave references to steel bands into their daily game singing.

# A Goosie Lost His Tail

Sung by a group of children at The Valley Elementary School,
The Valley, Anguilla.

*A goosie lost his tail,*
*And he lost his tail for a penny bread.*
*And a goosie, goosie,*
*And a goosie, goosie.*

**TO PLAY**   This is simply a song for frolicking and tickling. The Anguillan children who sing it break into a round of giggles at the end of each repetition.

**ABOUT THE SONG**   Some traditional songs seem to appear out of nowhere. We find no previous publication of this brief verse in either British or Caribbean sources. The goose has long been important in the lives of farming peoples because it is the largest domesticated bird, providing sizable eggs, tasty meat, down for goose-feather beds, and quantities of fat that can be rendered down for many uses. The figure of the goose girl, guiding her stately charges back and forth to the pond, was a familiar sight in traditional European villages. This impressive fowl has naturally assumed an important place in the folklore and folk song of European and Caribbean children alike—from Mother Goose to Aunt Rhody's goose, who so sadly perished, to the Grey Goose celebrated in the black American work song, to the Anguillan goosie who lost his tail.

Original key: D♭

♩ = 144

A  goo - sie lost his  tail,  And he  lost  his  tail  for a

pen - ny bread.  And a  goo - sie, goo - sie,  And a  goo - sie, goo - sie.  A

# SOMET'ING MAKE ME
# LAUGH HA, HA, HA

Sung by a group of older women in Brick Kiln Village, Nevis.

*Up in the garden day,*
*Dooma, dooma, dooma,*
*Up in the garden day,*
*Dooma, dooma, dooma.*

*Ah mean no lengé-lengé,*
*Mean no lengé for not'in',*
*Lengé-lengé,*
*Ah mean no lengé for not'in',*
*Lengé-lengé,*
*Mean no lengé for not'in',*
*Somet'ing make me laugh ha, ha, ha.*

TO PLAY   This song can be sung as dance accompaniment or just for the fun of the tune. If danced, the standard form of African-American ring dance should be used: an informal circle of clapping singers within which one or two dancers take turns in showing off their skills.

Various improvisational claps can be used with this tune as well as some of the rhythms transcribed for other songs in this book. The following is the basic pattern used by the Brick Kiln ladies (additionally spiced with their own personal variations, of course).

| Syncopated clap: | c | | c | | c | | c | c | | c | | c |
|---|---|---|---|---|---|---|---|---|---|---|---|---|
| On-beat clap: | C | | | C | | | C | | C | | | |
| (Ah mean no) | len | - gé | - len | -gé, | | Mean no len | - gé for | not' | - in' | | | |
| | 1 | & 2 | & | 1 & 2 | & | 1 | &2& | 1 | & 2 & | | | |

Practice each part separately before combining them.

ABOUT THE SONG   J. D. Elder notes that the Creole refrain word "lengé-lengé" means "tall and lanky" or "dry-bones," a term of satirical

Original key: E♭

$\downarrow = 120$

Up_____ in the gar - den day,  Doo - ma,_____  doo - ma,_____

1.

doo - ma,_____

2.

doo - ma._____  Ah mean no

len - gé - len - gé, Mean no  len - gé____ for not' - in',  Len - gé - len - gé, Ah mean no

len - gé____ for not' - in',  Len - gé - len - gé, Mean no  len - gé____ for not' - in',

1.

Some - t'ing make me laugh  ha, ha, ha._____

2.

Ah mean no  ha, ha, ha._____

Clap patterns: 1.
                2.                                    etc.

and, possibly, erotic significance. Overall, this dance song has a pleasantly
nonsensical text sung for its own musical sake and for the pleasures of
polyrhythmic clapping.

# PASS-PLAY SONGS

## FROM

## CARRIACOU

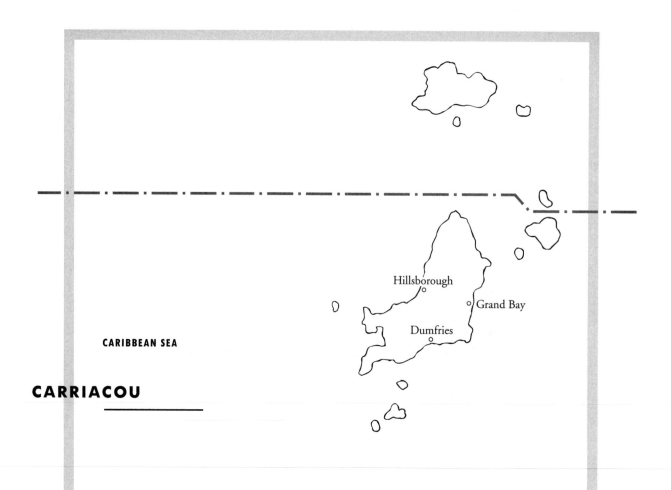

**CARIBBEAN SEA**

Hillsborough

Grand Bay

Dumfries

## CARRIACOU

**ATLANTIC OCEAN**

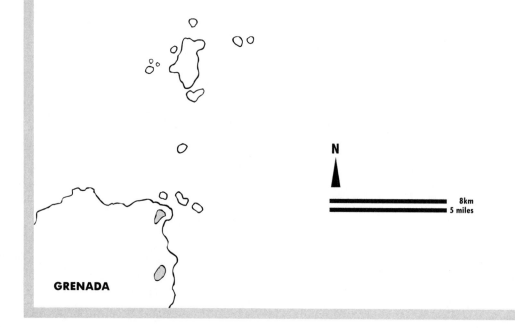

N

8km
5 miles

**GRENADA**

# CARRIACOU

~~~~~

Carriacou is a small island, rural and perhaps a bit out of the way, a part of the independent nation of nearby Grenada. Although early Scottish settlers have left a bit of a Scots snap in the local dialect, almost all Carriacouans are of African stock. In both language and custom, many Africanisms still survive.

The island itself is neither low nor high, with rolling hills and meadows, apple orchards, and small farms. It is some five by eight miles in area, and about 6,000 people live there. Much of the island is dry and scrubby with cactus, acacia, and bougainvillea, a weave of dry neighborhoods. Though most Carriacouan families farm or garden, raising corn, beans, cotton, perhaps a pig or chickens, the face of the islanders seems always turned to the sea. Carriacou men are known throughout the Grenadines as fine boatbuilders and expert seamen.

Carriacouans are also known as conservators of old custom, handed down to them by their ancestors—the Old Parents. The Big Drum Dance, or Nation Dance, is performed seasonally or at special events, but pass plays or wake pastimes may be called for any time of year. Throughout the Caribbean, and notably in Carriacou, ceremonial requirements link birth with death, childhood with maturity, growing up with growing old. Here, Alan Lomax and Winston Fleary, an important island cultural activist, are talking with an elderly lady (CW) on Carriacou.

WF: Children are usually shy and like to hold back. Pass plays teach them individuality and initiative and self-worth. Nobody's putting down one another; it's just everybody doing something and laughing so he doesn't feel terrible. The child who stays away, they put him aside. So in order not to feel put aside, he joins the circle and is creative. Everybody has a chance. And I think that's good for the world. It teaches them to wait, to emulate each other.

AL: But at the same time everyone was singing and clapping.

WF: So we are one brave world. The girl has a chance in the ring to turn to the boy she loves the best! Sometimes she's so blushed she turns to a girl, and they all laugh at her because she's supposed to turn to the boy she loves the best. Sometimes she turn to her brother because even though she loves somebody in the ring, or a cousin that is there she know, so she turn to her cousin. [laughter]

AL [turning to the old lady]: What happened to you when you came to that?

CW: They tell you hug and kiss the partner, you feel blush. [laughter]

AL: But you did it anyway?

CW: Oh, you have to do it. Yes.

AL: Sometimes he didn't want you to do it too, I bet.

CW: No, you know, he often too is shy.

AL: Do you remember the name of the little boy you used to want to kiss? [group laughter]

CW: Yes, I remember his name. His name was Prince. [The old lady, in her late sixties or seventies, broke into uncontrollable giggles and ran off into the dark to hide a "blush" that had lasted her since girlhood. When she returned, she said, still giggling]: He was a good-looking young man.

AL: Did you all go for walks together?

CW: Nonononono. You couldn't do that. You couldn't do that at all.

AL: How about coming home from school, nothing like that?

CW: Nowadays that could happen. But in those days we couldn't do it at all.

*Carriacou, 1959*

# Anana-O

Sung by a group of women in La Resource, Carriacou.

**W**hen Lomax asked the Carriacou women about the truth of the story behind this banter song, they explained: "It's a lady that went in Trinidad and she worked all over Trinidad, and when she came back to Carriacou, she only brought a jooking board to scrub clothes, to jook the clothes, and a tub to put water in." She had brought home her washerwoman tools, but no money whatever.

> *Ana went in Trinidad.*
> *When Ana come,*
> *What Ana bring is a*
> *Tub and a jookin' board.*
>
> *Anana-O,*
> *Anana-O,*
> *Anana-O, is a*
> *Tub and a jookin' board.*

**TO PLAY**  This rare and lovely minor tune with its occasional two-part harmonies accompanies adults as well as children in ring play. Cross-clapping makes the song go with a real swing.

**ABOUT THE SONG**  West African kings so much feared the satirical songs of talented local bards that they often employed them at court. The calypsonians of Trinidad continued this tradition, and their mordant satires on the antics of the British ruling class helped to win their country's independence. But there are many other local forms of such banter

Original key: F♯ minor

♩ = 132

A-na went in Trin - i - dad. When A - na come,

What A - na bring is a Tub and__ a jook - in' board.

A - na - na - O, A - na - na - O,

A - na - na - O, is a Tub and__ a jook - in' board.

songs current in the West Indies, all playing an important part in community life. A woman may launch such a song to bring an erring husband to heel or to wound a rival, and so potent are these musical weapons that the maker can be jailed for annoying or maliciously lampooning another. To avoid danger of arrest, the maker of banter songs follows the rule "No name, no warrant."

Highlighted in the banter song "Anana-O" is the crucial problem of the continuing migration of smaller-island people to work on the richer islands like Trinidad, and their subsequent return home, physically, emotionally, and economically impoverished despite their long sojourn in foreign parts. This is true also of rural folk who migrate to urban centers in search of better conditions. In both cases either the migrant is too ashamed to return home penniless and remains in exile, or he returns and becomes the laughingstock of his community. In this song the cruel criticism of banter songs all over the eastern Caribbean exposes Ana to open ridicule. She should have stayed home and bought these cheap little washday tools in her own town.

# ÉLÉ MISI-O

Sung by a group of adults in La Resource, Carriacou.

CREOLE

| | |
|---|---|
| Group: | *Misi, dit oui, dit non, yun fwa,* |
| Solo: | *Élé Misi-O,* |
| Group: | *Misi, dit oui, dit non, yun fwa,* |
| Solo: | *Élé ninnin-o,* |
| | *Misi, dit oui, dit non, yun fwa,* |
| | *Misi boulé kado,* |
| | *Misi, dit oui, dit non, yun fwa,* |
| | *Élé Misi-O, etc. [ad lib.]* |

SINGABLE TRANSLATION

*Missy, say yes, say no, right now [one time],*
*Hey there, Missy-O,*
*Missy, say yes, say no, right now,*
*Hey there, baby-o,*
*Missy, say yes, say no, right now,*
*Missy burned the cadeau [present],*
*Missy, say yes, say no, right now,*
*Hey there, Missy-O, etc. [ad lib.]*

TO PLAY This song is for general singing, or it can be used as dance accompaniment. Either way, it is deceptively simple; the rhythm is actually quite tricky and much depends on the leader's ability to come in at the right instant. Both the group and solo singers overlap extensively at the

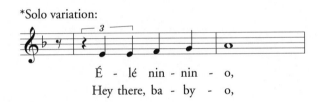

*Solo variation:

É - lé nin - nin - o,
Hey there, ba - by - o,

end of each phrase and, by prolonging the last syllable of each line, add to the wailing resonance of this enigmatic lament.

ABOUT THE SONG  Like "Anana-O" this is a song of local reference, about an event that happened long ago. Someone happened to make up a song about it, and now only the song is remembered. Who Missy was and why she burned up her present, no one can tell you for sure, but she is still remembered on the little island of Carriacou, and her story is still sung at dead-wakes, when the community comes together to think about the dead and celebrate the living.

# Meet Me on the Road

Sung by a group of adults in La Resource, Carriacou.

*Meet me on the road,*
*Meet me on the rollee rolla.*
*Meet me on the road,*
*Meet me on the rollee rolla.*

*If I dead, I dead,*
*When I dead, I bound to bury.*
*Meet me on the road,*
*Meet me on the rollee rolla.*

Verses are repeated in any order ad libitum, as long as desired.

**TO PLAY**  This song may be sung without any accompanying action; it is a good tune and the harmonic possibilities are interesting. Cross-clapping always adds an urgency, a typical Caribbean energy and vigor.

**ABOUT THE SONG**  The calinda was a dance similar to the bamboula dance in New Orleans, where the English composer Frederick Delius found the inspiration for his opera *Koanga*. Early New Orleans observers George Washington Cable and Lafcadio Hearn describe calinda dancing and drumming in Congo Square around 1900, but there is evidence that the calinda, as well as juba, counjaille, and other such African-derived dances, was known in the West Indies a full century earlier.

In the eastern Caribbean, "kalinda" (in the Creole spelling) is not simply a dance; it is a duel performed to drum and vocal music by experts armed with hardwood sticks. Stick-fighting (kalinda) tournaments occur

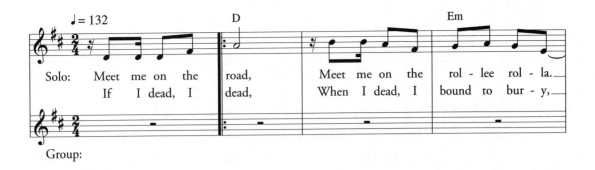

every Easter Monday, August first, and New Year's Day, when "kalinda kings" clash with others from surrounding villages. The fame of local kalinda kings spreads abroad, and challenges may be sent out as early as one year ahead of Carnival Day (Mardi Gras).

Once a stickman establishes himself as a "king," he is said to be "on the road" and he is expected to meet all comers. As he moves through a village, his supporters, men and women, sing boast songs in order to excite local experts in the art of kalinda. Messages are sent out days ahead—"Meet me on the road, Willie Doorley [Greyhound, Tiger, etc.]; I am Benbow [Lion Heart, the Razor, etc.]." The song speaks of the fighter's bravery and invincibility; the singer challenges his rivals; he does not fear death. The "rollee rolla" may perhaps be the "rolling roller," the train that will take the singer to his next bout.

In the pastoral tribes of the Sudan (source of much West Indian culture), *all* the men carry herding sticks of the same length as the kalinda sticks. Again one sees old African custom living on in the new world.

# VIO VIO LÉ

Sung by a group of adults in La Resource, Carriacou.

| CREOLE | SINGABLE TRANSLATION |
|---|---|

Solo: *Vio vio vio lé*

Group:    *Vio lé, vio vio la*

Solo: *Panyol pa sa mouté koko.*

Group:    *Vio lé, vio vio la*

   *Panyol pa sa mouté koko.*

   *Vio lé, vio vio la*

*Vio, vio*

   *Vio lé, vio vio la*

*Vio vio vio lé*

   *Vio lé, vio vio la,*

      etc. *[ad lib.]*

*Vio vio vio lé*

   *Vio lé, vio vio la*

*Spaniard, he can't climb the coco.*

   *Vio lé, vio vio la*

*Frenchman, he can't climb the coco.*

   *Vio lé, vio vio la,* etc.

TO PLAY   This is a ring game, played at wakes; in Carriacou such activities are called "pass plays." The song is to be sung by the ring of players, who support and urge on the turn-taking dancers.

ABOUT THE SONG   In one of the traditional patterns of the eastern Caribbean, a suitor may be invited to spend a few days in the home of his intended so that her relatives may size him up. He is well treated with bed and board, but one morning the mistress of the home may ask him to get her some "sky grease" (fresh coconut), basic to many Caribbean recipes. This means that the gentleman, at the risk of life and limb, must climb a tree with a smooth hard trunk that may well be from twenty to fifty feet high. If he fails, the girl's family may decide he cannot support

Original key: B♭

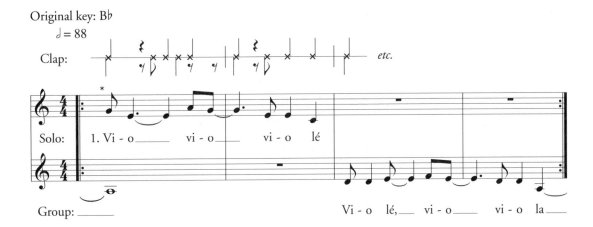

their daughter and send him away. In Tobago, rather than the coconut tree climb, the suitor is sometimes given a hardwood stump to split with an ax. Such real-life Caribbean tests recall those required in myths and fairy tales.

The unsuccessful suitor in "Vio Vio Lé" is a "Panyol," the Creole word for "Spaniard" (that is, "he who speaks español"). The refrain word "vio" is probably a contraction of the Spanish term "viejo," which means "old man"—another way of characterizing a suitor who cannot even climb a coconut tree. In this song there is scant sympathy for the foreign speaker (perhaps a black man from Venezuela) who fails to prove himself according to black Creole norms of manhood.

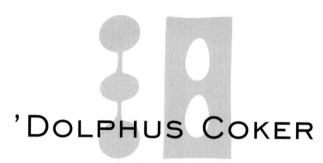

# 'DOLPHUS COKER

Sung by a group of adults in La Resource, Carriacou.

Solo:    *Say, who 'en killed the coolie man?*
Group:       *'Dolphus Coker.*
           *Say, who 'en killed the coolie man?*
              *'Dolphus Coker.*

           *Doris O, look the jaguar coming,*
              *'Dolphus Coker.*
           *Doris O, look the jaguar coming,*
              *'Dolphus Coker.*

           *Doris O, in the coco bwa [bois = tree],*
              *'Dolphus Coker.*
           *Doris O, in the coco bwa,*
              *'Dolphus Coker.*

**TO PLAY**   Make a circle of clapping singers, with anyone who wants to dance in the center. This is a hot and highly danceable tune.

**ABOUT THE SONG**   After the abolition of slavery in the Caribbean, indentured East Indian workers were imported in great numbers to work the sugar plantations on many islands. Today in such islands as Trinidad, East Indians form a significant part of the population and are now a prosperous and respected group.

    It was not always so. In the early days, East Indians were viewed as standoffish, and for many years they were exploited and mistreated by blacks and whites alike. They were called "coolies" and given miserable

Original key: A

*If playing a piano or guitar accompaniment, try playing C instead of Am for a different effect.
If you can't decide which you prefer, sing it without accompaniment; then it can be C and Am
simultaneously!

pay and bad treatment. Often, they were even found dead on the roads,
victims of hunger or cruel and careless violence. The mood of that
period is reflected in this wake song in which the singer asks "Who killed
the coolie man?" and the name of any man present might be given as a
sort of boasting joke. 'Dolphus Coker is the man chosen here, not
because he had committed the crime, but because the syllables of his
name provided good rhythmic material for the song. "Jaguar" is the
soubriquet for the song leader, the Bongo king (see "Meet Me on the
Road," p. 168).

# MARY AND MARTHA IS
# BOUND TO WEAR
# THE CROWN-O

Sung by a group of women in La Resource, Carriacou.

Solo:    *Mary and Martha is bound to wear the crown-o,*
Group:       *Mary and Martha, bound to wear the crown.*
        *If you want to see them, go behind the hill-o,*
          *Mary and Martha, bound to wear the crown.*
        *Mary and Martha, Mary and Martha,*
          *Mary and Martha, bound to wear the crown.*
        *Bound to wear the crown-o, bound to wear the crown-o,*
          *Mary and Martha, bound to wear the crown.*

**ABOUT THE SONG**   This spirited song is sung as accompaniment for dancing or, perhaps, for one of the typical Caribbean stone-pounding games in which players sit in a ring formation, each with a few stones or pebbles at hand. The leader starts play by picking up a stone in his right hand and placing it in front of the player to his right. All other players then begin imitating the leader's actions and following his rhythm exactly, so that the entire circle is picking up stones and slamming them down all together to the same, sharply accented, even beat. According to the leader's signals, the stones may reverse their route and go back to the left; the rhythm must still be kept even. Since the stone game is usually played after dark by the light of flickering lanterns, it is easy for a player to miss his stone and end up having his fingers painfully pounded. But this is all part of the fun—an experience consistent with the virile funeral games such as "limbo" played at dead-wakes in the Windward Islands.

Original key: E♭

♩ = 120

Solo: 1. Ma - ry and Mar - tha__ is bound to wear the crown - o,__

Group: _____

Ma - ry and Mar - tha,__ bound to wear the crown. _____

Solo: 2. If you want to see them,__ go be - hind the hill - o,__

Solo: 3. Ma - ry and Mar - tha,__ Ma - ry and Mar - tha,__

Solo: 4. Bound to wear the crown - o,__ bound to wear the crown - o,__

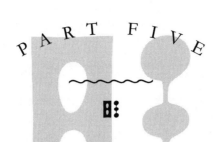

# PART FIVE

# I Recall . . . :

# Growing Up

# in Tobago

*by J. D. Elder*

recall a very interesting rhyme from my school days. It was a boy's song game, but with hardly a tune. One boy acted the role of "cousin"—a term that has nothing to do with blood relations, but was used to address anyone in the village to whom respect was due. In the game the players would stand before the "cousin" and put demands, and he would shout back the answers. And did we boys shout those demands in the school yard there at Bethel Church Hall!

> Cousin, lend me your pickney!*
>> What you want with me pickney?
> Pickney to work for money.
>> What you do with the money?
> Money for buy some lala [food].
>> What you do with the lala?
> Lala for to put in me belly.
>> What you do with the belly?
> Make one pickney.
>> What you do with the pickney?
> Pickney to work for money.

And then we would begin over again.

I remember my old aunty, Patsy Caria, coming down to my mother's house in Charlotteville and saying, "Eva, give me one pickney," and one

---

* "Pickney," meaning "small child," is a Creole word used widely and without disrespect throughout the Caribbean; it is probably derived from the Portuguese "pequenino," which also means "small child."

of us little shavers would have to go off with her and live in a little old dark house that her sea-captain husband had left her. Auntie needed a pickney to pick up, to run to the market, to find eggs, to do a thousand things that she had no more children to help her to do. Hers were grown up and gone.

Most of all, she needed company, somebody young and lively, to instruct and feed and pet. So Mama would give her one pickney; she had a house full of them. Thinking of it in this way, I can understand why we little boys shouted our ironic rhyme at the top of our voices, and our leader would shout back the facts of life at us.

> Come and give me one pickney.
> What you do with a pickney?

We knew what those adults would do. They would work that pickney. That pickney would be doing the tasks that he could manage, so as to leave the older hands free to do more money-making jobs. In the enterprise of getting and spending, children worked side by side with the adults—so it was in Charlotteville where I was born. A kind of junior partnership existed between the older people and the children. Rather than emphasizing the difference between the young and the old, this black ethic arranges for both to be involved in the work. You began very early. As soon as you could carry a little thing in your hands, it was "Bring it for Mama, bring it for Mama." As a dutiful child who knew where everything was in the home, you would run to obey. I can't imagine a child not doing that. Man, you love your mother too much.

The jobs for the little girls and boys differed in many ways. The little boys would go with their father to the garden and pick grass and weeds from round the corn and pea plants. In French this is called "ronde"—it's a task that a grown man finds it hard to do, to double himself up and get right down there and pick the grass so that the plant stands alone in a circle of pure soil. So the little boys do that job while their fathers are digging or hoeing or chopping wood—clearing the land for planting crops.

If his father was a fisherman, the little boy would go down and collect his father's fish, and take him his hot drink of cocoa or coffee when the boat came in. Each fisherman in a boat selects a mark—cut eye, shave head, one tail—that he uses to mark every fish he catches. All the fish go together in the gunnel of the boat, so when the little boy comes with his basket, he'll ask his father, "Daddy, what is your mark?" and he'll tell him, "Boy, shave head." So while the father be busy washing the boat and fixing the gear, the boy will pick out all the fish with the skin shaved off their heads, and when they get home and gut the fish, he has to go outside and dig a hole and bury the entrails.

If the family minds goats or sheep or pigs or rabbits, the little boy, before he goes to school, has to go and pick hog meat or rabbit meat or goat meat—that means greenstuff—to last the animals all day. The whole family rises early, at five in the morning, for a meal must be prepared for the man to go to work at seven. He must have his "wash-mouth," a so-called token meal. If the man is a heavy eater, he might eat five johnny-cakes and a mug of chocolate for his wash-mouth. But that's not his breakfast. He carries his breakfast of johnnycake and some kind of meat or fish and cocoa with him. So that woman has to be up early, frying fish and baking, and if there are little girls, they have got to be doing chores along with mother, parceling out the food for their father, demonstrating that they are interested in the breadwinner of the family.

As soon as the father leaves that home, the little boy's in charge, sort of. "Your father's gone to work, you're the man here now. Come on, feed the goats, get the hog meat. . . ." It's a happy thing for the little boy to stand in his father's shoes. By eight o'clock he has done his chores, eaten his breakfast, and has left for school. And this regime applies to the girls as well. Day for us was work—morning and evening—and in the middle of it, school. On Saturdays you put on your old pants and you scrub your mother's floor and pick up firewood. We were boys, but we had to wash clothes, we had to knead bread, we had to grate coconut, we had to pound chocolate on Saturdays because Sunday was the big day. Except on holidays, there was no time to play. The games like the ones in this book were played on moonlight nights. Full moon.

If you belonged to a large family, you'd play in your own backyard, and you'd sing so loud and so sweet that the neighborhood children would be attracted and they would join you, if your parents approved. You might go to your neighbor and say, "Cousin, I come to beg you to allow so-and-so to come and play with us." And then that person would use the occasion to come visit their neighbor and bring all the children. You see, parents don't want their children to be out playing and they're not there.

So on these moonlight nights, when the games were played, the parents would sit down there and watch and, if the game is not going according to the way they think it should go, they'd go in and demonstrate it. I have seen my Aunt Annie come to our house with all those girls of hers and demonstrate games we never heard of; my mother grew up in one part of Tobago and Aunt Annie in another.

So parallel to the involvement of children in adult work in black society is the positive way in which adults have been involved in the play activities of children. Although on the whole girls have played the singing games more than boys, there are many song games which are played by either boys or girls. In "Brown Girl in the Ring" there is room for a "brown boy in the ring," and, of course, the boys play the chasing games, the kissing and show-me-your-motion games.

When they sang "Show me your motion" in the game, then that child is supposed to wind his little bottom. If he didn't show his motion, his mother would call, "Come on, boy," and if he still didn't do it, she would come and hit him two slaps. But don't do that winding in public, *outside* that game. If someone says, "Mrs. Elder, I met your little boy down there winding his bottom," his mother would give him a beating. So that little child is very much aware of taboos and social approval.

All this points up the importance of the song games in the socialization process in Caribbean society. In my day, mothers and fathers were present at game sessions and directly instructed the young in how the games ought to be played. This gives the older folk the opportunity to influence the children's choices of play partners, to reinforce household pacts, and to emphasize cultural values and behavioral norms. And in the evenings fathers made toys for their children and on holidays accompanied them to the playgrounds and watched over them as they played the traditional games.

There were four traditional holidays, later sanctioned by government decree—Easter Monday, August 1, Christmas Day, and New Year's Day. On holidays each family, no matter how poor it is, sees to it that each child gets new clothes and shoes and spending money so that the children can share, equally with the adults, the pleasures that the holiday seasons bring. The community spends a considerable part of its earnings on fêtes. Children and the young claim an equal part with the adults in conspicuous spending on new clothes and on the food that is shared with friends and neighbors. In sum, the Creole family can be said to operate on an economy that is child-oriented.

In Trinidad and Tobago, rich and poor engage in "esusu"—a layaway savings system by which members of a savings ring contribute money to a pool and then draw their "hand" in time for Carnival, when they need a lump sum to buy new clothes and costumes for themselves and their children. These holiday customs, organizing work and play into a rhythmic cycle, have helped to establish a positive work ethic in the Caribbean. They have rubbed away some of the scars left by the plantation system, in which work and play were mandated. The people work hard and then they play hard. The children understand early the place in life of organized work and play—the work group and the play group, through which the balance between earning a living and recreation is achieved.

## Easter

My father was a great man. Nothing he couldn't do. He could play any-thing. He could pitch a top. He could pitch marbles. He could blow the flute. On Good Friday he had to go to church for three hours of service. He had to go in a white suit, white boots, and sing in the choir. When he comes home, you're eating. Olive oil and salt codfish and yams is all you are supposed to eat on Good Friday. Not supposed to shed no blood—no killing of no chicken, no beef, no pork.

Each holiday we race boats. Our Charlotteville harbor, called Man of War Bay, is exceptionally deep. As you face the ocean, the deepest part is on your left, called Bottom Bay, and on the right is Corner Rock. In the race you're rowing from Bottom Bay to Corner Rock. The best oarsmen were the men who worked on the seine boats, the boats used to carry the nets to surround the shoals of fish that swarmed the harbor. Any boat could enter the race. There were no regulations about boat size or num-ber of rowers. So a little boat, *Little Willie,* with only four men in it is rac-ing a big boat with eight men in it. They pay the same dollar to enter the race and they both aim to reach the winner's pole first. So you would be dressed up to see the boat race or the horse race on the beach, and, if you're little enough, you get a pig-a-back on your father.

But Good Friday is really marble day. You see them hang a purse round the waist. You hear them marbles shaking—"chuck-chuck-chuck." You have different kinds of marbles. You have chow and you have aggie, you have common. Common is a beautiful little marble, but the value is only one. Then you have twosy and fives—the value of that is not five penny but five commons. You have crystals, clear like a green bottle and beautiful. Then you have your taw, the master marble. If you have to sell your marbles, you never sell your taw. Some fellows use a solid steel sphere for their taw because it's heavy; some fellows use a big fives. When you pitch your taw and hit another man's taw, then every marble in the ring belong to you. You put them in your pocket and you pass.

All that knowledge about marbles comes to you from your father. He buys you your first set. Remember that first little bag of pretty marbles you had? Before you go to bed, you feel around, and if you don't have them, you can't sleep? Here's three boys in the family—my two brothers and me—we thief each other's marbles. When you sleeping, they thief your marbles, because each fellow is building up his own bank. My last brother was the greatest marble pitcher in the world. The man wasn't losing. Nothing. He have a gunnysack full of marbles and he hiding them in the ground and he would forget where he hide them and he was crazy for weeks, looking, digging. I think marbles is worse than alcoholism. It's an addiction.

Easter Monday was kite-flying day. Every family make its own kites. A man who had no time to make his children's kites would employ a kite maker to come to his home and make kites for a wage. But my father was a great kite maker, and on the evening before Easter Monday he would sit home the whole night making kites, my mother grumbling, "Charles, come nail back this door for me"—things like that.

And he would say, "Leave me with my boys." And we round him like a great god, while's he's making kites for us.

You use "cocoye-fex"—the midribs of the coconut palm fronds— for the kite ribs. You buy number eight Clark thread, strong enough to fish with, for the kite string. And you boil starch, cassava starch for paste, and put aloes in it because, if you don't, when you wake up Easter morning, these roaches eat up your kite—eat up the starch, that is, and you're in tears because you miss the competition.

So we're cutting paper in triangles, using my mother's seamstress scissors, cutting quiet, quiet, because if my mother come to know, she take away her scissors. We make the frame out of the cocoye-fex, run string around to form a hexagon or an octagon. Paste paper on kite frame, and make a jib boom right on top there, with two flaps made of contrasting colored paper. The compass is put on and the string attached to the center, and then the kite maker adds a "singer"—a paper fringe on a small cross string attached inside a curved funnel. When the singer flutters in the wind, it makes a steady booming sound. In Charlotteville a kite that did not sing was regarded as defective.

The final touch is the "zwill." Kite flying was competitive. So at the tail of the kite you hang a razor-sharp piece of glass, the zwill. Any kite attempting to outfly your kite will be "given the zwill"—you jerk your string and the tail will swing and the zwill will cut the string of the rival in midair. To be master of the sky full of kites is the aspiration of every little boy in the village.

After the kite flying and the horse racing, there were other village sports. Tug-of-war was for the grown-ups, both males and females. Greasy-pole was for anyone who was a good tree climber. Tree climbing is a common form of work for Charlotteville people—coconut trees, timber trees, cocoa trees, and the masts of sailing boats have to be climbed. On Easter Monday a huge pole some thirty feet in height and about eight inches in diameter was planted deep in the earth. At the top of it was the prize—a hamper containing ham, money, rum, and candles. The surface of the pole was larded with cart grease until it was slippery. Contestants were expected to climb this pole and dislodge the hamper. Whoever did it kept the prize.

## AUGUST DAY

The first of August was Emancipation Day, officially; we called it Freedom Day. Early in the morning on that day some of the old Congo people in the village would observe a ceremony in which they beat their mali-doun-doun, a heavy steel drum container for olive oil, and sang freedom songs like this one:

Ta la lie le-oh,
Freedom are come-oh.
Ta la lie le-oh,
King George, here you hoe-oh.

No one in the village would work on that day, no matter how high the wages offered. Anyone who did was regarded as disloyal and forgetful of slavery days.

August Day morning was devoted to the Sunday school anniversary meeting, when the teachers and pupils celebrated with Bible plays—the story of Ruth and Naomi or David and Goliath, or about Mr. Greatheart and the other characters in *Pilgrim's Progress*. In Charlotteville there's three books you have in your house—Sankey and Moody's *Sacred Songs and Solos,* the Bible, and *Pilgrim's Progress.* If a man lose his *Pilgrim's Progress,* he'll announce it in church from the pulpit. In time, the younger generation began to act in the drama of Dick Turpin, the great British highwayman, instead of the Bible stories, and secular plays like *The Sinking of the "Titanic"* crept in and the escapades of Brer Anansi, the trickster, were accepted. They all made good plays.

If August Day was a big day, it was a big day because of freedom. It was a very emotional time. People recounted all the sufferings of slavery and talked it over to their children, over and over again. My grandmother would come home especially to tell us all these slavery stories. Story after story after story about Congo Brown—the wizard who saw freedom coming and went from plantation to plantation telling the slaves the good news. Congo Brown—the slave who rose up in the air and flew back to Africa—is the great legend of Tobago.

And when I was a little boy, and my grandmother was telling us about Congo Brown, we had to lock up the house in the night, because this here man who could sail back to Africa, he could turn people into stone, he could take a long bamboo and chuck the moon, and we're frightened to death of this Congo Brown. The fact is that Congo's family still live in Charlotteville. All those people name Brown are kin to him, so that we can't disbelieve this Congo business as just my grandmother's own thing.

As you go from village to village in Tobago, the great things that Congo did, multiply. He is the hero of freedom, an active freedom fighter in our August Day dramas where children took part side by side with the adults, reciting poems about slavery and emancipation and singing old slave songs.

> Haddie Massa and haddie Missie,
> When you go home, say haddie for me.
> Oh, you Moma, way gie-ah we free,
> Oh, you Moma, way gie-ah we free.

A song like this would be acted out. Massa and Missie are leaving by ship for England. Black people, now free, stand on the pier and send "haddie" (howdy) to Queen Victoria (Victoria the Good), who "gie-ah we [all of us] free[dom]."

## CHRISTMAS

Work goes up to Christmas Eve, villagers making preparations for a two-day rest. The house gets a new look with wallpaper. The whole compound is properly cleaned. The best of the yam and plantain crop is selected and brought home late on Christmas Eve. Large stone jars of ginger beer are prepared, and the traditional sorrel drink is a compulsory item in all homes. It's a time of spending the money received from the cocoa crop and from working on the coconut estates at Starwood and Hermitage.

Your mother went to Scarborough about the Thursday before—walking. Walk one day. Sleep, get up early. Walk in to Scarborough, shop. Buy all the nice things and put them in a big canister (a trunk made out of tin). Put in all the toys, the clothes, the books, the shoes, and so on, and walk back.

So your mother coming back Christmas Eve night. You're not sleeping, you're sitting up and waiting for your mother. Your father had to go inside the kitchen and cook and clean the house. He don't want to touch things wrong inside that kitchen; so my father is gingerly touching, but he has got to feed the children.

He would sit up with us, and we would smell all the sweet smells of the city when my mother come with her perfume. As she burst through, we all grab her around her waist, lift down this canister, and she would lock us out of the bedroom, open up the canister with her husband, and we are wondering what has happened. She would bring a dancing man. For the boys she would bring cocked hats, which you can't touch until Christmas Day. And new clothes for the New Year, and books, town sweets.

Christmas Day you visit your grandmother. No work. You had Maypole, too. The Maypole was organized by the few Spanish people in our midst, Grenadian Spanish. There was a chorus and an orchestra of drummers, guitar players, and fiddlers. Le Roi Victor would compose his own songs, about village experiences and "comesse" (scandals), and there would be lots of eating and rum drinking in the fashion of the old Grenadine "cheerup."

The village shopkeepers stood the cost for the pole, the costumes, while the villagers threw up the money for the food and drink. The Maypole was made from a manioc tree trunk, peeled and painted red. From the top hung ribbons of different colors, and the person dancing a certain ribbon had to wear clothes of that same color. The man stood in the middle, holding the pole, was dressed in all the colors. And your hat had to hang down by a ribbon in the back of your head.

They would bring the Maypole into the village square. The whole village would be following them, and when they'd meet in the square, they'd make a space and all these people would sing and dance the Maypole until a fight break out, and everybody scattered and run and break up the Maypole. Next morning we see this pole lying down with all the ribbons. It was sad, very sad. We would take away a ribbon. Christmas done.

## NEW YEAR'S DAY

Boxing Day, the day after Christmas, was a lazy, quiet day. The people may visit each other, eating and drinking the leftovers from Christmas. On New Year's, we children play top, and sometimes the Methodist folk had a tea meeting. These were the occasions for benefits for the church fund, and they normally happen on New Year's.

The whole congregation divided into classes. Every class leader is given five dollars, and she gives out to her class members one shilling each. Five dollars is twenty shilling. So each class member must go take her "talent" and work the talent. You might make starch and sell. You might buy anything and work it. And then talent is called in, and all the money is put together and they use that to buy sugar and flour and things to bake bread and tea.

But don't fool yourself. Not a box of tea is bought. Tea is not tea, it is *cocoa tea* you're talking about. Chocolate. They boil huge pots of chocolate. These women would add spice as they pound the raw chocolate in their deep mortars—vanilla and cinnamon and coconut fat—so that when they boil that chocolate, it smells sweet for miles around, and the eaters come down.

Each class member is supposed to sell so many tea-meeting tickets. A tea-meeting ticket entitles you to come in and eat as much and drink as much as you can. Mug after mug after mug after mug of chocolate and bread after bread after bread. We had a fellow called Jonathan Gray. Jonathan would drink twelve mugs of chocolate and eat fifty loaves of bread, and he says, "That is just wash-mouth." You remember a wash-mouth is just a bite early in the morning to help wait for your breakfast. So nobody would sell Jonathan a ticket to a tea meeting.

Apart from eating, drinking, there's a concert, and then all those big people will play those same games we have in this book. There were people with calloused hands—fishermen, washerwomen. We children just stand up and watch; those big people had no time for children in this play. My Aunt Annie knew all the games, and if you played that game wrong, she would drag you out and say, "Go and sit down." My Aunt Annie was a very nice woman, but I seen her say, "You're spoiling the damn game, man," and she'd drag that woman right out.

So the big people playing the games, maybe the one chance they have that year. The little children would stand around and look at them and in "Drop, Peter, Drop" if somebody fall down, as a child you can't stand up there and laugh at that big person. Somebody would go and hit you one box from behind.

New Year's Day—if you didn't have a top when that day came, it was a reflection on your parents. We had a neighbor called Simon Felix who was crippled, and so his son didn't have a top. My mother used to say, "Charles, call Felix child and give him a top." It was sad to think that New Year's come, and a child didn't have a top.

You see, all our tops were homemade. Store-bought tops would have been useless in the top games we played, where the aim was to split the other fellows' tops. Your top was made of the hardest wood, well cured, and had a tenpenny nail in the end, ground to a chisel edge or a needle point. My father used to make tops for us, but when we became too many, my mother would bring home this famous top maker called Brightman Adams, and he would bed down in our house, eating our food and sleeping on his corn-husk mattress, making tops for us.

This Brightman was a giant who knew all the secrets of top making. A good top must be well balanced, perfectly conical so that it stands erect in play, and it must sing or hum loudly while it is spinning. Brightman used dogwood, a yellow-looking wood with a nice smell. And he would work a piece that had a knot in it, rather than a straight grain, not so likely to bust when somebody hit it. He taught us how to "quail," or cure, the wood by burying it in the earth. He showed us how to shape the top with a sharp penknife, how to smooth it with a glass-bottle cutter and paint it and decorate it.

You learned to play top slowly from older men. Practice consists of punching holes in a piece of board laid on the ground in one's own back-yard. To open the game a ring is drawn on the ground and several players aim to strike inside the ring. Those striking outside must put down the tops in the ring so the others can aim their blows at it. You whip your top, aiming to hit a top in the ring with the sharp pointed nail at the end of your top. A good blow is expected to chip the side of the top on the ground or to split it in half.

In Charlotteville tops was a game for boys and for man. You had no right to a top if you were a girl, although we had some Congo people, some Amazon kind of folk, whose daughters used to play top like men. We were afraid of them. When those girls attack, they were fierce women. In fact, top playing could even be dangerous, and parents insist that only age mates play together, since older boys had the habit of running over the littler ones.


## CARNIVAL

Today we hold Carnival for the two days before Ash Wednesday, on Lundi Gras and Mardi Gras, a period of freedom to roam the streets, dressed in new clothes, spending money, dancing, visiting with friends. Children are excited because they get plenty food, pops, balloons, special clothes, boots, hats, and on Sunday night there's Kiddies' Carnival. Children coming out for that are judged on five points—best dress, best acting, topicality, design of artwork, and spirit of Carnival.

You have all kinds of themes. One year it was the butterflies of Trinidad and Tobago. One year it was the sea gardens of Tobago, with all the fishes you see on Bocu reef. One costume was a sea porcupine and at the ends of every steel wire there was a fish knitted in wirework. Carnival draws out the genius in people. They had one costume made like the old British penny, thick enough to hold a little girl. The head of Britannia on the penny was the face of the little girl. When she touched a little button, the penny door opened up, and you saw a gold and beautiful child inside.

Monday morning, at six o'clock, there is a short pageant called J'ouvert (daybreak). In this "old mask" the people dress in rags, enact the comesse (local scandals), and lampoon the high and powerful in the country. And the bell goes eight on Monday and the bands come out and they're judged. They say Monday is no "mass" (masquerade), but yet Monday can be nice; they don't send the kings and queens, they send little samples from the big bands to compete.

Tuesday those big bands begin to come. They take two hours before the judges. The glory that was Greece—you have ten different categories of Greeks in authentic costume, and each category is a hundred strong, man and woman. The subjects of Genghis Khan; twelve categories of the people that were in Genghis Khan day. And each category is hundreds and all jumping to the tune of Sparrow music. The whole of China passing in front of you face, jumping in Trinidad style.

Wednesday morning after you take your ashes, you begin your esusu for next year Carnival. As you come out of the church, you say, "Boy, what we gonna play for next Carnival?" And you're getting ideas. You read in book in library to get ideas. Your head going round and say what we going to play? Who we going to play with? You're the whole year planning. This is a people who work like hell. They work hard, and they play hard. To see a factory man or a chief civil servant jump in that band or a senator winding on the road under his beautiful costume, people say, "Who is that?"

"Dr. Warden, man, it's Dr. Warden. He playing J'ouvert."

That's us. Play. Not by yourself at all. Always a group. All of us are friends, working in this office. We gonna play butterflies. Some black as the ace of spades, some fair, and they're all playing butterflies—black butterfly, big blue, all the butterflies of Trinidad. And when one of those little girls put on that costume of butterflies, man, you could eat them raw, they sweetness. But Wednesday morning she's sitting down there doing my files, as efficient as you want. Work and play, play and work.


## BONGO

In our village there were some women whom my grandmother called "quelbe people" who were great drummers. You could hear them by night drumming and singing old African songs and beating on their mali-doun-doun, as their drums were called in Charlotteville. Sometimes these women would get together with the younger people and teach them the songs, the drumming techniques, and how to mark rhythm with stamping tubes made of bamboo. They showed you how to clap, they showed you how to drum, they showed you how to dance. They were good church people; they used to come to church, but their names were not in any book. They were heathens, but because they were good dancers and singers, people would bring them down to do their thing at the wakes for the dead, because the Bongo, or wake-house rituals, with dancing and singing and feasting, was the area in which these old Congo women specialized.

The wake for the dead goes on for many nights, and every night there is singing and dancing. I don't think they even notice they are laughing and crying both. People outside telling jokes and laughing. People inside the house crying. A woman who has been watching over her dying husband, when she is sure her husband is dead, she is supposed to come and stand in her door there and bawl, loud, and people will run and say, "What happened?"

"Charles dead."

And then they run down the streets and carry the news, tell everybody, "Charles Elder dead, Charles Elder dead."

Everybody who hears that news who is a cousin or family must wail loud. All the family will take up the wailing. You will hear them wailing all over the village. They will come to the house of death and give their condolence to the widow.

By the time they begin to Bongo, man, nobody crying again. If that woman crying, she in the house. They done bind up her belly already. People have taken over in the yard. The coffin is being made. Food is being cooked. The women inside there sewing the shroud, they tell her, "All right, you don't interfere, Mrs. Elder. Sit down, keep quiet." So if she's crying, she is crying very quietly. Because people have taken over.

On the first Sunday night after the death, the wake takes the form of a sacred ceremony. The participants dress in Sunday clothes—white for females, black for males. Hymns are sung and speeches are made in praise of the deceased. In Tobago there is a folk eulogy called a "heartfelt," usually given by a friend of the family, in which all the dead person's virtues are reviewed and praised, the audience cheering from time to time.

To the very straitlaced, the nights of Bongo that follow are ungodly. My mother said that Bongo was the devil's business and a Bongo king couldn't pass across our yard, so that by and large we never knew very much about Bongo until we grew up. Some ministers denounced it. But a compromise was reached. Bongo was African, it was said, and the church should not interfere with things cultural as long as the people attended church and paid their dues. So the Bongo wakes continued and outstanding churchmen took part.

Everybody who comes brings rum, brings food, brings all kind of things. The Bongo in the traditional way goes on for nine nights. Over there some people are playing card. Over there some people are telling Nansi stories. Over there some people are playing ring games and stone games. Over here some people are dancing and singing Bongo. The man who boss all this—the best dancer—the one that know all the songs in his head—is the Bongo king. Every game have its own formation. He invites the people, he forms them up, he gives them the "croix croix" sticks, he starts up the song and demonstrates the dance.

There are about five basic Bongo steps, but dancers often improvise others as the music gets hotter. Men and women dance in pairs with much body contact. Often two men dance, each one trying to do steps the other cannot follow. In one, two men with knees full bent balance on their toes, hopping and kicking forward with each foot alternately to the beat of the music. In another, they balance the whole body on one hand and spin round and round as they kick outwards.

Bongo is open. It's one time when nobody pulls any punches at all. The children who come look at the big ones, they learn everything, really, at a Bongo. When the Nansi story come, they dig out all the children, bring them, sit them around to tell the story. But Bongo is for grown people. They will dance Bongo all evening. At midnight they will feed you, clear the ring, and the Bongo king will call out, "Boys, it's limbo now, limbo, limbo."

"All right, lend me your cutlass."

Man takes cutlass, he run in the bush, he cuts two forked sticks, he sharpen the bottom of these sticks and he drive them in the ground. Then he get a bamboo stick and he puts it across there, usually waist-high. None of this lowering down to six inches or so. I'm talking about the natural limbo. The dancers would be singing

Liza come lay lay lay,
Liza come limbo like-a me.

Each dancer tries to pass under the crossbar without touching it and without touching ground with his body or his hands. You balance on your toes with your body thrown backward. You keep your balance by opening your legs while you move forward under the bar. The open legs go first, the chest and head and arms last. Then you must straighten up without touching the ground.

When every dancer has passed under the crossbar, it's lowered one notch. You get fame according to the height of the stick you pass under. In the good old days it was a great thing to pass under at two feet— enough for tired man who had done a day's work. Sometimes the women pass under the bar, but limbo was a really a man's game—an exhibition of male virility in the face of death.

I know nobody can limbo like-a me,
Limbo, limbo like-a me.

All through the night the champions challenge Bongo kings from neighboring villages to the limbo tournament. The fame of champions spreads to other villages and they travel from wake-house to wake-house to compete. Pearl Primus was the first dancer to choreograph the limbo for the stage when she did research in Trinidad with students from Columbia University under Vera Rubin in the early fifties, and since then the limbo has become a popular public entertainment. Some professional dancers make it under the crossbar at fourteen inches, the limbo bar soaked down with paraffin, blazing, and fire dropping on the fellow's belly and burning him. That's showmanship, city business, not the real hard rock limbo in the middle of the bush, when I used to see it.

A session might last until one or two in the morning, and the Bongo king call, "Next game is the stone game." The stone game is played by young and old alike, but all men. They kneel on the ground in a circle. In front of the leader is a pile of stones, big as two fists, one for each man in the circle. The song starts.

> When I was in jail, I heard the bugle blow,
> When I was in jail, I heard the bugle blow,
>   Comin' back to my country to see you.

The leader starts beating the rhythm of the song on the ground with a stone. After a couple of bars he slaps down that stone in front of the player on his right. That player snatches that stone and slaps it down in front of the player on his right, and at the same time the leader slaps down another stone in front of him, all in time to the music. Each player repeats the action with each stone as it appears in front of him, till all those stones are moving around the circle in rhythm.

> Roll, boys, roll, you rolling like a drum,
> Roll, boys, roll, you rolling like a drum,
>   Comin' back to my country to see you.

Next the leader will stop passing stones till they all pile up in front of him. Then he'll pass them to his left.

> Fight. boys, fight, and never run away,
> Fight, boys, fight, and never run away,
>   Comin' back to my country to see you.

The stones go round and round the circle—bop! bop! bop! bop!—like a military drill. You mustn't miss the beat or a stone will catch your fingers and bust it up. I've seen them playing this thing with coconuts, wicked fellows. There's twenty of them and you can imagine the noise of those twenty coconuts going down—boom! boom! boom! Imagine those big slippery coconuts. You've got to grab each one and slam it down to your right and not miss a beat. If you do, your finger is in trouble!

The Bongo king carries all these games in his head. He's the dancing master, and so long as he stay, there's something happening on the grounds—they're building the coffin, they're scraping the hog, they're pounding chocolate, they're baking bread. Bongo go on seven to nine nights, and it gets sweeter every night. Maybe a visitor from a faraway village might bring in a new Bongo song or dance that nobody know. You Bongo until the people tired and begin to fade out. Towards daybreak the Bongo king reminds the dancers that they have to work the next day.

"Poor people want a little sleep. Let we go home."

One by one the crowd leaves, after a last drink of rum or coffee. To keep away the jumbies (ghosts) that may try to follow them, some may wash their faces with some rum and turn their shirts inside out before setting out along the dark roads and tracks that lead towards their homes.

Play and work. Work and play.

# PART SIX

# OBSERVATIONS

# ON THE

# SONG GAME

*by J. D. Elder*

*and*

*Bess Lomax Hawes*

## Social Setting*

One aspect of the evolution of tradition in West Indian villages is that the school itself acts to channel children's songs into the local community. Nursery rhymes and play-party songs taught by the teachers during singing lessons are taken out into the village backyards, where on moonlight nights children from different neighborhoods congregate and work the songs over, adding to them new words and local dramatics, thereby creating a local body of homemade music. There are in addition black native compositions that move from village to village through the children of migrating parents.

Besides learning new items from other village children, young village singers also get direct tuition from their own parents, who from time to time direct the moonlight games, themselves deliberately teaching the art of singing to the young and showing them how to organize the playing group in order to get the best performance. Thus the child very early understands the norms of song performance, the meaning of the words sung, and how to discriminate against texts that carry disapproved overtones—when to sing them, when to hum them or modify them. This aspect of song making and performing by children is part of the socialization process in which the young are directly initiated into a knowledge of village cultural and philosophical norms.

*These remarks are excerpted from a report delivered by J. D. Elder to the Twenty-first Conference of the International Folk Music Council, in Kingston, Jamaica, in the autumn of 1971.

What emerges as the final product of this process carries the approval of all. What then may look to the outsider like simplistic folk activity is very serious conscious action in the field of art and morality through which run the major features of popular culture.

## Song Origins

Throughout this book the editors explore a unifying observation: when two or more vigorously different musical systems meet and interact inside a series of small spaces, a vast range of glorious things can happen: the careful preservation of ancient and elegant cultural items; the reediting of others for a better fit with new circumstances; the bursting forth of brand-new artistic inventions impossible to predict. The text accompanying each song game comments briefly on this theme, devoting what might otherwise seem to be inordinate attention to the tracing of childhood pastimes along winding and misty historical and geographical paths.

There are reasons for this. As researchers often point out, childhood is a period of conservatism. Children simply do go on doing what they think is the proper child thing to do regardless of where they find themselves or when. Their attempts at modernization are generally only cosmetic—changing the names rather than the plotlines, for example. The repertoires of childhood are remarkably stable and often remarkably reflective of ancient times and of a kind of people's history. It is only in children's games that the battles between the Romans and the early Britons are still being seriously and actively debated.

Insufficient research time, however, has been given to African or Caribbean children's songs and games, and thereby our knowledge of paths of origin and distribution has been not only crippled but skewed. Perhaps further research may be encouraged by this book.

## Song Structure

In formal melodic and poetic terms, European songs are most often rhymed four-line verses, or *strophes.*

> There was a little sandy girl
> Sitting on a stone,
> Crying, weeping,
> All the days alone.

In sub-Saharan Africa, a two-line, only sometimes rhymed structure, *litany,* is more popular. Here a short, varied poetic phrase (roughly, what you can sing before you take a new breath) is answered by a short or long echoed refrain,

> Marry the girl one time,
> > Mamselle Marie, woy yoy yoy, Mamselle Marie
> Give her the wedding ring,
> > Mamselle Marie, woy yoy yoy, Mamselle Marie
> Look she ain't married yet,
> > Mamselle Marie, woy yoy yoy, Mamselle Marie . . .

Many of the game songs in this book are strophic, suggesting European origin. Such songs, however, are often performed in subtly African ways— for example, by singing so as to reduce a four-phrase strophe to a more comfortable litany-like two (for example, "How Green You Are," p. 144).

There is also the issue of the endless song, another possible demonstration of a preference for litany. Endless or circular songs are everywhere popular with juveniles; for if it's good enough to sing once, why not ten times, or a hundred, or until somebody makes you stop? Even so, within the Caribbean game repertoire, there is a truly remarkable number of melodies constructed so as to lure singers into singing them over again, and then again, and yet again.

This may perhaps prove to be just further evidence of a preference for litany, which is not constructed to come to a particular closure but normally just goes along until singers become bored or a new song takes over. Again, we see African style superimposed upon European form.


## VOCAL QUALITIES

Cantometric analysis demonstrates that the Caribbean children who performed the songs in this collection sing in near-perfect rhythmic unison; their diction is precise or very precise and they make remarkable rhythmic play with the texts of their songs, always together to the split second. Within this overall picture appear two patterned ways in which Caribbean children use their voices:

1. A loud, forceful, energetic vocal style with strong accents, some rasp, generally fast and accelerating, with occasional shouting.
2. A gently lyrical vocal style with relaxed voices, some glissando, some tremolo, sustained, moderate, with even tempos and soft-to-moderate volume.

It is tempting to say that the first style reflects African, and the second, European influences. However, there is a widespread lyrical soft-voiced singing style common to Africa south of the Sudan, and British children have themselves been known to sing stridently, if not raucously.

## VOCAL HARMONY

Relatively few of the songs in this collection were sung with other than occasional excursions into two-part harmony, most often in the form of vocal overlap. Cantometric research has shown that overlap—most often heard when a second voice begins a refrain before the solo voice has finished, achieving a kind of temporary polyphony—is one of the principal ways in which European and African musical systems differ, in both old and new worlds. European singers rarely begin before the lead singer has stopped; African singers almost always do.

Overlap produces a harmonic interval; it also stands for a habit of interaction notably African. In African tradition two or more individuals can speak, sing, or dance different patterns in overlap without interfering with one another; in fact, the overlapping of parts often results in an exciting ensemble effect. It is a warm and supportive musical style.

## ACCENT PLAY

Caribbean singers, who seem very much interested in the texts of their songs, tend to play not only with their meaning but with their onomatopoetic and rhythmic qualities. One of the games they enjoy, when dealing with repeated words, is to shift the accent from one repetition to the next for a kind of playfully hot effect.

O <u>bon</u> ti ka-<u>li</u>-ko, <u>ka</u>-li-<u>ko</u>.

Another favored game is to set up a consistently altered accent throughout a verse, so that the singer always feels just a bit offbeat and thereby automatically just a slight bit hot. This can actually result in a smoothly flowing effect, once the singers have gained some confidence.

Down to the car<u>pet</u> you must go,
Like a black<u>bird</u> in the air.
Oh, rise and stand <u>up</u> on your knees . . .

I have a tree <u>in</u> my right hand,
It bears ro<u>ses</u> in the month of May . . .

Strictly following the unusual accents in "I Have a Tree" allows children to sing quite easily in a complex ($\frac{5}{4}$) meter, or, while singing "One, Two, Three," to change the meter from $\frac{3}{4}$ to $\frac{2}{4}$ and back again as though it were commonplace. Even the astoundingly complex shifting of meters required in such songs as "Mwen Lévé Lindi Bon Matin" (see p. 124) was accomplished casually and in perfect rhythmic unison by a group of elementary schoolchildren.

Probably the key, as J. D. Elder points out, is to realize that the children had learned *directly from other singers,* which is the method of choice in almost every society in the world. No child or adult should ever feel ashamed of using this age-old and most reliable method of learning music.

## ACCOMPANIMENT

Almost all the songs in this book were recorded in situations of outdoor games or dancing, so there was no formal instrumental accompaniment. The editors have included optional guitar or piano chords for a few songs. However, the accompaniment of choice is the original—hand clapping—in which some surprising rhythmic features emerge,

Unlike their African-American peers in the United States, these children from the Lesser Antilles clap steadily on the downbeat: ONE and TWO and, or ONE two three, ONE two three. An interesting exception is "Early in the Morning," in which the children clap on the offbeats—One AND two AND—a hot effect achieved in this particular way by few other songs in the book, though it is a commonplace among African-American children in the United States.

These Caribbean children also frequently clap in rhythmic unison with the melody and stop when the melody rests between verse lines; they even turn a jump rope *with* the melody. (By contrast, in the United States both black and white child clappers forge steadily onward, filling in the rests at the ends of the poetic lines.) It is worth considering whether such a clear preference for rhythmic unison with the melody might well act as a learning drill preparatory to the later development of polyrhythm, that pre-eminent African musical behavior.

For Caribbean adults normally accompany their dance tunes with complex cross-clapping. This means that one or more varied rhythmic patterns are superimposed by individual clappers upon a downbeat or offbeat clap, so that several rhythms are being sounded at the same time.

This provides an aural effect that has much in common with the social supportiveness of vocal overlap.

Polyrhythm, however, can become aural muddiness if the beats are not clear and clean; the critical aesthetic quality is precision. Novices do well to leave improvisation and creativity out of it for the time being and get to be rock-solid in the basic repetitive simple patterns, absolutely precise and absolutely unflappable. This is what Caribbean children are learning to do in voice and movement as they sing and clap these "simple children's songs." This is what the steel drum orchestras of the West Indies work at without let-up. This is what all great drummers around the entire world practice without ceasing. It is not a childish exercise.

## Game Form

As the title of this book suggests, the primary form of Caribbean children's song games is the ring play. Over and over the same pattern is repeated: a ring of singing, clapping children led by a participating, possibly changing, song leader. One or more children are distinguished from the rest by being inside or, rarely, outside the ring, where they perform according to the dictates of the song text for a period of time that is strictly limited by the length of the song verse. A successor then takes over and the play is repeated until all children have had a chance at the central role or roles.

Perhaps the best ring plays for the smaller children or for new learners are those in which they can simply act out the directions given in the song text (e.g., "Little Sally Water"). Older, more experienced players can take on lead roles in song games that have advanced so far toward litany that they have no specific directions or endings (e.g. "Éliza Kongo") and can simply be danced by the improvising center player. Many games lie between these two—"Si Si Maria" or "Mamselle Marie"—where the lead singer gives only occasional directions to the center dancers: "Dance in the saga t'ing."

Besides ring play, clapping games are the particular favorites of little girls. While their brothers are challenging themselves to ever more complex solo virtuoso rhythmic flights by slapping any sound-producing article—an empty wastebasket, their own bodies, even a drum—the girls are enjoying pastimes that demand a series of rhythmic palm-to-palm meetings with their neighbors. Choreometric research indicates that the wide use of open palms in dance is associated with factors of cooperation and mutuality. Judging by the ubiquity of clapping games among girls,

Caribbean (and other) societies may have assigned this special responsibility to their female children.

There are also European-based dances with specific choreographies, such as "Round and Round the Village" or "Blue Bird." J. D. Elder observes that even such an apparently undemanding activity as a round of "Blue Bird" requires turn taking, stepwise procedures, maintenance of clear-cut formations, and transformations of group patterns—all valuable in the societal repertoire.

But always the ring play returns, ever the central formula. This may be because the basic qualities emphasized in the classic ring play—sharing social space, and group support of individual expressivity—are major African and African-American themes that identify socially desirable behaviors. Teachers may do well to point out these elements as important cultural universals.

## Song-game Content

Adults who want to "make use of" these song games, whether for educational or recreational purposes, need to remember that it is the adults themselves who are outsiders here. They have entered the children's world, and the children will ultimately make the important decisions. Adults can, however, help, and they can help best by practicing careful observation, good scholarship, and sincere respect,

For example, the kind of poetic initiative that causes children singing "Blue Bird" to change the bird colors to reflect the colors they themselves are wearing might well be encouraged by teachers or parents instead of insisting on the printed words as the "right" way. Such creative editing is important to the child's enjoyment of these traditional pastimes. It can also lead, and it often has, to significant and lasting variations, so that there may eventually turn out to be several "right" ways to sing a particular song. Confronting the existence of variation and difference is an important ethical as well as aesthetic experience for children; it fosters thoughtful analysis, judgment, and respect.

In cases where children already know variations on particular songs, their sharing should be encouraged. Perhaps a group of children could even come up with their own collection of different ways to recite "Miss Mary Mack" or play "Little Sally Water." It is a wonderful moment when one discovers for oneself that there are truly many interesting ways of doing exactly the same thing, and that each one has its own particular beauty, excitement, and value.

## FURTHER CURRICULUM CONSIDERATIONS FOR TEACHERS*

The actual verbal content of many of these song games can sometimes be fruitfully examined with the players. A round of "Roman Soldiers" may be vastly stimulated by the children's knowing that such "pretend" activities are reflections of historical reality, that the Romans and the Britons actually did fight, and that generations of children have since reenacted those ancient struggles. For some few children a realization of this kind may be their very first glimpse of the marvel of human historical memory that stretches back, in such apparently trivial forms as the playing of children's games, over centuries of time.

For children too old and sophisticated for "Roman Soldiers," the dead-wake song "Meet Me on the Road" could lead to discussions concerning the many ways any society controls violence by imposing order upon it. The tourney of medieval knighthood might be one example, the American game of football another, the kalinda (stick-fight dance) a third, the "rules of modern warfare" another.

Teachers of Caribbean history will find frequent and fascinating allusions in these songs to major sociopolitical issues within these small but strategically significant islands. The tracing of Spanish, English, and French influences as well as the development of the various island Creoles is only part of the picture.

"Coming Down with a Bunch of Roses," "Man o' War in the Harbor," and several other song games suggest excursions into naval history, a topic that may be especially important to include in a course on Caribbean history, for many islanders are themselves unaware of their historical prominence and international reputation as small-boat sailors, shipbuilders, and navigators.

Perhaps as important may be the numerous songs that deal with local historical events. The calypso—the Trinidadian national song form—stems from the African tradition of topical song, sometimes called the banter song, or the song of allusion. The notion of making up songs about things that really happen is an idea that many children will recognize; they can often cite examples from their own taunting and teasing songs.

In classes of older children the topical banter songs "Anana-O" and "Élé Misi-O" could serve to introduce the concept of oral history, leading to the interviewing of local elders on episodes they recall of the development of their own village or town—who moved in first, how the

*These comments are extracted from the many pedagogical essays of J. D. Elder, as well as from the introduction to his *Song Games of Trinidad and Tobago*.

streets were first laid out and named. Some classes in Trinidad have produced their own small "books" detailing such information.

This is the art of the expert teacher—making it possible for each child individually to perceive and begin to unwrap the intricacies that lie beneath the detail of everyday life, sharpening curiosity, beginning intellectual exploration, realizing that each has a role to play and gifts to bring, delighting in the quest.

# REFERENCES

~~~~~~

8⦂

## AUNTIE NANNY, T'READ THE NEEDLE

Various needle-threading games are known in Great Britain: Gomme 1964 (1894), vol. 2: 228–32 and 289–90; Opie and Opie 1988: 33–40 and 46–49; in the southern United States: Parsons 1923: 180 and 202; Jones and Hawes 1987 (1972): 81–83; and in Jamaica: Beckwith 1928: 38. The traditional dialogue "Neighbor, Lend Me Your Hatchet" appears in Brewster 1953: 175, as well in Jones and Hawes 1987 (1972): 81–83.

## BLUE BIRD

Though many assume this game is British in origin, the earliest printed versions of it are from the United States, where it has long been a favorite among both white and black children. Iona and Peter Opie report that the game came to Great Britain from the United States during the first decades of the twentieth century. Connections between the United States and the West Indies for this song game are its more complex cousin, "Round and Round the Village." United States: Lomax and Lomax 1941: 74–75; Newell 1963 (1903): 118–19, no. 41. Great Britain: Opie and Opie 1988: 364. Jamaica: Beckwith 1928: 69–70.

## DOWN TO THE CARPET

British versions include Douglas 1931 (1916): 54; Gomme 1964 (1894), vol. 1: 302–4 and vol. 2: 67–77; Northall 1968 (1892): 372; Opie and Opie 1988: 122–25. New Zealand: Sutton-Smith 1959: 14. United States: Chase

If a song game does not appear on this list, it is because no printed versions have been discovered.

1953: 4–5; Lomax 1960: 65; McDowell and Lassiter 1938: 66–67; Newell 1963 (1903): 60, no. 18, and 74, no. 17; Owens 1936: 1–2 and 344–45; Wolford 1959: 218–19; as a jump-rope rhyme, Abrahams 1969: 155, no. 445. Beckwith (1928: 75–78, no. 65) has discovered several uses of the verse in Jamaican song games.

### Drop, Peter, Drop

The lost-glove theme turns up in England: Baring-Gould 1962: 258, no. 647; Daiken 1976: 63; Gomme 1964 (1894), vol. 1: 109–12 and 305–10; Halliwell 1970 (1928): 145, no. 354. For general discussion of the "Drop the Handkerchief" theme, see Brewster 1953: 91–95, as well as Opie and Opie 1984: 114–15, 82–84 and 198–202. Newell 1963 (1903): 186–89, no. 117, includes early U.S. versions. For Jamaica, see Beckwith 1928: 29–30, no. 22.

### Early in the Morning

The history of "The Peanut Vendor" may be found in Fuld 1966: 350.

### Éliza Kongo

"For Ezilie Wedo," example 133 in Courlander 1988 (1960): 282, presents an interesting Haitian comparison.

### Fiolé

No other sources have been located for the song. The possible associations of the term "fiolé" can be found in Courlander 1988 (1960): 162 and Herskovits 1969 (1936): 53–55.

### Green Gravel

Great Britain: Gomme 1964 (1894), vol. 1: 170 and vol. 2: 46; Daiken 1976: 139; Halliwell 1970 (1928): 251, no. 651; Northall 1968 (1892): 362; Opie and Opie 1988: 239–42. Very frequent in the United States: Owens 1936: 8; McDowell and Lassiter 1938: 54–65; Newell 1963 (1903): 71, no. 15, and 242; Jones and Hawes 1987 (1972): 69. Baring-Gould 1962: 177, no. 326, reports it as a Mother Goose rhyme, while both English (Douglas 1931 [1916]: 31) and Americans (Abrahams 1969: 56) use it for jumping rope. It is known in Australia (Turner 1972: 55) and New Zealand (Sutton-Smith 1959: 16–17). In the Caribbean, Beckwith 1928: 62, no. 54, reports it as "Green Guava."

### Gypsy in the Moonlight

Elder 1973: 71, no. 8, recorded in Tobago; Scarborough 1963 (1925): 82; Ford 1965: 278–80.

## HERE WE GO LOO-BY LOO

This is described as a nursery rhyme by Baring-Gould 1962: 252, no. 637, and Halliwell 1970 (1928): 143, no. 353. It appears as a British song game in Daiken 1976: 155–57; Douglas 1931 (1916): 41; Gomme 1964 (1894), vol. 1: 352–61 and vol. 2: 430–31; and Northall 1968 (1892): 361, no. 68. In the United States, it is found among black children: Courlander 1963: 1578. Like so many other British games, it also appears in Australia (Sutton-Smith 1959: 13).

## HOW GREEN YOU ARE

For "Auld Lang Syne," see Fuld 1966: 96–97, and Ross 1887: 113.

## I HAVE A TREE IN MY RIGHT HAND

A French publication from 1883 (reprint 1967) by E. Roland cites three variants of this song. Gillington also contains a French variant. Newell 1963: 110 cites a Canadian version, as do Opie and Opie 1988: 12. Elder 1973: 71 prints a version from Tobago.

## IN A FINE CASTLE

This song is reported in the United States by Newell 1963 (1903): 44; in the Caribbean by Elder 1973: 63 and 67; and in Great Britain by Opie and Opie 1988, vol. 2: 370–73. The Lord Invader has recorded it on *West Indian Folk Songs for Children.*

## JANE AND LOUISA

Abrahams 1974: 88–89; Beckwith 1929: 73, no. 63; Elder 1973: 75, nos. 12 and 77.

## LINDI MWEN LARIVIÈ

This is described as a nursery rhyme in Baring-Gould 1962: 252, no. 637, and 143, no. 353; as a British song game in Daiken 1976: 155–57; Douglas 1931 (1916): 42; Gomme 1964 (1894), vol. 1: 353–61 and vol. 2: 4301; Northall 1968 (1892): 361; and Opie and Opie 1988: 392–95. In the United States, it is found among white children: Chase 1953: 609; Newell 1963 (1903): 131, no. 68; among black children: Courlander 1963: 1578. Like so many other British games, it also appears in Australia (Sutton-Smith 1959: 13).

## LITTLE SALLY WATER

British sources include Gomme 1964 (1894), vol. 2: 149–70 and 453–54 (seven tunes and forty-eight texts); Opie and Opie 1988: 167–71; Douglas 1931 (1916): 51; and Northall 1968 (1892): 372–78. Bolton 1888: 120 lists it as a counting-out rhyme and Baring-Gould 1962: 256, no. 644 as a nursery rhyme. For the United States, see Abrahams 1969: 114, no. 319; Newell (1903) 1963: 70, no. 13; and Wolford 1959: 210. For U.S. versions from black children, see Courlander 1963: 153–54, 275, and 278; Jones and Hawes 1987 (1972): 107–11; Johns 1944: 24–25. Caribbean versions include those from Jamaica: Beckwith 1928: 78–79, no. 66; Jeckyll 1907: 190–91, no. 99; from Trinidad: Elder 1973: 83, no. 14.

## LONDON BRIDGE
Combined variously with parts of the other old arch game, "See the Robbers Passing By," "London Bridge" is cited as a Mother Goose rhyme by Baring-Gould 1962: 254 and Northall 1968 (1892): 365–66. Other British versions: Daiken 1976: 94; Gomme 1964 (1894), vol. 1: 192–99 and 33–50; Northall 1968 (1892): 365–66; Opie and Opie 1988: 61–72. United States versions include: Brown 1952, vol. 1: 137–49; Newell 1963 (1903): 204–11; Randolph 1980: vol. 3: 388; and Wolford 1959: 221–22; for black versions see Jones and Hawes 1987 (1972): 1,979–80; Parsons 1923: 182; and Elder 1973: 107, no. 24. For Australia, see Sutton-Smith 1959: 21–22; Fuld 1966: 27–29 gives a brief history.

## MAMSELLE MARIE, MARRY THE GIRL ONE TIME
Elder 1973: 92, no. 18. The description of "dancing in the saga t'ing" comes from Aladdin 1974: 9.

## MARY AND MARTHA IS BOUND TO WEAR THE CROWN-O
For further discussion of stone-game songs, see "Me Stone Is Me Stone" and "When Ah Was in Jail" in Elder 1973: 87–88 and 113–14; also, "Balance Yay" in Courlander 1988 (1960): 185–86.

## MEET ME ON THE ROAD
For further discussion of the kalinda (calinda) dance, see Courlander 1963: 190–91 and Courlander 1988 (1960): 132–33.

## MISS MARY MACK
Great Britain: Daiken 1976: 65; Halliwell 1970 (1928): 238, no. 634; Gomme 1964 (1894), vol. 1: 7–8; Opie and Opie 1988: 469–70. Australia: Turner 1972: 43, no. 13007a and b. United States: Abrahams 1969: 64, no. 189, and 120, no. 334; Courlander 1963: 158–59; Lomax 1941: 73; White 1965 (1928): 288, no. 21. The riddle reference comes from Taylor 1951: 234.

## MISSY-LA, MASSA-LA

In an early British version, the lost object was a diamond ring (Gomme 1964 [1894], vol. 1: 96), but in the United States, the ring turned to gold (Newell 1963 [1903]: 150, no. 97; Jones and Hawes 1987 [1972]: 165). The theme proved popular in the Bahamas (Lomax 1941: 82) and in Jamaica (Beckwith 1928: 27–29, no. 21; Jeckyll 1907: 197, no. 95).

## MISTER RAM GOAT-O

For Jamaica, see Murray 1957: 39.

## MOSQUITO ONE

Newell 1963 (1903): 199; Turner 1972: 11009 and 11018. The section that begins "My mother say" is reported frequently: in Australia (Turner 1972: 44); in New Zealand (Sutton-Smith 1959: 85); in Great Britain (Opie and Opie 1988: 441–42; Baring-Gould 1962: 240, no. 603; Daiken 1976: 158); in the United States (Abrahams 1969: 134, no. 377). The last verse appears in jump-rope play in Great Britain (Daiken 1976: 70) and the United States (Abrahams 1969: 38, no. 108).

## ONE SPANIARD CAME

See Opie and Opie 1988: 92–103; Abrahams 1969: 190, no. 550; Gomme 1964 (1894), vol. 2: 25–79, including thirty-seven versions; Bolton 1888: 120, no. 845; Baring-Gould 1962: 250. no. 633; Halliwell 1970 (1928): 134, no. 333; McIntosh 1957: 98–99; Newell 1963 (1903): 39–45, no. 1; Northall 1968 (1892): 134; among others.

## POCO, LE' ME 'LONE

See Walke 1970: 8–9.

## POP GOES THE WEASEL

British references: Gomme 1964 (1894), vol. 2: 63–64; Opie and Opie 1988: 216–18. Except for one Australian version (Sutton-Smith 1959: 12), others located come from the United States: Fuld 1966: 363; Brown 1952, vol. 3: 130; McIntosh 1957: 53–55; Randolph 1980, vol. 3: 368–69; Wolford 1959: 231 and 206.

## RING A RING O' ROSES

Great Britain: Baring-Gould 1962: 253, no. 639; Bolton 1888: 115, no. 767; Gomme 1964 (1894), vol. 2: 108–11; Northall 1968 (1892): 360; Opie and Opie 1951: 364–65; Daiken 1976: 113. United States: Newell 1963 (1903): 127–28, no. 62. Australia: Sutton-Smith 1959: 12. A lengthy and fascinating historical review can be found in Opie and Opie 1988: 220–27.

## RING DIAMOND

This song game is found only in the Caribbean: see Elder 1973: 55, no. 6, and Jeckyll 1907: 194, no. 92.

## ROMAN SOLDIERS

Great Britain: Daiken 1976: 16–20; Gomme 1964 (1894), vol. 2: 343–63; Opie and Opie 1988: 280–85. United States: Newell 1963 (1903): 248–49; Chase 1953: 26–29. Trinidad: Elder 1973: 117–19, no. 28.

## ROUND AND ROUND THE VILLAGE

For British references, see Daiken 1976: 76; Douglas 1931 (1916): 41; Gomme 1964 (1894), vol. 1: 122–43 and vol. 2: 441–42; and Opie and Opie 1988: 360–64; for Australia, Sutton-Smith 1959: 23. For the United States, see Brown 1952, vol. 1: 119–23 and vol. 3: 108–9; Chase 1953: 14–15; Jones and Hawes 1987 (1972): 76–77; McDowell 1938: 60–61; Newell 1963 (1903): 128–29 and 229–30, no. 63; Owens 1936: 3–4; Parrish 1955: 97; and Randolph 1980: vol. 3: 337–38. Beckwith 1928: 67–68, no. 50, reports a Jamaican version.

## SALLY GO ROUND THE MOON

For Great Britain, see Baring-Gould 1962: 251–52, no. 636; Douglas 1931 (1916): 28; Opie and Opie 1988: 398–400; and Gomme 1964 (1894), vol. 2: 149. Abrahams 1969: 174, no. 505, reports it as a jump-rope rhyme in the United States. For two versions from black children in the southern United States, see Carawan 1966: 130 and Lomax 1941: 75.

## SANDY GIRL

Opie and Opie 1988: 170–71; Elder 1973: 83–84.

## SOME LIKE IT HOT, SOME LIKE IT COLD

Great Britain: Baring-Gould 1962: 237, no. 599; Halliwell 1970 (1928): 118, no. 283; Newell 1963 (1903): 132, no. 71; Opie and Opie 1951: 345, no. 400. Australia: Sutton-Smith 1959: 85. United States (hand-clapping and rope-jumping versions): Abrahams 1969: 15, no. 32, and 33, no. 84.

## THERE'S A BROWN GIRL IN THE RING

Trinidad and Tobago: Elder 1973: 45, no. 2; 24, no. 23. Jamaica: Beckwith 1928: 74, no. 64; Jeckyll 1907: 208. Roger Abrahams cites this song game as widely known through the Caribbean.

## TRA LA LA VOUM-BÉ

No other sources found for the Creole text. For "Ta-Ra-Ra Boom Der-e" see Fuld 1966: 462–63 and Spaeth 1959: 163–66. Elder, personal communication.

## WALKING UP THE GREEN GRASS

Great Britain: Gomme 1964 (1894), vol. 1: 153–69 and vol. 2: 426–28; Northall 1968 (1892): 381–83; Opie and Opie 1988 ("Green Grass": 116–20, no. 17; "Three Dukes A-Riding": 76–91, no. 11). For U.S. references: Newell 1963 (1903): 50 and 226–29; Talley 1980 (1922): 183.

## WHAT SHALL I PUT IT IN?

For British versions, see Gomme 1964 (1894), vol. 2: 321–22; also Opie and Opie 1988: 158–62. For U.S. versions, see Brown 1952, vol. 1: 132–33 and Newell 1963 (1903): 72, no. 16. Laura Ingalls Wilder refers to the game in chapter 21 of *On the Banks of Plum Creek*.

## WHO STOLE THE COOKIE FROM THE COOKIE JAR?

Traditional dialogue games from which this song game may be derived may be examined in Brewster 1963: 26–28; Gomme 1964 (1894), vol. 1: 301 and vol. 2: 79; and Newell 1963 (1903): 145–46. no. 90. Closer versions include those to be found in Courlander 1963: 150; Turner 1972: 48, no. 13014; and Opie and Opie 1988: 448.

## YOU LIE, YOU LIE

See Jeckyll 1907: 206, no. 107.

# BIBLIOGRAPHY

〰〰〰

Abrahams, Roger D. 1969. *Jump Rope Rhymes: A Dictionary*. American Folklore Society Bibliographic and Special Series, vol. 20. Austin: University of Texas Press.

———. 1974. *Deep the River, Shallow the Shore: Three Essays on Shantying in the West Indies*. American Folklore Society Memoir Series, vol. 60. Austin: University of Texas Press.

———. 1983. *The Man-of-Words in the West Indies: Performance and the Emergence of Creole Culture*. Baltimore and London: Johns Hopkins University Press.

———. 1992. *Singing the Master: The Emergence of African American Culture in the Plantation South*. New York: Pantheon.

Aladdin, M. P. 1969. *Folk Chants and Refrains of Trinidad and Tobago*. Maravel, Trinidad: MP Publishers.

———. 1974. *Folk Dances of Trinidad and Tobago*. Maravel, Trinidad: MP Publishers.

Attaway, William. 1957. *Calypso Song Book: Authentic Folk Music of the Caribbean*. New York: McGraw-Hill.

Baring-Gould, William S., and Cecil Baring-Gould. 1962. *The Annotated Mother Goose*. New York: Clarkson N. Potter.

Beck, Jane. 1979. *To Windward of the Land: The Occult World of Alexander Charles*. Bloomington: University of Indiana Press.

Beckwith, Martha Warren. 1924. *Jamaica Anansi Stories*. New York: G. E. Stechert.

———. 1928. *Jamaica Folklore*. American Folklore Society Memoir Series, vol. 21. New York: G. E. Stechert.

———. 1929. *Black Roadways: A Study of Jamaica Folk Life*. Chapel Hill: University of North Carolina Press.

Bolton, Henry C. 1888. *The Counting-Out Rhymes of Children: Their Antiquity, Origin, and Wide Distribution.* London: Elliot Stock.

Botkin, Benjamin. 1957. *The American Play-Party Song: With a Collection of Oklahoma Texts and Tunes.* Lincoln: University of Nebraska Press.

Brewster, Paul G. 1953. *American Non-Singing Games.* Norman: University of Oklahoma Press.

Brown, Frank C. 1952. *Collection of North Carolina Folklore.* Durham, N.C.: Duke University Press. 5 vols. (Vol. 1, *Games;* vol. 3, *Folk Songs*).

Carawan, Guy, and Candie Carawan. 1966. *Ain't You Got a Right to the Tree of Life: The People of John's Island, South Carolina.* New York: Simon & Schuster.

Chase, Richard. 1953. *Hullabaloo and Other Singing Folk Games.* Boston: Houghton Mifflin.

Conner, Edric. 1945. *Collection of West Indian Spirituals and Folk Tunes.* London: Boosey & Hawkes. Sheet music.

Courlander, Harold. 1939. *Haiti Singing.* Chapel Hill: University of North Carolina Press.

———. 1963. *Negro Folk Music USA.* New York: Columbia University Press.

———. 1988 (1960). *The Drum and the Hoe: The Life and Lore of the Haitian People.* California Library Reprint Series edition. Berkeley: University of California Press.

Daiken, Leslie. 1976. *Children's Games Throughout the Year.* New York: Arno Press.

Doerflinger, William M. 1951. *Shantymen and Shantyboys: Songs of the Sailor and the Lumberman.* New York: Macmillan.

Douglas, Horman. 1931 (1916). *London Street Games.* Reprint. London: Chatto & Windus.

Edwards, Charles. 1942. *Bahama Songs and Stories.* New York: G. E. Stechert.

Elder, J. D. 1969. *From Congo to Steelband: A Socio-Historical Account of the Emergence and Evolution of the Trinidad Steel Orchestra.* St. Augustine, Trinidad: University of the West Indies.

———. 1971. "Folk Song and Folk Life in Charlotteville: Aspects of Village Life As Dynamics of Acculturation in a Tobago Folk Song Tradition." Paper Prepared for the 21st Congress of the International Folk Music Council, Kingston, Jamaica, August 27–September 3.

———. 1973 (1965). *Song Games from Trinidad and Tobago.* American Folklore Society Bibliographic and Special Series, vol. 16. Philadelphia: University of Pennsylvania Press. Reprinted with photos. Port of Spain, Trinidad: National Cultural Council Publications.

Emery, Lynne Fauley. 1972. *Black Dance in the United States from 1619 to 1970.* Palo Alto, Calif.: National Press Books.

Epstein, Dena J. 1979. "African Music in British and French America." *Music Quarterly* 59: 61–91.

Ford, Ira W. 1965. *Traditional Music of America.* Hatboro, Penn.: Folklore Associates.

Fuld, James J. 1966. *The Book of World-Famous Music: Classical, Popular, and Folk.* New York: Crown Publishers.

Gillington, Alice. 1910. *Breton Singing Games.* London: J. Curwen.

Gomme, Alice Bertha. 1964 (1894). *The Traditional Games of England, Scotland, and Ireland.* Reprint. New York: Dover. 2 vols.

Halliwell, James Orchard. 1970 (1928). *The Nursery Rhymes of England.* Reprint. London: Dodley Head.

Harlow, Frederick Pease. 1988 (1928). *The Making of a Sailor; Or, Sea Life Aboard a Yankee Square Rigger.* Reprint. New York: Dover.

Herskovits, Melville. 1969 (1936). *Suriname Folklore.* Columbia University Contributions to Anthropology. Reprint. New York: AMS Press.

Hill, Donald. 1993. *Calypso Calaloo: Early Carnival Music in Trinidad.* Gainesville: University Press of Florida.

Hopkins, John Barton. 1984. "Jamaican Children's Songs." *Ethnomusicology* 28, no. 1: 1–36.

Hurston, Zora Neale. 1930. "Dance Songs and Games from the Bahamas." *Journal of American Folklore* 43: 294–312.

Jeckyll, Walter. 1907. *Jamaica Song and Story.* London: David Nutt.

Johns, Altona. 1944. *Play Songs of the Deep South.* Washington, D.C.: Associated Publishers.

Jones, Bessie, and Bess Lomax Hawes. 1987 (1972). *Step it Down: Games, Plays, Songs and Stories from the Afro-American Heritage.* New York: Harper & Rowe. Reprinted by Brown Thrasher. Athens: University of Georgia Press.

Lomax, Alan. 1960. *The Folk Songs of North America.* Garden City, N.Y.: Doubleday.

———. 1968. *Folk Song Style and Culture.* American Association for the Advancement of Sciences Publication no. 88. Washington, D.C.: McCall Printing Co.

Lomax, John A., and Alan Lomax. 1941. *Our Singing Country.* New York: Macmillan.

Manuel, Peter, with Kenneth Bilby and Michael Largey. 1995. *Caribbean Currents: Caribbean Music from Rumba to Reggae.* Philadelphia: Temple University Press.

McDaniel, Lorna. 1992. "The Concept of Nation in the Big Drum Dance of Carriacou, Grenada." In Carol Robertson, *Musical Repercussions of 1492.* Washington, D.C.: Smithsonian Press.

McDowell, Lucien, and Flora Lassiter. 1938. *Folk Dances of Tennessee: Old Play Party Games of the Caney Fork Valley*. Ann Arbor, Mich.: Edwards Brothers.

McIntosh, David S. 1957. *Singing Games and Dances*. New York: Association Press.

Murray, Tom. 1957. *Folk Songs of Jamaica*. London: Oxford University Press.

Newell, William Wells. 1963 (1903). *Games and Songs of American Children*. Reprint. New York: Dover.

Northall, G. F. 1968 (1892). *English Folk Rhymes: A Collection of Traditional Verses Relating to Places, Persons, Customs, Superstitions, etc.* Reprint. Detroit: Singing Tree Press.

Opie, Iona, and Peter Opie. 1951. *The Oxford Dictionary of Nursery Rhymes*. Oxford: Clarendon Press.

———. 1988. *The Singing Game*. Oxford: Oxford University Press.

Owens, William A. 1936. *Swing and Turn: Texas Play Party Games*. Dallas: Tardy Publications.

Parrish, Lydia. 1955. *Slave Songs of the Georgia Sea Islands*. Hatboro, Penn.: Folklore Associates.

Parsons, Elsie Clews. 1923. *Folklore of the Sea Islands, South Carolina*. American Folklore Society Memoir Series, vol. 16. Cambridge, Mass.: G. E. Stechert.

Patterson, Massie, and Lionel Belasco. 1943. *Calypso Songs of the West Indies*. New York: M. Baron. Sheet music for twelve popular songs.

Pearcy, G. Etzel. 1965. *The West Indian Scene*. Princeton, N.J.: D. Van Nostrand.

Randolph, Vance. *Ozark Folksongs*. 1980. Vol. 3: *Humorous and Play-Party Songs*. Columbia and London: University of Missouri Press.

Ritchie, Jean. 1955. *A Singing Family of the Cumberlands*. Oxford and New York: Oxford University Press.

Roland, E. 1967 (1883). *Rimes et jeux d'enfance*. Reprint. Paris: Maisonneuve.

Ross, John D. 1887. *Celebrated Songs of Scotland*. New York: William Fagan.

Rutherford, Frank. 1971. *All the Way to Pennywell: Children's Rhymes of the North East*. Durham, England: University of Durham Institute of Education.

Saxon, Lyle. 1945. *Gumbo Ya-Ya: A Collection of Louisiana Folklore*. Boston: Houghton Mifflin.

Scarborough, Dorothy. 1963 (1925). *On the Trail of Negro Folk Songs*. Reprint. Hatboro, Penn.: Folklore Associates.

Simpson, George E. 1954. "Peasant Children's Games in Northern Haiti." *Folklore* 65: 65–73.

Southern, Eileen. 1971. *Readings in Black American Music.* New York: W. W. Norton.

———. 1997. *The Music of Black Americans: A History.* 3rd ed. New York: W. W. Norton.

Spaeth, Sigmund. 1959. *Read 'Em and Weep: A Treasury of American Songs.* New York: Arco Publishing.

Stearns, Marshall. 1970 (1956). *The Story of Jazz.* Reprint. New York: Oxford University Press.

———, and Jean Stearns. 1968. *Jazz Dance: The Story of American Vernacular Dance.* New York: Macmillan.

Sutton-Smith, Brian. 1959. *The Games of New Zealand Children.* University of California Folklore Studies 12. Berkeley: University of California Press.

Talley, Thomas W. 1980 (1922). *Negro Folk Rhymes: Wise and Otherwise.* Reprint. Folcroft, Penn.: Folcroft Library Editions.

Taylor, Archer. 1951. *English Riddles from Oral Tradition.* Berkeley: University of California Press.

Turner, Ian. 1972. *Cinderella Dressed in Yella: The First Attempt at a Definitive Study of Australian Children's Play Rhymes.* New York: Taplinger.

Waddell, D. A. G. 1967. *The West Indies and the Guianas.* Englewood Cliffs, N.J.: Prentice-Hall.

Walke, Olive. 1970. *Folk Songs of Trinidad and Tobago.* Arranged by Gareth Walke. New York: Boosey & Hawkes.

*West Indian and Caribbean Year Book 1973.* 1972. Croydon, England: Thomas Skinner Directories.

White, Newman I. 1965 (1928). *American Negro Folk Songs.* Reprint. Hatboro, Penn.: Folklore Associates.

Williams, Connie. 1958. *Twelve Songs from Trinidad.* San Francisco: Pan Pipes Press. Most are of popular origin.

Wolford, Leah Jackson. 1959. *The Play Party in Indiana.* Edited and revised by W. Edison Richmond and William Tillson. Indiana Historical Society Publication no. 20.

# DISCOGRAPHY

## AFRICA

*African Songs and Rhythms for Children.* Recorded and Annotated by Dr. W. K. Amouku. Smithsonian/Folkways 45011.

*Children's Songs and Games from Africa.* Vol. 1. Kojo Fosu and Edwina Hunter. Folkways 77855.

*Children's Songs from Guinea and Senegal.* Game songs, message songs, and prayer songs. Arion CD.

## CARRIACOU

*Big Drum and Other Ritual and Social Music of Carriacou.* Recorded by Donald Hill. Folkways 34002.

*Big Drum Dance of Carriacou.* Collected and annotated by Andrew C. Pearse. Folkways LP 04011.

## JAMAICA

*Children's Jamaican Songs and Games.* Louise Bennett, vocals. Smithsonian/ Folkways 7250.

*Folk Music of Jamaica.* Ring play, work songs, kumina. Recorded by Edward Seaga. Folkways 4453.

*From the Grass Roots of Jamaica.* Mento, ring-play, nago, work songs, and kumina. Recorded by Olive Lewin. Dynamic Sounds LP.

## TRINIDAD AND TOBAGO

*Knock Down Calypso.* Performed by Growling Tiger. Rounder Records.

*Lord Invader: Calypso for Children.* Folkways 7262.

*Send Your Children to the Orphan Home: The Real Calypso.* Vol. 2. The Lion, Lord Executor, The Tiger, and others. Folkways RF 4.

## United States

*American Folk Songs for Children.* Collected by Alan Lomax. Atlantic 1350.

*Negro Folk Music of Alabama.* Vol. 6: *Ring Game Songs and Others.* Folkways 4474.

*One, Two, Three and a Zing Zing Zing: Street Games of the Children of New York City.* Folkways 7003.

*Play and Dance Songs and Tunes.* Edited by B. A. Botkin. Archives of American Folk Song L9.

*Ring Games: Line and Play Party Songs of Alabama.* Produced and recorded by Harold Courlander. Folkways 7004.

*Song and Play Time.* Performed by Pete Seeger. Smithsonian/Folkways 45023.

## Collections

*Caribbean Songs and Games for Children.* Compiled and edited by Edna Smith. Folkways 7856.

*West Indian Folk Songs for Children.* Sung by Lord Invader. Folkways 7744.

*You'll Sing a Song, and I'll Sing a Song.* Ella Jenkins with members of the Urban Gateways Children's Chorus. Smithsonian/Folkways 45010.